STAY WHERE YOU WERE

HARLAND PADFIELD
OREGON STATE UNIVERSITY

ROY WILLIAMS
INDUSTRIAL RELATIONS COUNSELOR

STAY WHERE YOU WERE

A STUDY OF UNEMPLOYABLES IN INDUSTRY

J. B. LIPPINCOTT COMPANY
Philadelphia
New York   Toronto

Library of Congress Cataloging in Publication Data

Padfield Harland
    Stay where you were.

    Includes bibliographical references.
    1. Hard-core unemployed—United States—Case
studies. I. Williams, Roy, joint author.
II. Title
HD5724.P26   331.1'37'0973   72-11972
Paperbound: ISBN 0-397-47280-3
Clothbound: ISBN 0-397-47289-7

To Eldridge, Jay, Tamu and Mary

Contents

Tables and Figures

Foreword

Even before the War on Poverty, some social scientists and anti-poverty experts argued that the best way to eliminate poverty was to create decent and well-paying jobs for the under-employed, the unemployed, and the so-called unemployables or hard-core unemployed; the men out of work so long that they are no longer counted as members of the labor force. Most of the work-related programs of the War on Poverty were limited to job-training schemes which did not include jobs, but after the ghetto uprisings of the mid-1960s, the National Association of Businessmen, responding to fear of further unrest by their corporate members, joined with the federal government to establish a job-creation program for the hard-core unemployed, giving them on-the-job training after they were hired but before they were put to work. Although the NAB program, which altogether employed about 300,000 people the country over, was effectively terminated after the end of the ghetto uprisings and the onset of the recession, it provided an opportunity to apply the idea that poverty can be eliminated through job creation.

Padfield and Williams' well-researched and well-written case study of one NAB project, in a San Diego plant they call Southwestern Aircraft, tests this idea and shows that it is valid. As far as I know, this is the first sociological and anthropological study of the effects of job creation, and its many practical and theoretical findings should be read by anti-poverty officials and researchers, industrial managers and union officials, and social scientists who deal with poverty, the ghetto, and the industrial enterprise generally. But Padfield and Williams' empathic account of the life of hard-core unemployed men in the factory and the community—much of it in the men's own words—should interest the general reader too, and it joins that small circle of recent ghetto studies; Liebow's *Tally's Corner,* Hannerz's *Soulside,* and Rainwater's *Behind Ghetto Walls,* among others, which report what life is really like for the underclass.

By constant observation, informal interviewing, counseling (by Williams) and other research methods, the two authors demonstrate that a group of hard-core unemployed men, mostly black or Mexican, poorly educated, often arrested, and frequent users of drugs and alcohol, had no trouble learning to do the required work and to work effectively. The authors also show, however, that the process by which men "who have learned to cope without work" become integrated into the labor force is far more complicated and beset with obstacles than I, for one, thought, partly because of a variety of off-the-job difficulties encountered by the men, but mainly because of shortcomings in the design of the job creation program, which in turn reflects the structured inequality of a society wanting, intentionally or not, that these men stay where they are.

Of the 28 men who began the program at Southwestern Aircraft as trainees, 16 remained on the job a year later, but they and the 12 who were fired encountered a variety of problems. As the authors indicate in Chapter 3, many of the men adapted to the society of the factory with the styles they had found useful in adapting to the streets of the ghetto and most were fired for this reason. Seven reacted with the familiar bravado of the street corner male, an aggressive but careful risk-taking which resulted in high-level performance on the job but did not endear the men to their coworkers. Another seven were unable to control their aggression at the critical moment—the authors call them the compartmentals—and most were fired. Eight became "dependents," so beset by feelings of inadequacy that often they could not cope with job success and the opportunity for advancement, and altogether only three of the 28 made what the authors call a natural adaptation to the plant.

Still, the men's major difficulties originated outside the shop. Almost all the men had been in trouble with the law before they went to work, and one of the book's unexpected findings is that these troubles—and their rate of arrest—increased after they became employed. When Padfield and Williams explain the reasons, however, it becomes clear that the increased arrests should have been expected, for they resulted from the men's having to live in two worlds: in the factory of mainstream society and in the underclass of the ghetto. Most of the arrests were brought on by traffic violations, and it is worth quoting the authors' poignant description of how these men, who needed cars to get to work, retained underclass ways of coping with car ownership and use:

> To most of the hard-core, traffic was not *a* problem but a problem syndrome. If a trainee had one citation, he usually had several. In some cases, this resulted from the police making several charges simultaneously, a simple moving violation or a faulty equipment charge combined with a no license, open alcoholic container, or concealed weapons charge. Sometimes, the emotional behavior of the trainees upon arrest . . . might lead to a charge of eluding the police, disturbing the peace or resisting arrest . . . there was the tendency to compound the charges by such coping patterns as ignoring tickets, mutilating out-of-date licenses or forging new ones, or simply driving without a license.
>
> There are numerous aspects of the hard-core situation which account for this mode of traffic behavior. One is their high exposure to traffic surveillance which comes from living in a high crime area. Another is their low economic standing. A hard-core . . . cannot afford accidents, expensive repairs, traffic fines, or attorney's fees. Therefore, his responses . . . are appropriate to his selfish interest in the situation which tend to be shortcut short-term-gain strategies for evading the formal rules . . . this leads to bench warrants, suspended or revoked licenses, which lead in turn to forced licenses, ticket fixing and so on . . .

And these difficulties lead finally to tardiness or absence from work.

A yet more harrowing effect was the increased amount of family strife—and arrests for it—after the men became workers. In what I found the most interesting chapter of the book, the authors show that the transition from unemployment to employment was at least as hard for the men's families as for the men. Almost all of the men were "marginal males," living either in a female-dominated household or in one in which they had to struggle to maintain their dominance. Often, their wives, girlfriends or mothers received welfare, which gave them not only a steady if low income but also economic and political control over the household. When the men became breadwinners, the women were faced with the loss of their control and took it out on the men, resulting in family fights which sometimes wound up in the police station or the court. Frequently, the causes of such fights were petty, as when a woman refused to make lunch sandwiches for her man because she had never been asked to do it before; sometimes, they were tragic, as in the sad case of Darrell and Justine described in Chapter 6. Even when family strife did not lead to arrest, it left the men tired the next day or angry and in a foul mood, which of course affected their behavior in the plant.

In addition, while coping with unemployment, the men had become participants in the street corner society of the ghetto so well described by Elliot Liebow; their closest friends were other unemployed men— and alcohol and drugs, and some had earned their living through pimping and other kinds of hustling. These old ties, which conflicted with the factory routine and time schedule, had to be broken whether the men wanted to or not, and all in all, they were broken or altered remarkably often and quickly. Sometimes, however, the men needed to retain these ties—and to rely on them when they got into trouble in the factory or at home—and sometimes, past ties created difficulties for the men through no fault of their own. For example, when the police killed an old friend and mentor of one of the workers, his grief and anger could not be bottled up at work. More often, the police, who did not know or care that the men had taken on a new work role, continued to pick them up on suspicion when they were looking for suspects, and this, too, caused trouble on the job.

Over and over again, the book reports how hard the men were trying to alter their lives, to put the job, job performance and job advancement, at the center of their lives, as all regularly employed people do automatically. Indeed, the men worked much harder at occupational success, both on and off the job, than most middle-class people. What defeated the men who were fired and burdened those who remained on the job was not the work; but the rest of their society; the job had liberated them from unemployment but had not allowed them to leave the underclass.

As a result, the study seems to give some support to the so-called Moynihan thesis that black family pathology interferes with the escape from poverty, and to the late Oscar Lewis's concept of the culture of poverty which interferes similarly. Padfield and Williams demonstrate, however, that the pathology and the culture do not develop in a vacuum; they are understandable and often rational responses to the situations which under-class men and their families must deal with, and these situations are structured largely by the ways in which mainstream society treats the underclass. These ways do not change the moment the men become breadwinners and competent workers, and so their responses cannot change quickly enough to meet the requirements of the factory—and thus of mainstream society itself. In a sense, the men were caught in a vicious circle; joblessness put them in the underclass, but the job alone could not move them out of that underclass at once, as the factory demanded, and so some were forced back into it. In an unequal society, the poor get few opportunities and when they get them, they are expected to adapt at once or the opportunities will be withdrawn; not enough time and other help are given to allow them to adapt more gradually. Nevertheless, the authors indicate that neither the pathology nor the culture of poverty were strong enough to prevent the men from doing their work competently, and in many, although not enough cases, both were weak enough that the men and their families could overcome them.

Moreover, perhaps the major reason that wives, old peers and others complicated the adaptation to the job stemmed from the fact that they were not sufficiently rewarded by the men's new role. The women, for example, had to pay a variety of social and emotional costs; they had to change their own behavior and to deal with new sources of stress and conflict. To be sure, the men brought more money into the household, but evidently this was not enough to offset the women's loss of familial power. Of course, it must be remembered that the book describes only the first year's experiences, and by now, women and old peers may have found—or have received—some rewards from the men's jobs, and the police may have informed themselves that the men are no longer to be treated as potential suspects for every crime in the neighborhood.

There was, however, another group which also suffered from the job-creation program and was also not rewarded: the coworkers in the plant and their union, and they were strong enough to object and eventually to terminate the program. Although both were initially sympathetic to the men, and remarkably so considering that they were often indulged and over-protected by management, the recession came just as the men began their training and some older workers were laid off. As a result, when a new union contract was negotiated, the union demanded and received a more stringent set of job descriptions and a retraining program tied to seniority, giving laid off older workers first rights to re-training, and thus ending management's incentive to hire and train more of the hard-core unemployed. Although Padfield and Williams are critical of the union, the real fault lay with the NAB program; it provided incentives to the hard-core unemployed and to management, but not to the men already at work in the factory, and they had to pay unexpected costs when the company tried to replace laid off workers with trainees. Even though the union did not want to hurt the trainees—who themselves became union members in short order—it felt that it had to protect its older members first.

The unequal pattern of rewards which I have described could probably not have been anticipated in what was, after all, a pioneering program, and if the program had survived, at Southwestern as elsewhere, this pattern might have been corrected. The program was terminated not because of the union—or in the nation at large, because of the end of the ghetto uprisings—but because of the recession. Ultimately, it ended because the American economy cannot provide jobs for all those ready and able to work even in good times, thus forcing it to extrude the so-called unemployables, the underemployed and others the moment a recession occurs. That recession, in turn, stemmed from the Vietnam war, for the American economy is simply not healthy enough to provide both full employment and finance imperialistic adventures overseas. To paraphrase the words with which the authors close their book, any effective policy to bring the ghetto back into mainstream society will find the illness of this economy far more formidable than the pathology of the ghetto.

HERBERT J. GANS
Columbia University
New York

Acknowledgements

This study was made possible by the generous support of the Rockefeller Foundation through Grant No. GA HSS 6865, awarded to the University of Arizona in 1968 and supplemented in 1969, and the equally generous matching support by the Bureau of Ethnic Research, Department of Anthropology, University of Arizona. Also, the authors appreciatively acknowledge the support of the Western Area Development Research Center, Oregon State University, during the final stages of manuscript preparation in the fall of 1972.

Individuals to whom we are indebted are Professor Thomas Weaver, Director of the Bureau of Ethnic Research and Professor John Howard, Dean of Social Science, State University of New York at Purchase, for their insightful criticisms of the initial drafts of the manuscript; Marianne Padfield for her family interviews and both Marianne Padfield and Ruth Williams for providing useful perspectives throughout all phases of the project; Edith Hallet, Olivia Smith, Jan Hastings and Anna Hicks for their patience and skill in text transcription and manuscript typing; and Mr. A. Richard Heffron and Ms. Val Rementer of Lippincott Publishing Company for their skillful editing and generous assistance in revising the manuscript.

Finally, we are indebted to those whose identities must remain anonymous—the company and the union; the managers, supervisors and workers; and most especially, the 28 men and their families whose private experiences and insights will hopefully contribute to a better understanding of a public problem.

"Agnew's Hour." Copyright *Newsweek*, Inc. 1970, reprinted by permission.

Charles J. Butler, "Must I Concern Myself." Reprinted by permission of the author.

Eldridge Cleaver, from *Soul on Ice.* Copyright 1968 by McGraw-Hill Book Company. Used with permission of McGraw-Hill Book Company.

Herbert J. Gans, "The Negro Family: Reflections on the Moynihan Report." Reprinted by permission from *The Moynihan Report and the Politics of Controversy* by Lee Rainwater and William L. Yancey. Copyright 1967 by The MIT Press.

James D. Hodgson and Marshall H. Brenner, "Successful Experiences: Training Hard-Core Unemployed." Reprinted by permission from Harvard Business Review, 46, 5 (September-October 1968).

Elliot Liebow, from *Tally's Corner.* Copyright © 1967 by Little, Brown and Company, Inc. Reprinted with Permission.

"Runaway Child." Copyright © 1971 by Motown Records, Inc. Reprinted with permission.

Charles L. Snaders, "Industry Gives New Hope to the Negro." Reprinted by permission of EBONY Magazine, copyright 1968 by Johnson Publishing Company, Inc.

Earl Warren, remarks at the Equal Opportunity Day Dinner of the National Urban League. Reprinted by permission of EBONY Magazine, copyright 1970 by Johnson Publishing Company, Inc.

Prologue: Runaway Child

In the summer and fall of 1968 an aircraft factory in San Diego cooperating in a National Alliance of Businessmen's program hired 28 hard-core unemployables as trainees in industry. A year later, 16 men were still working and well on the way to being converted to industry, and 12, unable to make the transition, were back on the streets. Tim Carter was one of the 12 for whom the program was too late.

We begin this book about the experiences of these 28 men with a remarkably intuitive statement in the form of a conversation between Tim and a factory counselor shortly after Tim's termination. The counselor is called "Brother" because this is what Tim frequently called him. Except for the use of pseudonyms and minor editing, the conversation is reproduced exactly as it occurred.

BROTHER. *Watcha say there, Tim?*
TIM. *Hi ya doin'?*
BROTHER. *All right. What's the trouble?* (Referring to a prior phone call from Tim)
TIM. *I jus' called to tell ya that uh ...*
BROTHER. *...you got a job.*
TIM. *Well, it's better than nuth'n. They pay by the piece work, by how many cars you put out.*

BROTHER. *What do you do?*

TIM. *Detailin'. I do pretty good; think I'll stick to it. What I called you for was this—I won't get paid till next week, but I wanna, I wanna . . .*

BROTHER. *. . . fold me up?* (Laughing)

TIM. *I need some money to carry me through. I didn't even have no lunch or nuth'n.*

BROTHER. *You haven't eaten yet?*

TIM. *Naw. I wanna know could I get ten or five dollars from ya till I get paid; then I could start payin' you, cause wasn't for you a lot of times I'da, I'da caught me somebody staggerin' and hit em on . . .*

BROTHER. (Laughing) *Let's hope not, Tim!*

TIM. *Yeah.* (Pause) *That's sump'n I ain't never did tho, you know, detailin'.*

BROTHER. *Uh huh.*

TIM. *Another partner of mine showed me how to do it. It's fun; you're outside. You learn pretty good things. I mean you learn about a car.*

BROTHER. *How'd you get this job?*

TIM. *Oh, through my partner. Another friend of ours wantin' us to work; you know, he was like a foreman out there. But since he took over and can kinda talk to the Man, he jus' went on and told us he wanted us to work, cause we ain't got no job. We ain't, you know, doin' too swift.*

BROTHER. *And he pays you by the car?*

TIM. *Yeah.*

BROTHER. *What he give you guys a car?*

TIM. *Four dollars and sometimes four-fifty for interior.*

BROTHER. *Four-fifty? How many can you do a day?*

TIM. *Right now I can only do two a day.*

BROTHER. *That's eight dollars a day; that's better than nuth'n!*

TIM. *Yeah, that beat no money in my pocket at all . . .*

BROTHER. *If you gotta have it, Tim, you gotta have it.* (Gives Tim five dollars)

TIM. *I wanted to show you that I really wanted a job.*

BROTHER. *Well, I'm glad you thought that much of me that you wanted to show me you wanted a job.*

TIM. *Cause I'm tired of these here streets.*

BROTHER. *I get the feeling it's not only you but some more of the fellows are tired of the street.*

TIM. *You know they had a big messup down here, and my little brother started actin' up, and I was talkin' to him. I'm trying to keep him in line. I say, "If you know like I know, you wouldn't do this!" I say, "You'd go on and go to school and finish!" Cause I wish a thousand times I had.*

BROTHER. *Wish a thousand times you had, uh?*

TIM. *Yeah. I'm still gonna finish, but first I want my clothes, my car. This here is jus' till I get me another job.*

BROTHER. *Okay, and if I see something, I'll get in touch with you. You know, the fact that you got a job is good; that'll let the next man know that you want a job. You see, when you quit this job and go for another job the man will say, "Well gee, you been working!" See? That's a good record. You know you might have changed in the past three weeks. Look like you been straight for quite a little while.*

TIM. *Trying to. I had that phase, man. I knew I was gonna break out of it, and I broke out. So I be gettin' on my feet pretty soon . . .*

BROTHER. *Well, what will the five dollars do?*

TIM. *It's gonna keep me sump'n to eat in my stomach the rest of this week . . .*

BROTHER. *Man, I was sure glad to hear what you told me today, you're working. That, that just made me tickled pink. In the meantime I'm gonna keep talkin' to Ted, cause if a better job comes up, you know; in fact I'll look for two.*

TIM. *Okay.*

BROTHER. *You and your partner.*

TIM. *We wanna get under a roof. I was thinkin' about movin' out on the beach for this summer.*

BROTHER. *Do you think if you could get out of this environment it would really do you some good?*

TIM. *Well, I jus' like havin' fun. In the summer during the evening it's gonna be hot. I can come in, relax, and look out cross the water. Me and him have a lot of ideas, you know. And he lost his wife, so . . .*

BROTHER. *Who, that other guy did?*

TIM. *Yeah. He got a wife and a son.*

BROTHER. *Where he lose her?*

TIM. *She stays over here, you know.* (Pointing to the house next door)

BROTHER. *Is that what caused him to go down?*

TIM. *She shot him twice. She shot him in the back and in the arm. He almost died behind that.*

BROTHER. *Other than being shot, did it really hurt him?*

TIM. *Yeah, it hurt him, cause he still love his wife. He tells me all the time that.*

BROTHER. *How about Angie, you still love her?* (Referring to the woman Tim is living with)

TIM. *You wanna know the truth?*

BROTHER. *Yeah.*

TIM. *It was never no love. I don't know what started makin' me mess with Angie. Well, at the time she was nice, you know . . .*

BROTHER. *. . . to be with.*

TIM. *Yeah. After I got to really know her.*

BROTHER. *Was your problem basically Angie?*

TIM. *It was part her and some of the things I was doin', see . . .*

BROTHER. *. . . some of the things you were engaged in. Does that worry you about being caught or what?*

TIM. *What, bein' caught by the police?*

BROTHER. *Yeah.*

TIM. *That don't bother me. But they got my name on the watch list, you know, like they see me doin sump'n, they write it down.*

BROTHER. *Yeah, they keep a watch list, I know that.*

TIM. *Well, they been watchin' me ever since I been out of work.*

BROTHER. *It's a fact though, Tim, if a man don't work he gotta do somethin'.* (Referring to hustling)

TIM. *Yeah. See, I wanna get my own house where when I come in I can jus' relax, put on my TV, and listen to my stereo, you know. So I'm not gonna move till I get a better job. Sump'n that I know I can make some money off of.*

BROTHER. *That will help you. If you get away from around*

some of the areas where it's so free, you know.

TIM. *Uh, uh.* (Pausing, then sarcastically) *Get out there in them white folks' area I might not know how to act.*

BROTHER. *You're not scared of white folks are you?*

TIM. *Nope, uh, uh, n-o-o-no!*

BROTHER. *You mean you just don't have anything to do with them either.*

TIM. *Well, the women. Yeah, the women.*

BROTHER. *You have something to do with the women? How come the women?*

TIM. *They female. Sometime I might catch a rich one. I had one when I got out of jail, but I jus' cut that alose.*

BROTHER. *White woman?*

TIM. *Uh huh. She was sending me money. That's who kept me with money and stuff, her and my mother, while I was in jail.*

BROTHER. *What's so fascinating about the white women?*

TIM. *What's so fascinatin' about em? Some of em look good; they ambitious. They want sump'n out of life besides jus' laying around havin' babies, that's all. I'm gonna mess with each race regardless of this here Black Nationalist and all that. Long as they don't bother me, I don't care.*

BROTHER. *What do Black Nationalists basically do?*

TIM. *Well, they basically is a study of black culture—history. You know they go back, then they come forward and tell you what's what and what the white man have did so many years against, you know, not only us . . . They don't mainly speak of the blacks, they speak of Indians, Mexicans . . .*

BROTHER. *What you're saying is that they bring all this out in what they say.*

TIM. *I'm looking any time now, it might explode around here. Now, back here in sixty-five when we was rioting and all, the old people used to always say, well why you guys do this and that? Well, now they see.* (Long pause) *See our people is tryin' to move ahead, this is what I'm sayin'.*

BROTHER. *It's about time.*

TIM. *And jus' like I told some white man, he was talkin' about black history, and I told him if I had millions—about two or three million dollars—I would build me a clinic, a medical clinic, and employ black people, nuth'n but black people.*

*Build me a supermarket with all this cut-rate food, where all
this food is so high . . . you go out there in their area that food
ain't as high as it is over here.*

BROTHER. *We know that. We know that so well.*

TIM. *There ain't no good apartments around here; I could put
up some apartments. See I think, these all the things I
righteously think about, if I had the money, what I would do.*
(Pause) *Like these youngsters don't have nowhere to go. I
would build them a better place. . . . I would tear that
building down, put up a new building where there's a band
comin' in every week playin' for em. There would be adults, a
bar, and all that. Where they got to go now?*

BROTHER. *The streets.*

TIM. *Streets. A little old public, a little old Black History
Library. Why can't a black man have the equal rights of the
white man? Who gots all the money, mostly the money?*

BROTHER. *White men.*

TIM. *That's right. Who got the biggest land around here?*

BROTHER. *White men.*

TIM. *Right. There's a white man who owns that store up here,
and if I had the money and whatever it would cost, I would
buy em out.* (Pause) *You see I started back to readin', you
know. I was readin' a lot when I was in jail. But now I got a
couple books that I wanna read, but I could never catch up
with em . . .* Drum *and* The Falcom of Hurst. *See, slave
breedin',* Drum *was a breeder.*

BROTHER. *Did you ever read Malcolm's story? I'll try to get
it for you.*

TIM. *I'll read it . . . Lot of times instead of goin' up here on
the streets I could be at home. This how come I wanna get my
own house. I could do like I wanna do. I can't have no friends
over here, cause we get to talkin', and we might get to
laughin', listening' to music, and that bother Angie. At my
house it won't bother me, cause we all be talkin' bout the
same thing.* (Changing the subject) *I read a book when I was in
the joint, bout a man, a lawyer right today in New York. He's
a Brother . . . he was tellin' about the ghetto in Harlem, his
friends, and so forth. And when I come back to San Diego, I
got to lookin' around, what he was sayin' and the people, and*

it's true . . . it's true. (Long pause) *Have you ever heard that song* Runaway Child?

BROTHER. *Uh huh.*

TIM. *Listen to it. It tell you a whole bunch . . .*

BROTHER. (Police car goes by) *Sometimes I think the cops are followin' me.*

TIM. *I don't know, you get outta here with that white shirt on they gonna think you a big business man.* (Pause, then changing the subject) *Now, they want me in that black organization. I don't want to be in it, because some of the things they say is not right. Like I say, one day I believe like it says in the Bible that the world gonna burn . . . I believe, you know, when it burn it will be because of the black people; they gonna set the world on fire.*

BROTHER. *That's a lot of torches.*

TIM. *That's a lotta black people, too.*

BROTHER. *You know something Tim, the more I'm out movin' around—and I move around quite a bit—the more I know that there's a great need for black people to help the black people.*

TIM. *What the white man care about you gettin' ahead? He don't care, he don't really care. I noticed they have made like they care, like Smathers.* (Official at Southwestern where Tim used to work) *He's one of them people, not cause he fired me or nuth'n. He was one of them people who hired me. When I first seen you guys, I was judgin' you then.*

BROTHER. *Padfield told me to tell you that you're right. I told him that you said he didn't understand.* (Being a black in a ghetto) *And he said you're right, he don't.*

TIM. *He don't and he never will.*

BROTHER. *That's one of the reasons I said it's going to take black people to rescue black people.*

TIM. *Somebody that's strong.*

BROTHER. *Yeah.*

TIM. *But what's gonna happen, uh, some big millionaires is gonna get together and do the same thing, hire somebody to kill em! Now I believe big business, the big businessmen is behind them Kennedys' murders and Martin Luther King's murder. Because Kennedy started off, he was for the blacks.*

You know, all the things he had put forth to start doing? Well, Johnson had to come along and make sure they was did. But some of the things wasn't really did that he had planned. Didn't nobody know what he had planned. But he was for the black. He had all the money he needed. Kennedy, he got killed, and his brother came along and he got shot. Well, they got Nixon in there now. They got who they want in there. They got Reagan.

BROTHER. *We know who they're for.*

TIM. *That's the way it goes. I studies that a lot. I don't know why I'm so interested, but I am.*

BROTHER. *You know, one of the things that sometimes I don't understand is why you would cross the races when you feel so strong about what has been done.*

TIM. *Why would I cross?*

BROTHER. *With the white woman.*

TIM. (Quickly) *That's not crossing. They use our black women to breed, didn't they? You can use white women to breed too.*

BROTHER. (Laughing) *All right, that sound like Angie, but Angie is Mexican.*

TIM. *Right. They can breed black too. Have you ever noticed the average child that is born outta mixed couples—outta black and whatever the woman, whatever she is—that it takes more of the black side that the other side.*

BROTHER. *Maybe it's more there.*

TIM. *This is what I'm trying to say, that we are breeders, you see.* (Shifting) *There's a lot to be did. Now if they had any sense, all these houses that been here for years, how come they don't come in and remodel or sump'n?*

BROTHER. *Tear them down and build some new ones, cause they're nothin' but fire traps.*

TIM. *Rats and mice and all. Some big ones!*

BROTHER. *Well, Tim, thinking like you're thinking now, if you can keep your head clear, you can get yourself together and do something about it. You know, that's been part of the Brothers' problem—they didn't keep themselves together long enough to do anything. Heretofore it's been every man go his own way.*

TIM. *I went over a girl's house back here about two or three months ago. Me and my buddy was jus' jivin' around. And I seen this baby din't have no milk, and so I jus' said well here. I gave her . . . I think it was eight dollars . . . to go and get sump'n, you know. And then lately since I seen her, she say, "You the first man that ever gave me something and didn't look for it in return." I say, "What for?"* (Pause) *Sex is the least important thing to me, cause . . . well, it's there.*

BROTHER. *You've done a lot of thinking lately, you know it?*

TIM. *Oh, when I be walkin' around here and my head be half clouded, I be thinkin'. And I be really thinkin'; I be rightfully down with it when I be like that. I be so far off in it, I don't know. Sometime people can talk to me, and they have to touch me. And I go up on the streets, and I be loaded—I go up there on the streets, and I jus' look . . .* (Pause) *look at the people . . .* (Pause) *look at the places where they can't go, and the white man gonna come along and tell em they have to go. Now last week, if they had somewhere to go, that little ruckus* (referring to police beating three blacks in a small riot) *they had would never had happen. Most of them was youngsters. I told em; I say, "You can't win!" and I walked off. I told my buddy, "You can't win!" San Diego suppose to have the biggest police force. You can't win!*

BROTHER. *Not that way.*

TIM. *Naw. Now you go to gettin' your machine gun . . . but you got to have all this stuff at the same time . . . you got to do it at the same time then maybe we will accomplish sump'n. Let them fall in the streets and hurt theyself a couple times, let em see how it feels—let them get hit with sump'n . . . let em see how it feels. Police that they sendin' out here now, they looks for trouble!*

BROTHER. *I know this.*

TIM. *And the people now begin to pressure. They put you in a bind while they pushin' you to make you do sump'n wrong. I look at how that started up there Saturday . . . they look for something.* (Pause) *People sittin' in they car, and the Man drove by and said, "Yuall loaded." Then after this a little ruckus, bottle throwing, so forth started. But why? Because of one white man—which was none of his business.*

BROTHER. *Wasn't violating any laws?*

TIM. *He was sittin' in his car as far as he was concerned; he didn't see him do nuth'n. And if you have a warrant for somebody's arrest, you suppose to show him some kind of papers. Now take that man and do him right, but the way they was doin' people up here—beatin' people across the head with sticks, chokin', puttin' the choke hold on em—ain't gonna get nuth'n right! Now if I'da been up there when they got my brother, I'd been in jail right today!*

BROTHER. *Where's your brother at now?*

TIM. *Oh, my father went and got him out. But I'da went to the joint—I'da been ready to go to the joint tomorrow.*

BROTHER. *Because you can't stand to see them abuse your brother, huh?*

TIM. *I couldn't stand to see them abuse them people, cause I walked off. I wouldn't stay around; I left. All I told em that you can't win . . .*

BROTHER. *Man you ought to keep yourself straight all the time; you think good.*

TIM. *I told you I think good when I'm messed up, too. I jus' don't say nuth'n . . .* (Pause) *I'll let you go. I know you ain't had no supper yet.*

BROTHER. *Yeah, I'll tell you, I been running all day.*

TIM. *Okay. I'll see you later man.*

BROTHER. *Okay, see you later.* (He walks away, leaving Tim standing on the corner)

(The following are the lyrics of the song, *Runaway Child*, to which Tim referred in the previous conversation)

RUNAWAY CHILD, RUNNING WILD

You're playin' hookey from school, and you can't go out to play today. Yeah.

Momma said for the rest of the week in your room you've got to stay. Yeah.

Now you feel like the whole world's pickin' on you.

But deep down inside you know it ain't true.

Chorus: Whole world pickin' on me.

You've been dismissed cause your momma won't treat you the
    right way. Yeah.
But you don't care, cause you've already made up your mind you
    wanna run away. Yeah.
You're on your way.
Runaway child, runnin' wild.
Runaway child, runnin' wild.
Go back home, where you belong.
Roamin' through the city, goin' nowhere fast.
You're on your own at last.
It's gettin' late, where will you sleep.
Gettin' kinda hungry, you forgot to bring somethin' to eat.
Oh, lost with no money, you start to cry.
But remember, you left home wantin' to be grown, so dry your
    weepin' eye.
Yeah.
Sorry screamin' down beyond Ladder Street you want your
    momma.
Oh, they're lookin' for you—
You're frightened and confused.
Run! Run! Run!
She's much too far away, she can't hear a word you say.
You heard some frightening news on the radio about little boys
    runnin' away from home and the parents don't seein' em no
    mo.
You want to stop and hitch a ride and go home—
But your momma tole you never to trust a stranger.
And you don' know which way to go.
Streets are dark and deserted.
Not a sound, no sign of life.
Oh, how you long to hear your mother's voice.
Cause you're lost and alone.
But remember you made the choice.
Oh runaway child, runnin' wild.
Better go back home where you belong.
Runaway child, runnin' wild.
Better go back home where you belong.

You're lost in this great big city.
Go back where you belong.
Not one familiar face, ain't it a pity.
Chorus: Go back home where you belong.

Oh, runaway child, runnin' wild.
You better go back home where you belong. Oh, yeah.

Oh, momma, momma, momma, please come and see about me.
Oh!
But she's much too far away.
Can't hear a word you say.
You're frightened and confused.
Which way will you choose?

I want my momma, I want my momma. Momma, momma.

Listen to your heartbeat
Listen to your heartbeat
It's beatin' much too fast.
Go back home, where you belong.
Listen to your heartbeat
Listen to your heartbeat
It's beatin' much too fast.
Go back home, where you belong.

PART ONE

Stress in the New Arena

1

Introduction: Set Up For Encounter

This book is a case study of an experimental program in a San Diego, California, factory to hire hard-core unemployables as part of a 1968 nationwide program to alleviate conditions in the urban ghettos. The factory is given the pseudonym of Southwestern Aircraft. In this chapter we discuss the structure of the Southwestern program and the background leading to it, the riots of 1967.

But there they were . . . . rich white men trying to understand, as best rich white men can, why the slums of their "model city" had stirred.

Ditto took them by their minds and led them through an hour or so of black frustration and black despair, and told them how really angry black people are. He told them, because they had come had come to Blacktown to find out, that they could either let black anger take its well-known course, or they could get busy and relieve that anger. "If you cats don't do it, it's never going to get done . . . ."

(Charles L. Sanders, "Industry Gives New Hope to the Negro," Ebony, *June 8, 1968, p. 193.)*

Nineteen sixty-seven was the culminating year of civil disorders in American urban ghettos, and Detroit was its climax. Although in the four preceding years, beginning in 1963, riots had erupted in various cities, including Watts, Los Angeles, in 1965, the number and magnitude of disorders in terms of death, injuries, and physical damage, made 1967 worse than all four years combined, and worse than any single year in recent U.S. history. In that year, by Kerner Commission criteria, 128 cities experienced 164 disorders with 41 ranked as serious or major, occurring in 39 cities. Eighty-three people were killed, nearly 2000 were injured and 50 to 60 million dollars worth of property destroyed.[1] Major disorders developed in eight cities: Tampa, Cincinnati, Atlanta, Newark, Northern New Jersey, Plainfield, New Brunswick, and Detroit. Cincinnati, Newark, and Detroit were the most catastrophic, with Detroit alone accounting for 43 deaths and 42 to 45 million dollars worth of physical destruction. To bring this riot "under control," in addition to the Detroit police force of approximately 5,000 men, 800 state troopers, 9,200 national guardsmen, and 2,700 federal paratroopers were required. Before the curfew was lifted, 7,200 people were arrested. Besides side arms, shotguns, and rifles, machine guns, tanks, and almost the entire fire fighting resources of the city were used.[2]

Commencing in the early Sunday morning hours of July 23, riot activity peaked on the twenty-fifth, subsided on the twenty-seventh, paratroopers pulled out on the twenty-ninth, and Mayor Cavanaugh lifted the curfew August 1. In the August aftermath of contagion of alarm and violence, the reactions of government officials and civic leaders were dramatic but sharply divided. Detroit officials began preparing for Armageddon. The Detroit Common Council drew up a million-dollar military shopping list for the following:

> 1,000 M-1 carbines
> 200 12-gauge shotguns
> 100 Stoner machine guns
> 25 sharpshooting rifles
> 25 infrared "snooper" scopes

500,000 rounds of ammunition
1,500 flak vests
1,200 gas masks
5,000 mace dispensers
9,000 sets of fatigues
8 armored personnel carriers
4 mobile radio equipped vans
2 prisoner buses

Quite a different response was developing among leaders at the national level. Organized largely by the newly formed Urban Coalition, leaders of all major social sectors—business, labor, church, civil rights, and government—1,200 in all, held an emergency convocation in Washington, D.C., under the chairmanship of Andrew Heiskell of Time, Inc., and A. Philip Randolph of the Brotherhood of Sleeping Car Porters. At this meeting the Urban Coalition went on record in favor of massive emergency job programs for ghetto unemployed, with major expansion of the private sector's efforts to train and provide jobs for hard-core unemployed.

In response to these recommendations, President Johnson in January 1968 called for a National Alliance of Businessmen (NAB) and appointed Henry Ford II as chairman. NAB was to be the private sector half of a massive cooperative effort with the government. The federal Job Opportunities Business Sector program (JOBS) was the public sector half. Under Ford's chairmanship, NAB set a goal of 500,000 jobs for the hard-core by 1971—100,000 of them by June, 1969.[3] Fifty of the largest cities were selected where local NAB offices were set up under the directorships of prominent local industrialists. These offices went to work urging private firms to find jobs for the hard-core unemployed—with or without cost-of-training subsidies. By early 1970, through the NAB—JOBS effort, 23,520 companies had placed 300,000 hard-core people directly into their work forces. Encouraged by a 66 percent retention rate, NAB leaders were aiming at placing 614,000 hard-core workers on the business payrolls by 1971, instead of a half-million as originally planned.[4]

PREVIOUS EFFORTS

It would be a distortion to give the impression that there had been no previous action by business or government to place ghetto people in jobs. Starting in the early 1960s, especially after Watts, a number of businesses across the country launched emergency direct-action programs. As early as 1962 the Yellow Cab Company and the Shell Oil Company initiated and subsidized training programs designed primarily for people on welfare. In the immediate aftermath of Watts, H. C. McClennan of Old Colony Paint Company made a direct appeal to 100 company presidents in the Los Angeles area that resulted in 12,000 jobs for Los Angeles blacks. The STEP program (Solutions to Employment Problems) promoted by the National Association of Manufacturers was another effort. But until the 1968 NAB program and the special emphasis on direct hiring of hard-core unemployed ethnic minorities, private business programs tended to be spasmodic and to stress ethnic recruitment *per se*. In cases where "unemployables" were the focus, training for jobs was stressed as distinct from actual job placement, and these efforts in the aggregate involved far fewer numbers of people.[5]

In the public sector, government had been active for a number of years in manpower training programs for the disadvantaged poor. In 1964, various programs were inaugurated through the Office of Economic Opportunity, such as Job Corps, Neighborhood Youth Corps, Operation Mainstream, New Careers, and so on. The largest government input into expanding opportunities for the unemployed came through the Manpower Development and Training Act (MDTA) enacted by Congress in 1962. Administered jointly by the U.S. Department of Labor and the Department of Health, Education and Welfare, it was the first major manpower program ever to be enacted in the United States. It was motivated initially by the coexistence of manpower shortages in the midst of large manpower surpluses and by congressional recognition of the existence of a large population of Negro poor entirely outside the labor force. The underlying assumption was that government supported *training* programs would equip unemployed workers and permanently unemployed people to fill existing job vacancies. It was also assumed that federal support under MDTA would stimulate private sector employers, who had traditionally assumed the responsibility for training their employees, to expand their on-job training programs.

In addition, MDTA financed institutional training of "unemployable" people to upgrade their occupational and occupationally related skills, the lack of which were regarded as "constraints." This training was supposed to reduce the constraint thus permitting "natural" labor market dynamics to absorb the people into the labor force. Again, as in the case of private sector programs, overall MDTA emphasis was on training and upgrading skills to employment standards, rather than special access to existing jobs with training and counseling service provided on the job. In fact it was not until 1967 that the numbers of workers in the on-job training programs financed by MDTA equaled those in programs to prepare the unemployed prior to job placement. Up to that time, the ratio had averaged one on-job to four pre-job trainees.

By 1968 and the beginning of NAB, nearly 700,000 had been trained in some capacity by MDTA supported programs. If one adds other public financed programs like Neighborhood Youth Corps, Work Study, Work Experience, and Community Work and Training, several million disadvantaged people had received some form of special employment-related attention.

Precisely how many people enrolled in more than one program, or carried over from one year to the next or, more significantly, were becoming professional (repeater) trainees, no one really knows. What is significant is that on the eve of the 1968 crisis, the overriding emphasis in manpower training was on upgrading peoples' skills *prior* to job placement in business and industry. In 1967, for example, out of 1,434,900 people enrolled in all types of federally assisted manpower programs including MDTA, only 115,000 were on-job trainees in the private sector. The rest were enrolled in training programs *per se,* or in the Neighborhood Youth Corps, which for a number of reasons cannot be considered viable employment, although its training aspects must be considered.[6] Also, after five years of entirely new, large scale public policy experimentation in manpower resources, the public and private sectors were experiencing a rude awakening which revealed the profound depth of the problem. This awakening produced new insights which converged naturally with rhetorical interpretations of the catastrophic events of 1967.

Government people were beginning to see that although manpower training was effective in getting large numbers of people on the labor market, there remained a significant percentage who could not keep entry level jobs. When added to the numbers who could not succeed in getting viable jobs in the first place, this group became an enormous residual population sifting through the manpower training system. Just as criminal courts were confronted again and again with repeat offenders, manpower and welfare people were confronted with the repeatedly unemployed person.

In the private sector, hiring personnel became aware of the environment of the urban ghetto through interacting with people they might normally have seen only on television or encountered if their cars broke down in the slum section of a cross-town freeway. Out of these experiences came a more realistic concept of hard-core unemployment which implied basic changes for manpower training in the urban ghetto context. First, veteran public and private personnel workers were beginning to realize the population of hard-core unemployed was much larger than they had originally supposed. Rather than hundreds of thousands, there were millions—an estimated 4 to 5 million among disadvantaged minorities alone. Second, consensus was forming that in terms of measurable results, it was more practical to train the hard-core *after* employment than before. Third, it became evident that the effectiveness of on-job programs was related to how well industry met the special individual and cultural needs of the hard-core trainees while still maintaining *work-related* performance standards. In brief, two distinct social realities had to be dealt with. Finally, experience revealed that training the hard-core was not primarily a matter of teaching skills but a matter of deep social reorientation.

These insights formed independently in the context of steady experiences prior to the crisis of the summer of 1967, substantially reinforced the intuitions of Urban Coalition leaders and the deductions of the Kerner Commission. At different levels, and for different reasons, a large group of leaders were now saying essentially the same thing: The problem of the ghetto is enormous in terms of sheer numbers of people and their degree of social alienation from the economy. If any progress was to be made, huge numbers of people had to be assimilated into the economy rapidly. Direct job placement in business and industry was one of the major funnels for this transition, requiring extensive commitment of the private sector, special programming, and the willingness of government to help subsidize the extraordinary training costs involved.[7]

THE NAB-JOBS SYSTEM

Proposed in President Johnson's Manpower Message to Congress in January 1968, NAB was launched as a cooperative government-business program based on a radically new principle: hire first, then follow with on-job training and remedial counseling. The national NAB office selected 50 of the largest urban areas in which to establish local teams composed of a metropolitan chairman, local businessmen on loan from their respective firms, and a representative from the Department of Labor. The teams then went to work securing pledges from local firms to provide jobs for the hard-core. The overall objective was to gain commitment from a broad and expanding group of companies from all fields of business and all areas of the country.[8] NAB staff members also worked with local public and private organizations to identify and recruit hard-core applicants. In addition, where government training subsidies were involved, local offices expedited the paper work. Companies could receive cost subsidies for training by contract agreements with the Labor Department's office of Manpower Administration (MA). Amounts reimbursable ranged up to $3,500 per trainee per year, but cooperation by private business and government Manpower offices to hire the hard-core with or without formal contracts to help subsidize training costs came under the general rubric of JOBS.

Actually, the JOBS emphasis had an experimental stage preceding the formation of NAB. In June 1967, the Manpower Administration implemented an experimental program with private industry, asking companies in 10 major cities to bid on the training of 6,000 hard-core. Contracts were on a cost-reimbursable basis, running for 18 months and were entered into by private agencies who then subcontracted with businesses to train and permanently hire the trainee when they were satisfied he could do the job. The latter was an expectation but not an obligation of the subcontracting business firm. This JOBS program was known as MA-1. An extension of the program, MA-2, was started in November 1967, in five major cities. The MA-2 phase was also experimental and had a number of new features. It focused on incentives to move and expand industry into ghetto areas to take advantage of the ghetto labor pool; and the MA-2 contractor, unlike the MA-1 contractor, was the eventual employer of the people he was training. The contract was for a fixed price for 21 months instead of cost reimbursable for 18 months. There was also a 50 trainee minimum. Finally and most significantly, a bonus feature was added providing $3,800 per man for retaining hard-core as employees for at least six months beyond the 21-month period.

The MA-3 phase of JOBS coincided with the formation of NAB in January 1968, becoming an adjunct to the NAB program. The MA-4 program, following six months later, was basically a continuation of MA-3 but with new funding. Both programs eliminated the 50 employee-trainee minimum. The incentive factor was also eliminated because companies now had to agree to hire employees *prior* to training. Also, companies could form a consortium to enter into contract. The prime contract period was lengthened to 24 months with the training period subsidized by MA limited to 12 months per individual. Recruitment of the hard-core under MA-3 and 4 contracts was normally done by the Concentrated Employment Program (CEP) of MA.

But regardless of the numerous and varied recruitment practices that could be used to meet the terms of the contract, all trainees had to be certified by CEP offices or by state employment services as being hard-core. While on-job training had to be done by the contracting company, pre-job training and supporting counseling and training could be subcontracted to public or private agencies specializing in those services.[9] Thus with MA expertise in business-incentive programs sharpened by six months of experimentation combined with NAB organizations in 50 cities across the nation, the JOBS hard-core effort was enormously expanded and improved in terms of sheer numbers of hard-core hired and the *real* change in job opportunity it afforded them.

In order not to present too idealistic an impression of the national impact of the NAB-JOBS program, some analytical comment may be useful here. We cite Janger and Shaeffer's study of more than 100 NAB programs two years after NAB was launched.[10] On the plus side, these analysts include establishing the convention that hiring the hard-core is a necessary condition for preserving a favorable climate for business. The fact that NAB raised the JOBS target from 500,000 to 614,000 hard-core and that the number of companies making pledges increased from 500 to over 20,000 are also measures of success, as were the hundreds of thousands of hard-core actually hired and the 66 percent retention rate.

On the minus side Janger and Shaeffer cite the fact that companies employing more than 2,000 workers accounted for only 23 percent of MA-3 contracts. They show that a good part of the MA-3 effort as well as services of associated federally supported programs have been centered on moderate and smaller-sized companies and on forming training consortia of companies that employ less than 500 workers. This kind of emphasis, they say, raises the fundamental question of how much real opportunity is being provided the trainees in these positions. They reason that many smaller businesses already employ relatively large numbers of the marginal work force and consequently have openings that cannot be filled because these jobs do not pay enough to attract even the hard-core. They cite as evidence the complaints of some smaller company executives that it is harder for them to fill lower-level jobs since the NAB program opened the way to more desirable employment for the more able and ambitious disadvantaged.

In addition, Janger and Shaeffer remind us that NAB figures on hard-core placements and retentions include noncontract hard-core programs. Unlike the subsidized MA programs, no control procedures exist for validating the numbers pledged with the numbers actually hired or whether the hired individuals in fact meet the Department of Labor criteria of hard-core unemployed. They indicate that NAB figures are in fact challenged by some company executives on this basis.

A more fundamental but debatable criticism concerns the performance of the NAB program vis-à-vis the underlying philosophy of moving people into the labor force who are defined as permanently out of the labor force. Clearly this is a gray area of definition. How unemployed or underemployed must a person be before he is considered hard-core? Janger and Shaeffer conclude from their data that NAB figures do not in themselves reflect automatic deduction from the ranks of the "unemployable." They support this by citing the fact that some of the people hired in the special hard-core programs they studied were not unemployed but were instead working in jobs "below their capabilities." Moreover, they add that of the rest, "many observers" tended to believe most would have obtained jobs on their own eventually.

Arguing on the other side one can ask, what kind of jobs could they get? Low level, dead-end work, as this study demonstrates, is part of the experience of marginality which is what the concept of the hard-core unemployed is all about. Janger and Shaeffer themselves vitiate this criticism by concluding that the primary effect of the NAB program is to enable both the unemployed and the menially employed " . . . to move into better paid, more permanent, more challenging jobs, with better working conditions and opportunities for advancement." They quote Labor Department statistics on the national hard-core population hired as of November 1968, indicating that educational level averaged below the eleventh grade, unemployment averaged 24 weeks in the prior year, and annual family income averaged less than $3,000. Still, Janger and Shaeffer conclude that while some of the truly "unemployable" types—"individuals with police records, or no formal education to speak of, or severe mental or physical handicaps"—have been hired into NAB programs, "they have not been at the core of the effort" among the programs they analyzed.

At this point there are three facts we need to emphasize. The first is that jobs, or making people more occupationally mobile, is not the only type of development strategy for the urban ghetto. There are programs to increase entrepeneurship, such as those promoted by the National Business League and the Urban League. There are income maintenance programs, housing programs, special health and educational programs, all aimed at making the ghetto environment more viable. In addition, we must not forget the philosophies and strategies of militant separatists such as the Black Muslims, the Congress of Racial Equality (CORE), and the Manifesto of the National Black Economic Conference, which seek development outside the institutional structure—indeed, development by means of radical change *in* the existing capitalistic structure.

Second, in the emphasis on jobs, hard-core unemployed are not the only group receiving attention. An important example is the program organized by the Reverend Leon Sullivan called the Opportunities Industrial Center (OIC), designed to increase the employment options and mobility of all classes of black people. In mid-1969 more than 80,000 people were involved in various OIC training programs which are privately run and for for the most part privately funded.[11] We must also include the recent MDTA emphasis in its MA-5 program on the upgrading of minority and previously disadvantaged workers already in industry.

Finally we must emphasize that among programs by definition aimed at the hard-core unemployed, the NAB-JOBS program is but one of a multitude of public or private efforts of various scales and intensities and of varying local, regional, and national scope. In the private sector, there are businesses going it alone. In the public sector, there are government agencies training and employing hard-core unemployables independently of business. Also in the area of public-private sector cooperation, especially at the level of local businesses relying on state employment offices for identification of hard-core people, effort to hire hard-core may be entirely independent of the NAB program. That is, cooperation may consist in private businesses using the JOBS procedure of the Labor Department independently of NAB. Moreover, in the NAB program, efforts to employ the hard-core may not include MA contracts. Such efforts may be part of the NAB effort in terms of pledges and publicity, and reliance on state employment office hard-core certified applicants but without a government manpower contract and training subsidy. So the whole emphasis and effort on hiring the hard-core is broader than in the

NAB-JOBS Manpower Administration contract type of program that forms the basis of this case study.

All this aside, the NAB-JOBS program is the largest single program by almost any measure—numbers of hard-core people hired, number of businesses and state employment agencies involved, and money allocated to its purpose.

We stress another important characteristic of this program. In the closing days of 1967, in the atmosphere of emergency and alarm which prevailed, the program was a revolutionary idea. A fundamental restructuring of the labor market was implicit in its initial conception and operation in this atmosphere.

Southwestern and its parent corporation were among the first to respond to what they considered to be a call to emergency action. In actual practice, Southwestern, as did many companies, made a 180-degree shift in its screening practice to admit the hardest of the hard-core unemployables—people with police records, little or no formal education, and some with severe social-emotional handicaps. The principle underlying these practices may be termed the principle of compensatory opportunity, and we shall refer to it as the NAB principle.

HARD-CORE PERSONNEL SYSTEMS

Implicit in the NAB principle is a basic change in existing personnel practices in industry, because these practices constitute the mechanism of discrimination. Whether criteria are racial, cultural or simply economic, the consequences of existing systems of hiring, managing, training, and upgrading workers has been to "weed out" the same kinds of people. In fact the very concept "unemployable" derives its meaning from prevailing personnel practices.

How drastic a change in personnel systems was envisaged by the NAB program is evident in the numerous articles appearing in trade journals and special reports to business following the inception of NAB. Excerpts from a special report to business by the Research Institute of America in June 1968 illustrate this point:

An unprecedented challenge has been hurled at American business: to cooperate with the Federal Government in a bold national experiment to find jobs for 500,000 "unemployables".[12]

The report goes on to say that the experiment will work if industry " . . . is willing to *put aside* its selection standards, *relax* its discipline policies, *redesign* its entry jobs, provide *fundamental* training, cushion the impact of personal *frictions,* set guidelines for supervisors and absorb the *backlash*"—in short to effect an abrupt about-face in their personnel systems.

Almost two years later, summarizing the personnel practices of the 100 NAB programs they studied, Janger and Shaeffer[13] state that although there are companies who made basic changes in recruitment and selection procedures paving the way for a continued and significant influx of hard-core persons, these companies are at the extreme end of a continuum. "At the other extreme is the company whose NAB commitment carries with it no change whatsoever. It has always hired a certain number of marginal people, and this is the number it pledged to NAB." The majority of programs fall somewhere between these extremes and are characterized as experiments in hiring people "a cut below" existing minimum qualifications, but effecting no basic changes in normal recruitment and selection procedures.

Actually there are two issues here. One is the issue of systems through which the hard-core make the transition to industry and to what extent these systems differ from previous practices or, for that matter, from ongoing "normal" practices. The other issue concerns the degree to which hard-core systems are temporary or become integrated into personnel practices generally. If new systems are designed for the hard-core, does industry then have a dual system which lasts only for the duration of a specific program with reversion once again to a single conventional system when the program runs out? We contend that in industry generally, basic personnel systems changes are required for hard-core programs even if they are peripheral and temporary. Janger and Shaeffer themselves bear this out, showing that extraordinary practices obtained in every instance of their seven case studies.[14] With few exceptions, all testimony we have recorded on NAB and the hard-core, including firsthand accounts, tends to support our contention.[15]

Generalizing on the basis of Southwestern's experience and reports on NAB programs generally,[16] we see a need for three new systems designed to make the hard-core unemployables inputs instead of shutouts. First, the in-labor-force, or job-seeking population, has to be redefined. Put another way, a special system of communication has to be developed between the labor market and the newly defined "job seekers." This system boils down to on-the-scene recruiting, using professionals and semiprofessionals who themselves are members of ghetto communities. Different cities may use different combinations of agencies to accomplish this, for example, state employment offices located in ghetto communities, mayors' committees, churches, settlement houses, community action agencies, civil rights organizations, and even militant black and Mexican-American groups. Interviews with the 100 or so applicants for positions at Southwestern indicate that this type of recruiting had not altered their motivation for meaningful work. What was lacking was motivation to work at unsteady, low paying, low status jobs such as dishwashing, yard work and carwashing. The function of this recruiting system is obvious: to bring to the young ghetto population the message of the accessibility of jobs formerly unavailable to them.

Based upon criteria directly opposed to those normally used in screening applicants for industrial occupations, the second new screening system would employ a key concept: "subject to special obstacles to employment." These obstacles include being non-anglo, a history of being on welfare, long-term unemployment, job histories in obsolete skills, and arrest records. Because the NAB program with Manpower Administration contracts is federally subsidized for the nonproductive period of training, an industry must either hire applicants who are certified as "hard-core" by the state employment office or must see that the prospective trainees it hires through other channels receive this certification. Screening can be as simple as looking merely for the best of those certified or it can be a highly sophisticated, conscientious effort on the part of a company to develop a system that implements national strategy for meeting what many consider a national emergency.

Southwestern's screening system had three important characteristics: (1) it admitted those with arrest records (ranging from crimes of violence to nonsupport); (2) it screened out applicants who were "too qualified"—those certified as hard-core but who could, in the interviewers' estimations, eventually get stable employment; and (3) the interviewing staff took time—averaging an hour of intensive interviewing per applicant. The process allowed selection of not only the meek poor, but also the rebellious and the potentially violent poor as well.

The third new system would be training procedures. At Southwestern there were three stages: one month of classroom training, six weeks of on-job training, and job assignment. The daily classroom program in the first stage included one hour of remedial English using shop materials, plus a remedial reading series prepared by *Science Research Associates* and *Reader's Digest.* Another hour was given to remedial math, using shop blueprints and individually paced workbooks. Four hours were spent on shop instruction related to specific, potential job classifications. The shop courses were taught by the foremen who would supervise the trainee during his on-job training phase. One hour was also devoted to social problems with a focus on social legislation, civil rights, and the problems of minorities in general and of blacks in particular. Finally, there was one hour of group counseling focused on personal identity and personal decision-making. Southwestern also employed a program counselor who maintained close contact with each trainee throughout the program. He had to possess an inner toughness, an understanding of the trainees' situations and mentalities, and a knowledge of shop problems as well.

Training programs vary considerably. Most smaller companies, those with work forces of 500 or less, have no vestibule training, as the classroom phase is called. With quotas of only four or five hard-core, new employees are put in on-job training with special support, perhaps in the form of a work counselor.[17] Companies such as Lockheed, which is much larger than Southwestern, may have as much as 12 weeks of special classroom training.[18] Some companies may draw their hard-core trainees from government agencies or multicompany consortia who specialize in pre-job training. As a general rule, classroom training geared to the special needs of the hard-core is an integral part of NAB programs, and the social psychological aspect is a vital part of these programs.[19]

THE HARD-CORE PEOPLE

Who are the hard-core unemployed? In bureaucratically precise terms the NAB-JOBS definition is as follows:[20]

Poor persons who do not have suitable employment and who are either (1) school dropouts, (2) under 22 years of age, (3) 45 years of age or over, (4) handicapped, or (5) subject to special obstacles to employment . . . .

School Dropout. A school dropout is a person who was not graduated from a high school . . . .

Handicapped. A handicapped worker is one who has a physical, mental or emotional impairment or chronic condition which could limit work activities.

Special Obstacles to Employment. Individuals who are subject to special obstacles to employment are (1) unskilled workers who have had two or more spells of unemployment during the past year totaling 15 weeks or more, (2) workers whose last jobs were in occupations of significantly lower skill than their previous jobs, (3) workers who have family histories of dependence on welfare, (4) workers who have been permanently laid off from jobs in industries which are declining in their region (e.g., agricultural, coal mining) and (5) members of minority groups.

Poor Persons. A person will be deemed "poor" if he or she is a member of a family which (1) receives cash welfare payment, or (2) whose annual net income in relation to family size and location does not exceed the following income criteria:

Family size (number of members)	Income (nonfarm)	Income (farm)
1	$1,800	$1,500
2	2,400	2,000
3	3,000	2,500
4	3,600	3,000
5	4,200	3,500

Family size	Income (nonfarm)	Income (farm)
6	4,800	4,000
7	5,400	4,500
8	6,000	5,000
9	6,600	5,500
10	7,200	6,000
11	7,800	6,500
12	8,400	7,000
13	9,000	7,500

Person Who Does Not Have Suitable Employment. People who do not have suitable employment are (1) the unemployed, (2) the underemployed, and (3) those who should be working or seeking work but for various reasons are dissuaded from doing so.

(1) Unemployed. Unemployed persons are those who have no employment and are available for work and,

(a) Had engaged in any specific job seeking activity within the past four weeks, including registering at a public or private employment office; meeting with prospective employers; checking with friends or relatives; placing or answering advertisements; writing letters of application; or being on a union or professional register.
(b) Were waiting to be called back to a job from which they had been laid off.
(c) Were waiting to report to a new wage or salary job to be scheduled to start within the following 30 days.

Persons who would technically be classified as "not in the labor force" will be counted as "unemployed" the instant they say they are available for work and are registered through a component of any manpower program.

(2) Underemployed. Underemployed persons are those working below their skill capacity, or those who are or have received notice that they will be working less than full time in their industries or occupations, or, those who have received notice they will be unemployed because their skills are becoming obsolete.

(3) Those Not Seeking Work But Should Be. People not seeking work who should be are potential labor force participants. These are the individuals who would be working or looking for a job if they thought jobs were available. Also included in this category are those persons who do not seek employment because of their attitudes or motivational problems.

Member of Minority. Members of the minority are: Negroes, American Indians, Japanese, Chinese, Filipinos, Koreans, Polynesians, Indonesians, Hawaiians, Aleuts, Eskimos, Mexican-Americans, Puerto Ricans, and other people with Spanish surnames.

The "typical" hard-core person this definition covers:

Has a sixth grade education.
Has been unemployed for 18 months.
Has no skill training.
Has parents who were unskilled.
Lives with one-and-a-half families.
Is married with three children.
Needs eyeglasses and dental work.
Has seen a physician only once in his life.
Can afford to eat only twice a day.
Has no transportation.
Has had serious contact with the law. [21]

Some characteristics of the national hard-core population acutally participating in JOBS programs as of December 1968 are as follows:

Seventy-five percent were black.
Ten percent had Spanish surnames. (This includes Mexican-Americans, Puerto Ricans and some American Indians.)
The average level of education was below the eleventh grade.
Unemployment in the last year averaged 23.7 weeks.
Annual family income averaged $2,790.
Seventy-five percent were male.
Sixty-six percent were between 20 and 40 years of age, 23 percent under 20 and 11 percent over 40. [22]

Twenty-eight people were hired in Southwestern's hard-core program.

This group formed the basis of this study and is made up as follows.

1) Ethnic composition:

> Twenty-two black
> Two Mexican-American
> Two white
> One Puerto Rican
> One Italian-American.

2) All male.

3) Age:

> One under 20
> One over 40
> Twenty-six between 20 and 40
> Average age 28.

4) Education:

> Range fourth grade to twelfth grade
> Average 10.1 years of schooling.

5) Family household composition:

> Fifteen conventional husband/wife
> Seven cohabiting
> Two married but living singly
> Four single and living with mother.

6) Number of children:

> Seventy-seven children totally in all households
> Average of three children per household.

7) Income support:

> Only five of 28 households were *not* receiving public assistance.

8) Unemployment during year prior to NAB placement at Southwestern. The 28 trainees:

> Averaged 24 weeks without any work.
> Averaged 22 weeks underemployed—menial short-term jobs like dishwashing, busboy, carwashing and poverty program work.
> Averaged six weeks of mainstream-type of employment.

9) Arrest record excluding traffic citations and suspicion arrest with no charges:

> Only four of the 28 men had *not* had serious contact with the law.
> Twenty-four men had a total of 82 arrests on charges ranging from drunk and disorderly to strong arm robbery.

It is important to point out that all definitions presented here, official definitions by their very nature, derive from inside the social and economic mainstream and reflect only one set of facts about the hard-core. But a basic proposition of this study is that there is another set of essential facts that must be defined and digested before the hard-core experience can be understood. This set of facts springs from another vantage point—hard-core status and experience from the point of view of the hard-core themselves, from *outside* the social main-stream. This point of view has been discussed in a previous report on this study.[23]

Hard-core people possess a number of important American main-stream values in common with the working and middle classes. They aspire to meaningful occupations, good homes, and education for their children, and distinguish between rational and irrational behavior in terms of its effect on achieving these goals. But the essential difference between most hard-core participants and hard-core observers' view-points is the extent to which the hard-cores' failure to achieve their mainstream goals is judged to be a consequence of their own cultural system *per se* or a result of the normal operation of the American social system. The ethnic minorities who comprise the overwhelming majority of the hard-core unemployed, especially the younger ones, possess a strong rationale substantiated by numerous firsthand experiences that underwrites their own conception of themselves as colonized peoples. They see the NAB-JOBS program as one effort to undo the consequences of an unfair system.

All of the trainees . . . both black and white, are satisfied in their own minds as to why the NAB program was started; and my observations support their view. The furor caused by young revolutionary blacks has contributed immeasurably to the attention now being paid to the problem of the Negro poor. It reminds one of the revolutions that have shaken the European Colonies one by one. Just as peasants and tribal peoples in those revolutions gained recognition and a sense of their strategic value, so today poor blacks in American ghettos are important for the first time in their lives. Each of them now has a real choice between becoming part of a powerful separate element and becoming an integral part of American society. Suddenly they are wanted in that society because most Americans do not want them to go the other way. Being in such a strategic position means something in terms of personal and ethnic pride.[24]

This view is in direct opposition to the views of many, if not most, blue-collar workers.

The NAB program thus set the stage for the encounter of two culturally different classes of people—the working and the permanently nonworking—on a scale surpassing any previous engagement. It was not just the numbers of people thrown into contact, but the peculiar natures of the different classes and the nature of their contact which makes this experience significant. First, the contact occurred between two classes of people whose criterial social definitions and experiences were in direct opposition to one another. That is, the distinctiveness of each depended upon the existence of the other, and, more importantly, upon the continuance of their physical, social, and economic separation. Second this interaction was complex, occurring on both formal and informal levels between people of various ages and both sexes; it was prolonged and real as opposed to temporary and artificial, occurring every working day; and most significantly, in the work environment, the two classes interacted as *equals*.

There was another and equally important encounter: the juxta-position of the hard-cores' new industrial roles and relationships with old, ongoing relationships in the ghetto.

Both spheres of experience are examined in this case study.

2

The Plant: A Closed System Too Long?

Industry in the United States now is facing up to a task of awesome proportions, the task of realizing the National Alliance of Businessmen's goals of finding jobs for 100,000 hard-core unemployed by June 1969 and for 500,000 by June 1971 . . . . Few people questioned the advisability of undertaking this effort or the enlightenment and dedication of those companies supporting the NAB program. It is a job that necessity dictates and conscience supports.

(James D. Hodgson and Marshall H. Brenner, "Successful Experiences: Training Hard-Core Unemployed," Harvard Business Review, *46, 5 [September-October 1968] : 148.)*

Certainly neither a university, a business firm, nor a labor union . . . should discriminate among applicants upon any basis other than aptitude for learning and practicing its craft, but it *should* discriminate on this basis. (Italics added)

("Agnews Hour," Newsweek, *February 23, 1970, p. 24.)*

One of the implications of the NAB program was that industry contributes to hard-core unemployment by its personnel practices, and that converting the hard-core to industry depends in part upon changing these practices. However, this task is complicated by the fact that barriers to the hard-core exist at all levels; in screening, training, and discipline policies; in entry, upgrade, and layoff rules; and ultimately in the minds of the people already in the system whose self-interest may seem threatened by changes in the rules.

In the best of NAB programs under ideal conditions, planners and training personnel could not foresee let alone accommodate all major barriers. Such was the case for the planners at Southwestern. Although the company had access to training manuals developed and tested at the parent corporation's plant, its entire personnel, including training staff, foremen, and workers, were novices, faced with a new learning experience. But analyzing this experience reveals more than a collectivity of sympathetic and naive people learning together. It reveals the emergence and clash of economic interests, and the initial problem of naive people learning to be more effective in facilitating the hard-core's transition into the labor market evolved into the more complex issue of people learning to be more effective in preserving their relative advantages within the labor market.

The hard-core entered the factory organization by stages, and their impact on the factory evolved as they moved from the outer periphery to the center of the organization. Since these developmental stages of interaction were largely a natural consequence of the different phases of the training program, we discuss them as they evolved through time, from job application to job assignment.

SCREENING FOR WHAT?

Gary Nolan, a young white, was Southwestern's first applicant. His record included three prison sentences, two for marijuana possession and one for receiving stolen goods. An orphan almost from birth, he had spent much of his life in circuses, working with barkers and con men. Interviewers spent the first 20 minutes discussing Gary's background in terms of Southwestern's qualifications, and he responded by trying to convince the interviewers he would be a good risk. Midway through the interview the screeners began discussing the problem of whether or not he was really hard-core, probing to determine why he wanted the job. Gary became confused. Realizing that he had been building himself up too freely, he began tearing himself down, stressing how badly he needed the job. At one point an interviewer asked him to tell why he had used drugs. He answered that he lacked self-confidence and felt he wasn't a man because he could only get menial work such as carwashing, janitoring, or door-to-door selling, and he was desperate for a job that had status and stability. On the basis of his lack of normal qualifications he was hired.

Ambiguity is inherent in the hard-core screening process for obvious reasons. Industry, geared to a reward system based on efficiency, hires people who can produce the most for the least cost. Suddenly a national emergency confronts it with a new task: hiring people on the basis of their *lack* of qualifications and their need for help. Does one stress qualifications or lack of qualifications? Initially job screeners at Southwestern had to grope with this problem on their own with relatively little feedback, except that gained from exchanging their own experiences and the experiences of others engaged in job development and rehabilitation. This was the social philosophy phase. The second phase began when hard-core employees began to perform in the production line. Feedback then became harsh and direct, with comments like, "Are you guys scraping the bottom of the barrel?" "Can't you find better employees?" Thus the conflict inherent in the process was intensified. But this opposition from Southwestern's production-oriented people was a sign that the job screeners were fulfilling their responsibility to the NAB program, because if job interviewers had succumbed to this kind of pressure, the program would have been defeated. By definition all hard-core men are greater risks than normal; if these risks are not accepted the arrangement is fraudulent.

Obviously not all hard-core unemployed belong in a factory. For some, on-job rehabilitation is too late, or depending on one's optimism, premature. Sid Owens was a case in point. Sid had been in prison for six years—in county jails, in nonsecurity prisons, and in maximum-security prisons like San Quentin. He had a number of narcotics convictions and finally an armed robbery conviction with a sentence of five years to life. When Sid was interviewed, he perspired heavily, but remained calm and spoke slowly and deliberately.

> INTERVIEWER. *Now, since you've been out, you've been looking for work?*
> SID. *I did off and on, but I've never been able to get a job enough to support me. If I can get some substantial employment, I know I can make it, cause I've been out 16 months . . . .*
> INTERVIEWER. *Has anything in particular kept you from getting a job?*
> SID. *Well, I could have a job. I could be still doing a lot of these little jobs, dollar-fifty, inferior pay; and this is one of the things I guess I shy away from, because someday I want to get a decent job and be able to get married again and have a family.*
> INTERVIEWER. *Do you blame others for what has happened to you?*
> SID. *It's my own fault.*
> INTERVIEWER. *Can you look back and see at what point your attitude changed, and what caused it to change?*
> SID. *Seein' those guys in the institution, guys who never will get out. See guys goin' in the gas chamber, you know. You look at them and then look at yourself. And then you know. If you're intelligent enough, you can tell. Every type of motive that motivated your life, they've got a certain individual there that's carrying out that part. You see him walk in the yard.*

Sid was a tall, handsome black man. His attitudes and responses in the interview seemed sincere, and he was hired. He came to work Monday morning under the influence of heroin and by noon had been discharged. A month later he was arrested and charged with possession and selling of heroin.

Later, when Sid was interviewed in jail, he said that if this chance had come just a little sooner things would have gone differently. "I want to tell you that the moment they picked me up, the faces of you and those two white fellows appeared on my mind because I knew then that this was the chance that I had muffed." He confessed that he had been under the influence of heroin at the interview. This was his fourth day in jail, and he was still shaking. He had been forced to withdraw without medical aid. The only thing he had for relief was cigarettes.

He kept repeating, *"I only wish that you had reached me in time."*

Eventually the first five hard-core trainees for the first class at Southwestern were hired; four black and one white, all with records and very little employment experience, and all risks.

CLASSROOM: RELEARNING VS. LEARNING

If we extend familiar logic, that is, deeply ingrained thinking habits, to new experiences, do these experiences teach us anything? Or does learning involve a reshaping of the very mental and emotional structures that turn experience into knowledge? The concept of a classroom suggests the first proposition, that the barriers to social mobility are lack of knowledge and wrong knowledge rather than how experience becomes knowledge. The way the hard-core are defined and the broad outlines of NAB objectives tend to support the second proposition.

Monday, July 29, 1968, the first class of five men started classroom training.

All of these men had had experience in formal classroom settings. For most it was experience in failure. An argument could be made that this aspect of the program tended to reinforce that failure. Certainly the whole philosophy of the traditional classroom setting in hard-core training must be rationalized in a way that is consistent with the concept of hard-core unemployed. By definition the hard-core are fugitives from traditional learning. They are turned off and shut out by the system of transmitting knowledge from an expert to a novice with the latter being graded in a competitive situation in terms of how well he can remember or manipulate the ideas of the former.

But classroom setting was only one dimension of the trainees' learning experience; course structure was another. Courses such as Basic Skills and Shop were objective in content, but courses like Social Problems and Personal Affairs were subjective and, depending on their structure, ran the risk of casting the trainee in a demeaning role, another all too familiar experience for him.

A third dimension was the teacher, in terms of whether or not his personality and social philosophy offset or reinforced formal settings and pedantic, patronizing tendencies in courses. The effects of some courses were harder to offset that others. Personal Affairs especially, was permeated with white middle-class bias. As taught by Mr. Solomon, the first of its three instructors, it was a vivid stereotype of the trainees' classroom past.

Solomon was timid, formal and polite, referring to the trainees as "gentlemen" and "Mister." They in turn called him "grinner" because he had a frozen grin most of the time, especially when irritated. His subject matter was appropriate to a junior high school, and he made frequent use of films to project middle-class values. On the fourth day of class, Solomon showed a 15-minute training film featuring a white teenager living in an upper-middle-class, suburban neighborhood with a kind and understanding father who wore neckties and suits in his own living room. The boy in the film asks for an advance on his allowance because he can't afford to take his girl to the high school prom. The father refuses because the boy is spending more money than he should. The boy sits pensively in his room looking at a half-dollar. Gradually the image of Ben Franklin on the half-dollar dissolves into a dream where Ben Franklin comes to the boy and tells him how he should save his money and budget his expenditures. In the dream Ben Franklin points to an example in "modern" (1939) life of a frugal person who goes to the bank every two weeks to deposit his savings so he can accumulate the total needed to buy a new car *before* buying the car. When the amount has been accumulated, he withdraws his savings, presents it in its entirety to the dealer, and ceremoniously drives out with a brand new car. From this daydream, the boy learns his lesson and revises his conduct.

In the course of the movie, trainees Tim Carter and Bobby Hill peppered the class with raucous comments on the actors' queer mannerisms. Solomon apologized for the movie's age, but dutifully summarized its object lessons. During this recital Bobby and Tim had a mock argument as to whether one should go around with a written budget in his hands or whether the budget should be in his head. Solomon interrupted his lesson and rebuked them. Bobby ignored the rebuke and continued to argue. Tim simply pulled down his shades. Solomon didn't like Tim's copout any more than Bobby's belligerence and began to call on him in teacher-pupil fashion. Each time, Tim would grunt that he hadn't heard the question. Solomon would repeat it, and Tim would respond with a one-syllable answer. After some time, Solomon tired of the repetition and gave up.

In contrast to Solomon, Jones, a shop instructor, had a style the men liked. He appealed to each man directly by patting him on the shoulder or handing him a tool as he mentioned him by name. Of course, shop instructors had the obvious advantage of concrete subject matter, and shop learning was more clearly relevant to the workers' role. But success reinforcement is decisive in hard-core rehabilitation, and Jones, in common with many line foremen, had learned that the reward system of supervision gets the best results.

Shutler, teaching a course called Social Problems, had an altogether different style and philosophy. Like Solomon, he was white, and some of the black trainees resented him because he lectured on black problems. His loud voice earned him the nickname, "Loudspeaker." He had an informal lecture style that contrasted sharply with Solomon's dull style. One day, following Solomon's class, Tim and Bobby continued to sleep in Shutler's class as they had in Solomon's. In contrast with Solomon's petulant concern for such behavior, Shutler paid no attention.

At first, Shutler's attempts to speak to black problems were resented by the black trainees. Tim would say, "He really doesn't know. Those are just works that he is using." But gradually, Shutler changed from lecturing on the black point of view to dwelling on the alternatives to violence. He spent weeks explaining the legal and social means powerless people could use to obtain their rights. For example, during one class he discussed the industrial growth of the United States as it related to major wars and the Negro migrations out of the South.

On this day Tim jumped into the discussion with the comment, typical for him, "None of these wars are gonna be like the next war!"

Shutler queried, "What war?"

"The one between the black and white!" Tim responded. And instead of arguing the point as Solomon would have done, Shutler launched into an analysis of how such a hypothetical war might be waged.

One benefit of Shutler's teaching was his demonstration that a white person could be sensitive to minority problems. Another benefit was a developing group consciousness of the problems different ethnic groups had in common. But there was an even more important consequence: Shutler cleverly exploited the potential of old social realities to develop new insights into the trainees' experiences.

Dillon, a third instructor, used a full range of reading and math materials from first grade to college level. His class was completely unstructured. The men could work or not work, talk or be silent, sit or stand, so that the class became a voluntary tutorial program. In the classes we observed, half or more of the men consistently refused to participate. The assumption underlying Dillon's method was that the inherent motivation of the individual would be sufficient to lead him to get the help he needed. For a cross-section population, perhaps, this assumption might be valid. For a population defined in part as school dropouts, the assumption was logically inconsistent.

ON-JOB TRAINING AND LINE

The first contingent of five hard-core trainees arrived at the Plant Maintenance Department on Monday, August 30, 1968, for six weeks of on-job training. News of the NAB program had leaked out before the company had started constructing the classroom facilities on the second floor of building 39, creating the first of many problems to follow. One of the department heads who had waited a long time for new office space protested on seeing the space he coveted being converted into classrooms for the NAB program. Rumors circulated as the facility was built, until the training department held an orientation session with the foremen of Plant Maintenance a week before the first class was scheduled to meet.

At this session one of the foremen told Harper, vice president of Personnel, that some of his men were saying that they had been at Southwestern for varying numbers of years and had therefore earned the special privileges that were being given to the newcomers.

Harper explained, "These people have not had any way of upgrading themselves, whereas the old employees have. If any of the older employees want to go to night school, the company will help with their tuition and arrange their work schedule to allow free time."

In addition, six foremen in Plant Engineering had also served as shop teachers, and their biases were conveyed to the men on the line. During the final week of classroom instruction, management held two more orientation sessions.

In one way or another, everyone was conscious of the gut issue, the issue of a compensatory opportunity whereby a special group of people were being given economic advantages that blue-collar workers were being denied by virtue of their success. A management-union confrontation seemed inevitable as the trainees moved out of the classroom to on-job training and to sharply altered roles. This transition also affected the roles of those directly concerned with the trainees' progress. The role of counselor became more complicated as pressures on the men sharpened and spread. He became more deeply involved in the men's personal lives, getting them out of jail, counseling in domestic squabbles, getting licenses, settling traffic tickets and credit problems, and so on.

However, the most drastic transition was felt by the foremen, who initially were openly skeptical about the program. But as they became teachers they began to identify with the trainees, and when the latter moved to the on-job training phase, the same foreman often would find himself in a combined tutorial and supervisory relationship, responsible for production, but responsible also for teaching his students.

LAYOFFS!

Two weeks after the beginning of on-job training, seven men in Plant Maintenance were laid off; an event, as it turned out, equal in magnitude to the advent of the hard-core program itself, for it signalled the beginning of a general slowdown in industry. The issue of compensatory opportunity became compounded with the issue of diminishing general opportunity.

The union reacted immediately. On the formal level it pressured the company by filing grievances with management, arguing that the layoff should affect the trainees first. The company's general position was that if it complied, the program would end. The "general helper-learner" category was the key element in the on-job training phase, permitting trainees to work at a variety of jobs. But layoffs had occurred in the area of mechanics, plumbing, and electricians and carpenters—basic on-job training areas. The union ruled helpers to be forbidden from operating powered equipment or doing any task normally assigned to mechanics, plumbers, electricians or carpenters. If the company wanted the trainees to do such jobs, it would be obliged to hire back the men who had been laid off.

Management's response to the union was to manipulate the job placement process in such a way that the hard-core could be retained.

By October 7, 1968, the eleventh week of the NAB program, the first contingent of men were assigned to the production line, the second class of men began their third week of on-job training, and the third class of trainees started their third week of classroom training. The issue of compensatory opportunity raised in the beginning was now linked with another issue—rising general unemployment—greatly increasing initial tensions. What was happening at Southwestern reflected the national economy in microcosm. To underline the importance of this issue and to show why it became more critical to the union than it might otherwise have been, we will explore national and local background.

MANAGEMENT—THE FIRST FAMILY

For better or worse, Southwestern's management took the primary responsibility for initiating the hard-core training program. The union was informed but was not active. This is not surprising when one looks back on the thrust and tone of the NAB movement. The NAB's appeal was not from the black community to elected political leaders at the regional or national levels, nor was it to the unions. By and large these avenues of influence were closed to the black community. The 1967 message was direct, urgent, and dramatic from the urban ghetto to the corporate mentality of industrial America, and for one brief summer the black community had the attention of the entire United States.

Black leaders took advantage of this to appeal directly to those in the topmost positions in the industrial economy. The message was clear: "Do something!"

The result was NAB, a kind of high-powered United Community Campaign, with pressure beginning at the top of the industrial economy and trickling downward in chain-of-command fashion. Commitment to its principles varied from organization to organization and among individuals in those organizations. A sincere commitment to the ghetto in terms of restructuring priorities from efficiency and profit to human rehabilitation was implied in the rhetoric of black leaders, but the business world saw a clear threat to profits that impelled it to bring the ghetto into the industrial labor force. Both blacks and corporate leaders recognized institutionalized inequality. The cure was believed to be compensatory opportunity, administered by the captains of industry, the capitalists.

But two essentials were overlooked: (1) the capitalist in America had long since yielded much of his control of the industrial system to organized labor and (2) capital as well as labor had a stake in institutionalized inequality. If compensatory opportunity was to achieve its goals, the issue had to be resolved by the institutions who exercised powerful control over the industrial system to which the black community was seeking access.

Many of the officials at Southwestern were opposed to the NAB program. To many of the people in various levels of management, "hard-core" simply meant people who preferred welfare to work, in short, unworthy people. It is doubtful that Southwestern would have started the program if the corporate offices had not applied pressure directly on the president of the company, which was transmitted to lower executives and department superintendents. Many individuals in the process of carrying out their assignments, became personally committed. Others resisted any commitment.

Southwestern management's NAB activities fell into three natural periods: the pre-layoff period, the immediate post-layoff period of initial union confrontation, and the period of quiet confrontation. The pre-layoff period ran from June 1 to September 13. Management put the program into gear, built the facility, organized the NAB administrative structure and gave it a name: "Direct Opportunity Training Center," DOT for short. Class instructors were assigned, union officials were briefed, and initial orientation sessions were held with the foremen of Plant Maintenance where DOT on-job training was to be centered.

Action was simple and direct, setting a pattern. When Don Miller, DOT director, lined up his foremen, he did so with no input and a minimum of communication. Kenneth Johnson, one of the key foremen in the program, said that when DOT was being planned, Miller asked him to teach a class. Johnson thought the request involved simply an upgrade training class for workers in his shop, and he agreed. However, he knew no details of the training program until a memorandum and a class schedule were issued a week before the first class.

When Johnson saw that he was to be responsible for four hours of instruction, he protested to Miller that this would conflict with his responsibilities in his shop. Miller then rescinded the plan and spent the remaining week hastily seeking the cooperation of other foremen to teach the extra hours.

Management's pre-layoff relations with the union had slightly different and perhaps more subtle repercussions. A number of people in management claimed the company intended to bring the union into the situation only at some later date, others insisted that the union was informed every step of the way.

Informants in the union hierarchy had a different interpretation, saying that management informed them early in June, at which time union officials agreed in principle to the program. But they insisted they were not given all the facts, which became clear only much later.

There were numerous signs confirming the fact that the DOT program was primarily management's responsibility. For example, there was no union representation during the orientation sessions. Although communication between management and union did exist, there was no pattern of unity between management and union in a common cause, and no public display of such unity. Another indication was the fact that Southwestern trainees were not members of the union during the classroom phase. This meant that for four weeks DOT men, employees of Southwestern, a closed shop, were nonunion members.

Despite high level consultations on formal matters, DOT operational policy fell far short of an honest dialogue with the union. DOT men moved between two clearly marked domains in dealing with union and management, and this pattern continued throughout the program. The union thus felt free to put its self-interest ahead of the program, and it did so with impunity.

UNION AND THE WORKING MAN OR WHAT "THESE HARD-CORE GUYS DON'T REALLY WANTA WORK" REALLY MEANS

Like environmental pollution, the key issue today in unequal opportunity is not racism as much as how to liquidate our investment in racism. Like the cleanup of our air and water, compensatory opportunity means transforming the social and economic infrastructure by which upper, middle and even the working classes have achieved the differential advantages they enjoy. This fundamental reality goes beyond simply saying, "We're against pollution or against racism or unequal opportunity." It means classes giving up some of their advantages. It means refusal to honor promises implicit in class structure, many of which originated in racist practices. This strikes at the heart of union interests. Management can ignore this reality more easily than the union, whose chief business is the protection of a system of screening, job entry, and upgrading that favors its clientele.

Before the September layoffs, union officials saw the NAB program as a threat in theory, but after layoffs, it loomed as a threat in fact. It became a *personal* issue. There is no way to determine whether the union would have taken this same attitude, had it been involved in the planning of DOT from the beginning. The chances are that its conflict of interest would have been too great to surmount. Perhaps Harper knew this intuitively and took the only available course that would give management maximum latitude in the maneuvers it would inevitably have to make to protect the trainees. In addition, it seems reasonable that Harper suspected in advance that layoffs were coming. Knowing this, he would also suspect that when the layoffs did occur the union could only act as it had done. Of course, this line of reasoning is highly deductive.

The union's first move after layoffs was to file verbal and written grievances. The first grievance protesting nonmembership of trainees while in the classroom, was written, and filed about mid-July and was still not yet resolved by the end of October 1968. The second grievance was filed toward the end of August coinciding with rumors of layoffs which took place in fact on September 13. This grievance protested the classification of trainees as general helper-learners and the tasks they were performing in Plant Maintenance. The union's position was that *general* helper-learners could carry tools and clean up, but could not perform any operation of any *particular* job classification. This they could do only by being assigned as learners in that classification.

More verbal and written grievances were filed in October. Most centered on the use of power tools. In addition to laying men off, the company downgraded a number of men in job classification. These men were especially bitter about seeing trainees doing "finished work," a definition which they extended to include the use of hand power saws, jackhammers, hammers to put boards in place, and almost any job except the carrying of tools and the use of brooms, shovels, and rags. Management accepted the tool grievances and prohibited trainees from using any tools in finish operations in job categories where layoffs had occurred.

By October 21, the thirteenth week of the NAB program, the confrontation between union and management had reached its peak. The third class of trainees were beginning on-job training, and a fourth group were starting classroom instruction. There were now 17 trainees assigned to production, 15 of whom were working in the department where the layoffs had occurred. The union continued to attack the concept of general helper-learner. It filed grievances against the trainees for using tools, working alone, performing unauthorized tasks, and so on. If the company wanted a trainee to gain experience in a particular job, the union insisted that he be classified as a learner for *that* job rather than a *general* helper-learner. Union strategy was based on seniority procedures outlined in the 1966 contract which would force the company to rehire the men who had been laid off.

In addition, committeemen and union activists carried the battle directly to the trainees. They accused the trainees of being responsible for the recent layoffs. They made oblique references to striking and patrolled areas where trainees worked.

Paul Galvão's experience was an example of such union pressure. Paul was being trained as an automobile service attendant. Union men patrolling his area warned him that he could not work on motors, touch any wrench, or perform any job other than changing spark plugs, batteries, fanbelts, and tires. Paul was furious.

(Padfield.) I discussed the situation with a union committeeman: "It looks at this point that if this continues, the only thing the company can do is cancel the program and fire the trainees."

He argued, "Well, no, I don't think so. They could put them in jobs in the plant where no layoffs had occurred, and if they want, they can upgrade them to job classifications which would authorize them to do the work which they were beginning to do now. My only complaint is that the company had them doing work out of their classification. If they want to call these men mechanics or have them do mechanics' work, let them upgrade them to mechanics."

Another committeeman then interrupted, "Well sure, and then they've got to hire back all the mechanics that have been laid off—That's all they have to do!"

The first committeeman then added that if such placement problems had been worked out with the union in advance there would have been no confrontation. He said bitterly, "Lack of communication is our biggest problem in this company!"

I asked him, "What are we going to do about the millions of hard-core people that we've got in the United States?"

He replied, "Well, that's not my problem. My problem is simply to see that the contract is adhered to." He then argued, "If you're going to solve this hard-core problem, then at the same time, you're developing another hard-core problem. Look at those kids that can't find jobs—the ones that got out of high school and aren't going to college. They are good kids, and they're trying to find work too, and they can't find it! Pretty soon they're going to have records, then what are you going to do?"

Illustrating his point, he added, "My daughter is friends with some of those kids. They are good kids otherwise. But I won't let my daughter go with them. I tell them if they can't find jobs, to start washing dishes—which these fellows (the trainees) won't do .... They've got to work at something!"

"Do you think there's racial prejudice involved?" I asked.

The committeeman snapped back, "We've got some colored people in the union; they agree with the union position. There's Ernie Hicks who is deputy shop steward. He backs the union position now against the training program. Even though most of the trainees are Negro, this doesn't matter to Hicks because he's a union man!"

Union tactics, formal and informal, had completely altered the training program. The concept of general helper-learner was dropped. Now management's primary objective was keeping the trainees. Training was secondary. Management's defense, just as the union's offense, was based upon interpretations of the 1966-1969 contract. According to this contract, longevity procedures were specific to occupational categories. For instance, an individual with five years of seniority in a specific occupational category, such as maintenance mechanic, might rank relatively high in seniority in terms of the company's work force as a whole but still be the junior man in maintenance mechanics and hence subject to the next layoff in that classification. He has the right to request a transfer to another occupational classification, but if transferred, he loses what longevity he has accumulated in his previous classification, and he takes precedence over a new employee only if the senior man requests his transfer prior to the new employee's date of transfer.

At this point in the training program, management concentrated on placing trainees in departments where layoffs had not yet occurred. The union counteracted by anticipating these categories and advising its members who were threatened by layoffs in other categories to request transfer at a lower grade *before* management transferred the trainees. This strategy meant having access to information that only management had. As a result of this and the seniority rules in the 1966 contract, the union was limited to a relatively narrow range of tactics in protecting its aggrieved members. But as we shall see in Chapter 8, strategic plans for the long range battle were beginning to take shape within the union council chambers.

MANAGEMENT RESPONSE—THE "FIXTURES"

By mid-October, Plant Maintenance had absorbed all of the trainees for on-job training. But because Plant Maintenance had also sustained all of the layoffs, the trainees in this department were too localized, too visible, and hence too vulnerable to union pressure. Now a third class of seven men were ready for on-job training, and a fourth class were beginning classroom instruction. In order to find openings for these trainees before the union could react, DOT had to divert them as rapidly as possible to other departments.

Miller hastily improvised a supplemental classroom program for the new trainees, arranged for minimum blueprint instruction, and kept the trainees marking time while he searched Southwestern's entire operation for jobs. With the help of the personnel employment section, some jobs, such as fixture cleaners, assemblers, material processing, and machine tool operators were found. However, none of these jobs was taught in the classroom phase. When the nine trainees in Maintenance were prohibited from using tools, on-job training was effectively dissolved. Now the pre-job training program was partially obviated, making the whole training aspect of the program a casualty of the union's attacks.

(Padfield) At this stage in the conflict, I asked Jerry McClure, the head of Line Relations in the Personnel Division, if it wouldn't have been better if management had discussed the entire program with the union from the beginning. He answered that he didn't really understand my question because this *was* done, and the union officials had found the program acceptable.

I asked if the company had asked the union for suggestions for placing the trainees. He said, "No!"

I also asked if they had talked to the men on the floor and in the shop. He responded, "We can't sell the individual union members on any program that may have certain areas of disagreement with the union. Otherwise they would jump on us for that. The company had assumed the committeemen had talked to the men on the floor, but there must have been a breakdown in communications."

In his opinion the layoffs were the sole cause of the disagreement. He also pointed out that in the near future the local union would be nominating a new slate of officers, and all of the members wanted to appear responsive to the floor and especially to the men who had been laid off.

He also stated that Larry White (chief shop steward) was convinced that the trainees were going to remain in the company for a year anyhow, and every time a disagreement between management and the union arose concerning trainee placement White would say, "Well, we can look for the fixtures to be reclassified."

McClure concluded, "The program has been forced to change and perhaps for the better."

This last point is difficult to accept. To even the most casual observer it was apparent that management had made basic concessions to the union without going to National Labor Relations. Perhaps these concessions were necessary to save the trainees. Perhaps the company acted for important reasons unrelated to the hard-core programs, such as the impending negotiations for the 1969 contract. But to most participants and observers, including the authors, these concessions had weakened the program considerably.

Another event that coincided with the October showdown was the withdrawal of Harper from the training center's decision-making operation. At the beginning of the union confrontation, Miller was consulting with Harper on almost every detail. But by the end, Harper had withdrawn almost entirely from the situation, leaving the major decisions of job classifications to Miller.

By the end of October as DOT began shifting trainees in and out of departments and job assignments, Miller began taking them into the company's confidence and revealing to them the tactics management was using to thwart the union. Handling the men in this way made them even more visible and vulnerable than before. They soon assumed all the aspects of being "fixtures" owned by management.

There were many such displays of management paternalism. Some of the job classifications were above the initial competence of the trainees. In addition to the regular classes, special blueprint reading instruction was initiated to help the trainees qualify as learners for assembler or machine tool operator. Also, pressure was exerted on the screening interviewers in these programs to accept the trainees. Management paternalism frequently carried over into union affairs. The DOT staff and occasionally even the director of Line Relations urged the trainees to pay their union dues, and also encouraged the trainees to set up a credit union savings program with payroll to accumulate capital for these dues.

Because of its protective policy, management soon found itself being manipulated by the trainees. For example, one morning in November the foreman of Material Processing called the DOT staff to complain that Darrell Johns hadn't reported for work. The following day when Darrell's wife called to ask if someone could come and take him to the hospital, Miller drove out immediately and delivered Darrell to the hospital for an examination.

Miller was not only protective; he was possessive. He moved his trainees without following the established procedures or consulting with supervisors, foremen, and superintendents. This led to morale problems in the supervisory circle, even among those who were staunch supports of the NAB program.

SUPERVISORS—THE MEN IN THE MIDDLE

Communications between management and the foremen were as lax as those between management and union. All foremen, supporters as well as opponents of the program were equally uninformed. Most of the foremen were interested in the trainees. Moreover, sooner or later, the trainees would have to relate to their foremen and vice versa, and Miller's unilateral actions did little to foster these new relationships. Ironically these actions frustrated the supporters of the program more than the opponents or the neutrals.

One such supporter was Kenneth Johnson, a foreman who sympathized completely with management's effort to keep the trainees. He realized that it was essential to assign them to jobs which the union could not touch, but he believed in doing so according to the rules.

He insisted that part of the reason for union-management difficulties was that " ... 90 percent of the supervisory people at Southwestern had never been informed of this program, let alone what the intent or operation of it is! None of the shop workers have ever been given any information on this, and suddenly the shop looks up and five hard-core workers walk in ready to go to work!"

He added, "When Miller talks to the supervisors in Plant Maintenance it's only by accident—many times. We finally assign them so that Miller is given in to; then he will change his mind without anyone knowing about it."

An example of this came in mid-October when Miller was moving men from job to job, the same man sometimes twice a week. Johnson had just begun to make headway with Gary Nolan and Jack Davis when Miller informed him that they were being transferred. Johnson had reached the end of his patience. He refused to allow the transfer and threatened to resign. In this instance, Miller conceded.

Johnson continued, "There are procedures in transferring people. There is no problem in transferring so long as procedures are followed. No one would block it. People have to know where their men are. Doesn't Miller know that? They should be contacting the union on these things. I've found the union cooperative in every case where we've needed to transfer a man to a certain job or change his status—I can't understand this business!"

Johnson voiced another criticism: "Miller is telling these men that they are going to go here and they're going to go there, and they're telling them this when this hasn't been worked out, and they know very well that it hasn't been worked out! A man shouldn't be moved or shouldn't be told anything until it's all settled, otherwise you're going to get a breakdown in morale. That's no way to handle men!"

Communication with management was not the only source of stress in the supervisory system. The hard-core and the controversy surrounding them were challenging foremen to develop new sensitivities and new relationships with the trainees and among themselves. Regardless of how one stood on the basic policy implication of the NAB program, the actual presence of people from the ghettos, and the necessity of dealing with them as individuals created a new dimension of experience for the foremen. Just as layoffs and rumors of layoffs personalized the NAB issue for the union and the wage worker, person-to-person encounter and personal involvement began to flesh out the bare bones of the program for the participating supervisors. It was only natural that the dimension of personal experience would be for them quite different from that of the union or management because of the differences in their respective roles and responsibilities. In addition, the initial philosophy and attitudes of each foreman toward the issue of compensatory opportunity and its class and racial implications would help to determine the kind of personal experience he would develop.

Some foremen who were intellectually committed to the NAB principle and minority causes were too naive to be effective supervisors. Others who supported the principle saw it chiefly as a gracious gesture on the part of the government to enable under privileged people to become upstanding middle-class citizens. Their effectiveness was limited primarily to the more docile kind of trainee who was used to hard work but simply lacked the technical skills necessary for industry. Such hard-core types were in the minority.

Some foremen were decisively opposed to the whole concept of NAB and were reluctant participants in the supervisory teaching system. Others were ambivalent. Like the naive foremen, they could not interpret much of the behavior of the men, but unlike the naive foremen, they felt threatened by their unfamiliar attitudes and mannerisms. Others were uncommitted but cooperated for political reasons.

The most effective foremen were committed and were able to set standards without insisting upon cultural and racial conformity. Kenneth Johnson belonged in this category. Originally against the program, he nevertheless taught classes and supervised a number of men on the floor. He began taking a personal interest in his men and by October was strongly supporting the trainees as well as the program. Above all, Johnson knew his role. He was a foreman—not a union or a company man. He identified with the trainees, but did not let them use him. During the height of the union conflicts, Johnson often said, "This is a bunch of nonsense, because how are they supposed to learn anything if they don't handle tools!"

It was in Johnson's shop that the union warned Paul Galvão against using tools as an automobile service attendant. Regarding this incident, Johnson said that he knew he had Paul doing work not specified in the job classification, but said he believed in pushing the union a little, not necessarily for the sake of harrassing it, but to accomplish the work that needed to be done and to test the trainee. Furthermore he believed it was the union's responsibility to know what these jobs entailed.

Johnson wasn't anti-union. He simply wasn't pro-union. He understood the union point of view, but with regard to using tools, he said, "It hasn't a leg to stand on because a general helper can use tools according to union contract, and this is just another indication that the union is focusing on the training as a sort of scapegoat for cutbacks and layoffs which Southwestern would have regardless of whether it had a hard-core training program or not!"

Johnson cited two workers in his shop who had received down-grades. This represented a drop in their wages. "They are bitter! And they're directing their bitterness toward the training program. But they're not really against the training program itself. They are simply sensing in it a desire on the part of the company to put cheaper labor into doing some of the work that they have been doing as skilled journeymen. And of course the union resents this!"

Ken fought for his trainees. He fought union pressure, he fought Miller's transfer strategy when he felt it disrupted their training, and occasionally he fought his own instincts to keep from terminating them. Gary Nolan was one of Johnson's men. Gary's background was as traumatic as that of any of the trainees at Southwestern and included heroin addiction. Being white, was perhaps, his only advantage. He was in the first class and had stayed on the job improving until his eighth month (March, 1969), when he suddenly started missing blocks of days. Everyone who knew him, including the DOT counsellor, knew what this meant.

(Williams). During one of his prolonged absences, I drove out to his run-down apartment where I found him crashed out with two of his friends. Gary argued that he had a cold and an ear infection. I argued that he should come to work. Finally he agreed, and the next morning he punched in.

But within a matter of days Gary was back on the ropes. He had now accumulated over two weeks of absences. At the plant, Johnson was as disturbed as we have ever seen him. He said he felt Gary was "messing him over," because he had given Gary as much of a break as he'd given anybody.

He stressed that Gary had missed 13 days since he had been working and added, "You know this wouldn't be so bad, but here I gave another guy four days suspension and a warning when there are other people in the department, and I don't seem to take offense when they take off!"

The next day Gary still wasn't at work, and Miller and Harper went to his home to see what they could do. They returned completely resigned.

Miller suggested to Johnson that perhaps he might be able to help Gary. Johnson responded emphatically, "I'm only interested in these people after they get inside the gate!"

Finally the inevitable happened. Gary came to the plant and asked to be let go. He said he wasn't worth it. Johnson took him to the front office to sign the termination form. It was a charged atmosphere. Everyone was emotional. The division foreman was shaking so badly that he had great difficulty writing the termination paper. The director was there with tears in his eyes, and I (Williams) felt the same way because I knew that Gary really wanted to make it.

Abruptly the following Monday, Johnson arrived at the plant with Gary Nolan. He had brought him back to work! Johnson explained to Harper and Miller that Gary's termination had bothered him all week to the extent that he had lost sleep over the weekend, because he felt that Gary was a kid he really should help.

Gary came into the shop. He was happy, and all the people in Johnson's shop were happy.

In talking about it later, Johnson said, "Roy, I look tough, but underneath I'm real tender." (In my memory [Williams] this is the first time any foreman had left the job and gone out to bring a man back to the job.)

Johnson's style, his decisiveness and strong identity, contrasted sharply with that of John Harrison, another foreman in Plant

Maintenance. Harrison's first contact with the hard-core occurred the first day the first class arrived for work. Bobby Hill, a member of the class, was using a large pocketknife to clean his fingernails. This disturbed Harrison.

He drew me (Padfield) aside saying, "Did you see it? Did you see it?"

"See what?"

"Bobby's pocketknife!" I asked him if it was against the company rules to carry knives and if other employees carried them.

He admitted, "Well, yes they do." But then he added gravely, "You have to realize these people are not like regular workers, and they have pretty rough backgrounds!"

Harrison told Johnson about the incident. Johnson laughed and responded, "Aw, I wouldn't worry about it. If they pull a gun, then that's something else again!"

Bobby Hill was both black and aggressive. To many white people a black person's aggressive personality traits cannot be separated from his race. But the confusion of personality traits and the race issue is two sided. On one hand, Bobby tended to feel that anyone who did not accept his aggressiveness was prejudiced. Conversely, certain types of personalities could not cope objectively with Bobby's aggressiveness because he was black. This was especially true of those foremen who could not separate their normal disapproval of insubordination from their deep-seated needs for caste relationships where blacks were involved.

Harrison had a deeply ambivalent attitude about race. In his reaction to the trainees, he was defensive and seemingly fearful that his race feelings were being expressed in his supervisory behavior. If Bobby disturbed him in one way, other black personalities disturbed him in other ways. Indeed, almost all of the black trainees disturbed him for one reason or another.

When Bobby was assigned to Harrison, it took only a few days for these latent tensions to surface.

(Padfield). During the second week Hill was working under Harrison, the situation reached a climax. About midmorning John approached me. His face was tense, his head cocked to one side.

He said that Bobby had just walked off the job, refusing to work in the backup in the sewer outside. He exclaimed, "We can't have this. Bobby has a chip on his shoulder. He's got to go to work in some of the dirt and filth that the rest of us have to work in! Bobby refused to do it and said he could do this shit at home and didn't have to do it here and walked off!"

About 15 minutes later John found Hill in the office area of Plant Maintenance. He said very little to him and walked up to me and demanded, "How long do we have to go along babying these people?"

This conversation with Hill shortly after the incident gives another view of the subtle interplay of personality and race attitudes on the part of both trainee and supervisor:

DOC (The trainee's name for Padfield). *How did it develop?*
BOBBY. *Oh, when I was over there, after he got the hole unplugged, you know, old John come running over there to me, "Hey, Bobby, here, get something and git the water up over there." So I started getting the water up, you know; these guys called me and say help them do something. Okay, so I put my squeegie down, and I start helping them. John walks back over there, "Hey, Bobby, get the water up around this area right here." Okay, they got snakes, they got all this gummy oil and all this stuff that the people use to sweep the floors with, all over the floor, and then they got the snake machine itself, and John wants me to sweep water up!*
DOC. *What did you say?*
BOBBY. *I didn't say nothing. I started sweeping the stuff up and he say, "Hey, don't dump that stuff in that drain." Got a big old sewer there, (sarcastically) we can't dump it in the sewer. Big old sewer, people shit in it and everything else, we can't dump that little old crap in there. Big old hole go right down to the street, into the sewer line.*
DOC. *Then what did you say?*
BOBBY. *I didn't say nothing. Then he said take that stuff up and put it in a box; I just looked at him like he was crazy.*
DOC. *Did you do it?*
BOBBY. *Nope . . . I brushed that stuff all in a little pile, but I didn't pick it up.*

DOC. *Then what did you do?*

BOBBY. *I say, "Shit, if I want to sweep and mop floors, I could do this shit at home!" I felt like this about it, if we make the fuckin' mess, we clean it up. Shit, we didn't make the mess . . . That's why I really protested doing it, because I know we didn't make the mess.*

DOC. *Who shoulda done it?*

BOBBY. *The oilers shoulda done it. They the ones dumping that shit in there.*

DOC. *You went back to the job?*

BOBBY. *Went to see John to see what he had for me to do.*

DOC. *What did he say?*

BOBBY. *So he say "Me and you can work together Bob." All that old kinda draggin' talk.*

DOC. *Well, What did you say to him? . . .*

BOBBY. *I didn't say shit to him. This morning he come telling me about he was making a cabinet last night, and I didn't say "Oh yeah," or nothing cause I don't feel like hearing it, especially from him. He try to cut your throat.* (Cynically) *Old John!*

DOC. *How about Hoffman* (the lead man Hill was assigned to), *you ever have words with him?*

BOBBY. *Nope. I don't argue with neither of em. Cause if I do, I'll tell em a thing or two . . .*

DOC. *What is it you don't like about em?*

BOBBY. *I don't like that scar-face guy's* (Hoffman's) *attitude. He act like he's kinda prejudiced or sump'n.*

DOC. *How does he show it?*

BOBBY. *All kinds of ways. All kind of little old funny ways—I might be doing something—"Hey, don't be doing that; you might break that." All that old kinda shit, like I don't know my own strength or like I don't know what I'm doing . . . . You know what? Jack* (another trainee) *put the light on me about that other sucker. One day I was coming along there, and I had a big old fuckin' wrench, and Jack he say the scar-face guy had this little old fuckin' wrench. I bet it weighed about 50 pounds, about 35 or 40 pounds. Anyway, I had it on my shoulder, and Jack was laughing because he had the little wrench, and I had the big one, you know . . . . That's the way it went til yesterday.*

DOC. *How did it change yesterday?*
BOBBY. *Instead of me carrying all the shit, he carried some of it. He carried a little more than I did.*

Tim Carter's behavior and Harrison's concern for "the women in the plant" led to another minor confrontation. Tim was tall, muscular, and extremely black with perfect white teeth and natural hair. Harrison complained repeatedly about Tim's watching white women and twice included it in his job evaluation.

He often spoke of this particular "weakness" of Tim's saying, "He looks at women as if he were undressing them." The DOT staff lost no time expressing its disapproval to Harrison for his written complaints. Confronting him with his evaluation, it accused him of prejudice.

After this incident, Harrison defended himself for the next few days. He explained that one of the women had been courted by one of the other machine operators, a man named Harry, and she had turned him down. This rejection had angered Harry, and whenever he saw Tim staring at the woman he would go over to her and say, "Look at that! You won't accept a date from me, but you'll stand there and let that black man look at you and eat it up!"

Harrison explained that what hurt him most about this incident with Tim was " . . . I've tried to do so much for this program, and the reason I'm trying to do so much is that I feel I know *these boys'* problems. I've been poor. My Dad never had a job where he earned over four thousand a year in his life." He added, "These fellows are like a little dog kicked in the tail all the time."

He stressed his relationships with colored people and how he had come to know them in the plant. He said that he'd been to the homes of almost every colored person in the plant. He insisted, "They are free to come to my house!"

Harrison was continuously in doubt—doubt about himself, doubt about the trainees, doubt about the company doing right by the men. He argued strenuously that he supported this type of program, but on the other hand he occasionally sympathized with the union workers who had been laid off. During the height of the union-management confrontation in October, he had said that he thought the company was unfair to the trainees because, as he explained, "They're building up these fellows' egoes and then the company is going to turn right around and lay them off." John worried about this.

There were many similar signs of racial attitudes in Plant Maintenance. Two other supervisors in particular were quite outspoken against the NAB program. They consistently used "they" and "them" and "their kind" derisively. One could never be sure whether "they" and "them" referred to hard-core trainees or blacks. Nevertheless it was evident that these supervisors considered the hard-core as undeserving. It wasn't always clear whether this was because they were black or because they hadn't devoted their lives to being apprentices and working their way up as the supervisors had done.

However, one thing was clear. These expressions of racial attitudes by Harrison and the other general foremen centered on keeping "them" in a certain position until "they" had proved themselves worthy of advancement. It is in this manner that ethnic and class biases insinuate their way into screening practices and become subtly interwoven with "standards" and "qualifications." Racism is thus suppressed and extruded into a more acceptable mold.

The neutral or uncommitted foreman was another important type in the plant supervisory system. George Ryan belonged in this category. In many ways he seemed to consider the hard-core program as a temporary interlude which was irrelevant to his job. As a result, George never got involved. In some ways this was an advantage; in other ways it was not. One disadvantage was his tendency to provide very little feedback on the men's performance. He felt that it was the trainees' responsibility to perform and that evaluations and feedback were superfluous.

In many ways the hard-core and the issue they personified tended to divide supervisors within and across departmental lines. In some cases they set foremen against division foremen and division foremen against superintendents. Moreover the program occasionally became a divisive issue in areas not directly involved in its operation. At high levels of the supervisory system some people treated it as a pawn in interpersonal politics. But the hard-core issue did more than divide supervisors. It polarized the entire plant.

PLANT-WIDE POLARIZATION

By January 2, 1969, the last class of trainees were beginning on-job training. The full contingent of 25 men was now on the floor (Tim Carter, Leroy Fry, and Henry Boice had been terminated). The trainees were scattered throughout Southwestern in seven departments and two plants. The NAB issue was now personalized plant-wide. Instead of encountering the natural organization of the plant, the trainees were confronted by two conflicting systems of values typifying not just the social structure of Southwestern but that of society at large.

The NAB principle of compensatory opportunity was both an ethnic and a class issue. It was a class issue insofar as it implied the social rearrangement of the availability of opportunity. It was an ethnic issue insofar as it was precipitated largely by blacks in the ghettos and by the fact that nationally the majority of hard-core participants in NAB programs were black. Reactions to this principle by plant personnel guided both their attitudes and actions toward the trainees and toward one another. A certain amount of friction developed throughout the company—between union and management, within the ranks of management, and among supervisors. Friction even developed between the Main Plant and North Plant, eight miles away.

We are not trying to magnify these divisions in terms of their representativeness of the plant-wide picture, but considering there were only 25 hard-core in a factory of more than 3,800 workers, their impact was far in excess of the relative size of their numbers.

Of equal importance was the effect of this divisiveness on the trainees. Some of them were stifled by these tensions. They related to the individual or supervisor who favored them as opposed to the ones who did not. This produced an unreal atmosphere, one without sufficient feedback to learn plant etiquette. In fact, this atmosphere was too indulgent, a carryover of the trainees' identification with management. Some of the more aggressive trainees like Bobby Hill gravitated to the highest favorable authority attempting to work this to their advantage.

Bobby was permanently assigned to North Plant as an oiler under the supervision of Tom Morrison, foreman. In less than a week Bobby found a more favorable ally in Philip Gore, the general foreman. Gore took Hill directly under his wing, and Bobby used Gore's paternalism to his advantage. Morrison, a naturally timid man was intimidated further, and showed his hesitancy in numerous ways. Shortly after Bobby went to work at North Plant, Morrison called him aside, and with the DOT staff counsellor present, carefully explained that he shouldn't have left the oil out of one of the machines ". . . just to test whether or not the night oiler would do his job." Although Morrison was mild in his criticism, Bobby argued with him.

Afterwards Bobby remarked to the counsellor, "Morrison is just prejudiced. Morrison is scared!"

After Christmas vacation, Bobby was summoned to an interview with Gore over Morrison's head. It concerned an incident in which a machine operator who was about to pour the wrong oil in a machine was stopped by Bobby just in time. The incident and subsequent interview caused rumors of an upgrade for Bobby which he was quick to magnify. Despite this, progress reports came through signed by Gore that made no mention of such problems and that stated that he was progressing very well.

(Williams). A few weeks later I was talking to Morrison when Hill came up and abruptly pulled me off to the side to tell me about another trainee who was sleeping in his car during working hours. Noticing Bobby dressed in street clothes, I asked him why.

At that point Morrison reentered the conversation saying, "You know Bobby leaves here every Friday."

Bobby countered, "Naw, not every Friday; just about."

Morrison warned, "Bobby, you're going to have to stop that, because I'm not going to let you leave here every Friday!"

Bobby turned his back on Morrison and walked away. Then he stopped and looked back at Morrison saying, "Morrison, you know you're dying!" Morrison looked embarrassed.

Bobby walked back to him, looked him straight in the eye, and repeated, "Morrison, you're dying!"

Morrison replied, "Well, Bobby, everybody is."

Bobby walked off and threw back, "Morrison, your problem is you have too many credit cards in your pocket!"

Aside from Hill, there were four other trainees at North Plant. Three were assigned to Philip Gore's department. In all three cases, Gore dealt with them directly and paternalistically, bypassing the foreman.

The NAB issue with its racial or ethnic overtones affected the plant society in other ways. There were numerous complaints from time to time about trainees who dressed too flamboyantly, with natural hairdos, beards, and so on. One trainee, Carl Brown, wore a natural and hippie jewelry. His foreman disapproved, because he considered this a sign of association with militant groups. We had no way of assessing how general this current of distrust and superstition about black militancy was or even how important. However, it was there, and it was not localized in any one department.

In fact there was a disposition to believe almost any stereotyped rumor about the trainees. In some instances, these rumors were generated by the supervisors.

Rumors about narcotics were the most pervasive. In some cases the rumors were true, in other cases they were not, and in some cases we simply did not know. But regardless of the facts, those opposed to the program tended to believe the rumors; those who supported it did not.

The most persistent and dramatic stories about narcotics came from North Plant where Leon Smith was working with lead man (immediate supervisor) Leo Steiner. Smith dressed like a Black Panther but had an easygoing, friendly personality. He had no complaints about his lead man, but Steiner certainly had complaints about Smith. The situation reached a climax one day in January when Bobby Hill made an irregular appearance on the night shift. This irregularlity was enough to arouse Steiner's suspicions of narcotics activity between Hill and Smith. Steiner went directly to his foreman with a story he had documented with surveillance. He said that Smith was always making pipes out of copper and as Steiner put it, "I asked him what the hell was that?" Smith said (these are Steiner's translations), "I uses these when I smokes my marijuana to hold my reefer in my mouth."

Steiner referred to numerous conversations he had had with Smith and Hill, translating these conversations into stereotyped imitations of black speech. It is interesting to note that in the case of Bobby and

Leon, there was no resemblance whatever between Steiner's imitation and the dialect these men spoke.

Steiner spoke of other incidents—some involving private conversations with Leon, some involving suspicious activities around Leon's locker. He said that he had been studying about narcotics and had carried on extensive conversations with narcotics agents. But despite Steiner's surveillance, he was unable to find any evidence of marijuana on Smith. However, this only proved to Steiner that Leon was a clever operator.

He emphasized, "I would bet you any amount of money if you went out now and searched him you would find some on him!"

Steiner added, "If I am going to criticize a man, I should tell good things about him, too. These guys are good workers. Leon doesn't give any backtalk and works and does what you tell him to do." But he explained, "There are three things I don't like—I don't like Communists, I don't like dope addicts, and I don't like hippies!"

Such attitudes were symptomatic of deeper issues. Steiner did not hide his distaste for the hard-core program. He considered it a personal threat. He talked about working his way up from the bottom, using the phrase, "Sweat of my brow."

He challenged, "Why can't these people do it?" "Why must they drop out of school, give teachers a bad time, give police a bad time, goof off and draw welfare, and then suddenly get an opportunity for a job like this and an opportunity for training when we never got it?"

It did not help Steiner's ego that his general foreman paid no attention to him. Gore claimed the narcotics rumors were merely traps set by the union to catch the trainees.

Management's paternalism further aggravated blue-collar resentment. Later in the year at North Plant a foreman found a hard-core trainee, Dennis Timbers, asleep in the ladies' restroom. The foreman recommended immediate dismissal, but line relations persuaded him to reconsider. The foreman agreed to give Dennis a written warning instead. This caused a wave of resentment in his shop. A delegation of workers confronted him with a written protest which said among other things, "All one had to do was to be black and he would be protected." The foreman said there had been a similar incident in which a white worker had been found asleep. He had been given three weeks suspension without pay.

For many of the plant personnel, the NAB issue and the race issue blended indistinguishably. Statements verbalizing these issues were repeated over and over:

"Why didn't they have this kind of program in our day when *we* needed training?"

"Why are all these hard-core trainees Negro?"

These questions were not confined to the workers and committee-men. Although less visible, the race issue permeated the higher ranks of management.

However, on the basis of extensive conversations with many of the supervisors we could say that more than half of them supported the NAB program. But as we've seen in a significant number of instances this support tended to intensify the division in the plant.

PERSISTENT QUESTIONS

February 1969 was the high water mark of Southwestern's hard-core program. The maximum number of men were on the job, all of the major moves seemed to have been taken, and tentative rules for adjustment had emerged. As we evaluated the situation, we were still faced with a number of persistent questions.

The first was: What was happening to the training system? It was obvious to everyone that a union-management rapproachment had been at least temporarily achieved. While this rapproachment was in some measure satisfactory for both union and management, it was damaging to the trainees. It diluted their training and hurt their morale. No tools meant less technical training and less work, causing boredom and the feeling of futility.

Trainee morale was affected in other ways. Shop instruction was no longer directly related to job assignment. This intensified the trainees' feelings of inadequacy. Occasionally men were placed beyond their capacity, or their *felt* capacity. In addition, management's handling of trainee placement during the union confrontation, as unavoidable as it may have been, also weakened the trainees' morale.

Finally, the polarized atmosphere created a distorted image of the plant's social environment. Instead of learning a normal set of role expectations, the trainees were learning an abnormal set. Instead of learning to relate to the union and to the foremen, they were relating to management. To a certain extent this was inevitable even under the best of conditions in an on-job rehabilitation program such as NAB. In this case it was magnified by union pressure and management paternalism. Identification with management put the trainees in an awkward and exposed position. The longer it was prolonged, the longer final adjustment was delayed.

The extent of the danger depended upon the personality of the trainee. The weak individual tended to be confused. The more aggressive trainee used this distorted map of social relationships as an invitation to resist normal instruction and discipline from his supervisors. Such rule infringements as absences, lateness, early departures, early standing in checkout lines, using the phone during working hours, talking on the job were pushed by the more aggressive trainees, partly because of their false sense of security which stemmed from their identification with management. They were thus denied an essential experience in being rehabilitated or converted to industry—learning to understand their social environment and their social position in it.

The lack of communication between union and management posed other problems. Union officials claimed that management had not given them the complete facts about the program, and officials in Line Relations accused the union of trying to undermine the program. Management's contention seemed to have been supported by the fact that it chose Plant Maintenance, the center of union activitiy, as the organizational center of the on-job training program. It is doubtful that management would have chosen this area for training if it had anticipated a confrontation with the union.

A set of key questions which leads us to the major issues posed by the Southwestern experience was: Could the union attack on the general helper-learner concept have been successfully fought? Were management's concessions made simply because the union's position was correct, or were they made in order to enhance the company's position for the coming contract negotiations?

THE PLANT: A CLOSED SYSTEM TOO LONG?   71

(Padfield). I questioned Harper about these issues: "Have you sacrificed the training program in order to maintain your posture in a strong position against the union in the coming wage negotiations?"

Harper was quick to respond, "They (trainees) are there working. We have them, and we haven't fired them and we are not going to! It doesn't matter if we have lost the general helper-learner classification. We may have lost the battle, but we are winning the war. We must protect seniority, but the union must support training." He added, "Another point is that the minute these trainees pay their dues, the union also has to protect their rights. My feeling is that the union is not after the program, and that it must accept training, but it cannot afford to allow us to erode away the value of the job in terms of wages and this is really what it is interested in protecting."

This conversation suggests a larger theater of operations in which management and union were engaged, and it raises another important question: was the war Harper referred to the same as the war being waged by the NAB program? Harper's logic depends upon what we define as the war—simply protecting a given quota of trainees from being laid off or keeping the doors open to a *class* of people against whom the doors of industry have been closed.

What war was the union trying to win—protecting the rights of just the seven men who were laid off or keeping the doors of industry open only to a class of people represented by their clientele?

Management did not rehire the seven men, and it did not lay off any of the trainees, but it did concede to severe restrictions in the opportunities these trainees had in the job structure at Southwestern. It could be that management's battle was actually the union's war. Therefore, the basic question is what was *the* war?

Actually there were two wars—the NAB war and the union-management war over who got how much of the benefit of their production. The NAB war was not primarily between union and management. It was between two classes of people—the working middle class and the ghetto. The ghetto had appealed to management to be a protagonist in this war. It was only logical that the union who represented the working middle class would strategically link the two wars together, and say to management in effect, "If you persist in trying to keep doors open to the hard-core, this is going to cost you in the new round of wage negotiations."

Why did Harper remove himself from the front lines in the floor skirmishes between DOT and the union? To some, ourselves included, this was partly to minimize his identification with the NAB issue. In other words, while making clear his determination to keep the hard-core the company had agreed to hire, he was willing to negotiate the larger issue. In the early spring of 1969, this was a moot point. One could say only that management had *not* lost the NAB men but they were beginning to compromise, perhaps unavoidably, the NAB principle.

The added factor of layoffs (diminishing opportunity) at Southwestern was crucial. Because of this, management perhaps had no choice. Maybe the potential cost in terms of counter compensation to the union was greater than the company was willing to pay. Answers to these questions would have to wait until the coming round of contract negotiations. At this point there were a number of signs indicating that an old familiar conflict was beginning to cloud the basic NAB issue.

We leave the plant to return to it in our final chapter. We leave it with a question we consider fundamental to the understanding of what was happening at Southwestern: Had opportunity been increased for a class of people or had opportunity been increased simply for 28 men from the ghetto who by some historic accident had gotten through briefly opened doors?

3

The Hard-Core: Dignity Too Late?

In the hierarchy of human rights there are few to compare in importance with that of equal opportunity . . . . because so many other rights are implicit in it—the right of human dignity; the right of education; the right to a decent home; and the opportunity to obtain a useful job which will enable one to feel that he is a needed member of society. It is hard to believe in this advanced stage of our civilization and the general standards of affluence that these rights would not be afforded to every citizen in accordance with the American ideal.

(Earl Warren, Remarks at the Equal Opportunity Day Dinner of the National Urban League, New York, November 19, 1969)

To the average American ten years ago, "hard-core unemployed" was an alien term. Today it is an integral part of the American vocabulary, but universal usage does not mean universal cognition. On the contrary, its meaning is controversial because it identifies people whose lives in one way or another seem to personify discrepancies between the American ideal and the American reality. As the benefits derived from the American economy vary enormously, so do interpretations of any concept which draws attention to this variation. But drawing attention is the first step in alleviating the problem. The term hard-core unemployed communicates two indisputable facts: one, an enormous population of employable but *un*employed people *not* reflected in the monthly unemployment index does exist; and two, somehow the experience of being unemployed adversely affects the employability of these people in a progressively negative relationship through time.

The world of the hard-core unemployed, however, remains an alien experience to most Americans, as foreign to them as the culture of an Amazon tribe. Perhaps it is more so because the *needed* member and the chronically *unneeded* member of society live out most of their lives in deceptively similar social relationships and institutions. They go to similar if not the same schools, shop at the same stores, listen to the same music, watch the same television shows, and talk over the same telephone lines, using a common language. Yet in the midst of apparent uniformity there is a diversity as profound in some ways as differences between peoples divided by time and space.[25] This division is similar to that between two brothers—one who has been loved and accepted all his life and the other who has been hated and rejected. Each occupies the same house and sits down at the same table, but each plays out a different role. With the advent of the NAB program, this picture changed superficially. Suddenly, the hard-core unemployed were being told they were needed. This was the situation at Southwestern Aircraft in July, 1968, when the 28 hard-core trainees were hired and moved into statuses totally unrelated to their life experiences.

UNEMPLOYMENT HISTORIES

By definition, the attributes of the trainees at Southwestern conformed to those described for the national population of NAB trainees (see Introduction). A closer examination of their employment profiles will give a better understanding of the unemployment experience (see Table 1).

Low status, low wage, high instability, and extended length of unemployment are the common denominator on all of these profiles. Of the occupational categories listed in Table 1, only three or four can be regarded as acceptable goals according to the norms set for these young men by public school, the mass media, and other American

Table 1

EMPLOYMENT PROFILE OF TRAINEES PRIOR TO JOB AT SOUTHWESTERN
(MILITARY SERVICE AND GOVERNMENT TRAINING PROGRAMS EXCLUDED)

Occupation of Most Experience	Longest Continuous Employment	Starting Wage	Terminal Wage	Age at NAB Interview	Time Elapsed since This Employment
Carwasher	5 mos.	1.25	1.25	25	2 yrs.
Fisherman	9 mos.	by share		41	1 yr.
Laborer, mattress factory	6 mos.	1.40	1.40	23	2 mos.
Busboy	5 yrs.	1.50	1.50	29	4 yrs.
Truck driver	1 yr.	3.00	3.00	23	2 yrs.
Porter	2 mos.	1.50	1.50	19	8 mos.
Hotel handyman	2 mos.	1.50	1.50	25	3 mos.
Short-order cook	3½ yrs.	1.65	2.85	25	2 yrs.
Spray painter	5½ yrs.	2.25	2.25	32	2 yrs.
Burner helper	8 mos.	2.18	3.28	25	1 mo.
Machine welder	6 mos.	2.05	2.05	25	2 yrs.
Leg skinner, slaughterhouse	4½ yrs.	1.50	2.15	33	12 yrs.
Milker	6 mos.	1.50	1.50	36	3 yrs.
Garbage truck driver	2½ yrs.		1.75	34	2½ yrs.
Book salesman	1 yr.	commission		23	1½ yrs.
Seasonal farm worker	1 yr.	1.25	1.25	21	2½ yrs.
Janitor	9 mos.	1.50	1.50	34	1 yr.
Delivery truck driver	8 mos.	1.50	1.50	25	2½ yrs.
Automotive painter	12 mos.	....	....	35	4 yrs.
Salt packer	15 mos.	2.42	2.90	25	4 mos.
Carwasher	13 mos.	1.25	1.50	33	none
Hospital orderly	9 mos.	1.50	1.50	25	2 yrs.
Dishwasher	1 yr.	1.65	1.65	23	2 yrs.
Janitor	1 yr.	1.50	1.50	26	6 yrs.
Entertainer	1 yr.	...	...	26	2 yrs.
Furniture mover	3 mos.	1.50	1.50	27	3 yrs.
Laboratory aide	6 mos.	1.25	1.49	20	7 mos.
Machine operator, ice cream	2 yrs.	2.20	3.90	28	6 mos.

experiences. Where longevity of employment does appear (in terms of a year or more continuous employment on one job), in most instances (9 out of 15), the jobs are menial, low paying, and nonunion.

Lester Banks was a case in point. Lester washed cars in San Diego for 13 years for $1.25 an hour, and finally was raised to $1.50, a salary which is clearly below the minimum wage standard. Lester's average take home pay was $9 to $15 a week because he was continually in debt and forced to draw advances on his salary to meet his obligations. Lester said that the carwash owners did not inform their employees about company policy or wage scales, although the owners had an association where such policy was decided. He said the foreman of the carwash was the sole individual making commissions and that regardless of how much work an employee might do—he might wax, buff, and polish up to seven cars a day—he would not get a cent beyond his hourly wage.

In addition, these companies intimidated their employees. If an employee quit and attempted to collect unemployment, the company would inform the employment office that the individual had an extremely poor employment record. This would not only delay payment of compensation, but also served as a negative recommendation for future jobs. Lester mentioned a carwasher by the name of O'Malley who had had 15 compensation checks held up because of this tactic.

The frustrations caused by these injustices affected Lester's home life. According to his wife, "Lots of times he'd come home this way (frustrated) when he'd have someone drive in in a Cadillac and say, 'Hey boy, clean out the back of my car real good!' And he'd go back and see that there was dog crap or dog vomit all over the seat, but he would have to clean the car anyway. And he just held it inside and came home and raised hell with the kids."

The hard-core experiences of trying to find employment were deeply personal accounts of discrimination and frustration. Reactions to these experiences varied. Some men were frustrated and fatalistic, accepting closed doors as a fact of life. Some were incredulous that the NAB program was sincere. With others the frustration found expression in cynicism, anger, or addiction to drugs and alcohol.

In the course of the job interview, Andy Manners expressed his opinion of the employment opportunities afforded a black high school graduate.

INTERVIEWER. *When you came out of high school as a graduate, did you look for work?*

ANDY. *Yes, I did. I was workin' for my father, you know, doin' uh . . . janitor work, you know; we had our own janitor service.*

INTERVIEWER. *Where did you have the machine operators' training?*

ANDY. *At, uh, San Leandro City College.*

INTERVIEWER. *How did you do in that?*

ANDY. *Well, I got a diploma.*

INTERVIEWER. *Did you ever try to get a job doing that?*

ANDY. *Yeah, I put a application in at Southwestern. . . .I think I talked to you once . . . .You tole me to check back witcha. I never did check back, cause I thought you was jus' jivin', you know; I knew I wasn't gettin' no job.*

ROY (Williams). *Do you actually feel that way even now, that a lotta these people are jus' jivin'?*

ANDY. *Yeah, I do, I figure they feel I'm not good enough for the job, or sump'n.*

INTERVIEWER. *How do you make it now?*

ANDY. *Well, I, uh, paint part time, and I'm still on welfare.*

ROY. *You want to get off that?*

ANDY. *Yeah, I would like sump'n now, get me a job so I could get me a paycheck every week, you know. I got six kids; I jus' gotta make it.*

Once they were hired and knew us better, the men talked more freely about their unemployment experiences. Dennis Timbers, a veteran of the Vietnam War, contemptuously recalled some of his postwar opportunities:

ROY. *Prior to Southwestern, what did you do for work?*

DENNIS. *I worked at the Scripps Memorial Hospital . . . .*

ROY. *How much did you make out there?*

DENNIS. *It was about $120 every two weeks. Averaged out to $60 per week. See, it was all right for me then . . . right after I* *came out of the war. See, that was the first job I had . . . and I didn't have no kids, and I was livin' in her (wife's) grandmother's apartment, so I never had rent . . . .*

ROY. *When you got out, did you expect findin' a job to be easy?*

DENNIS. *When I got out, there were 370 men that got out with me, that day. And they all lookin' for jobs. They tole me it would be hard.*

ROY. *Where did you go first?*

DENNIS. *I went down to the employment office one day, and they came up with this little job. Get there, man say, "I'm sorry, we jus' hired a dude off the street." I went down there one day on a NDTA thing, one of these government sponsors. They offered to pay me while I went to school for, uh, what they call a male nurse aide. At that time I was gettin' kinda desperate, cause my unemployment was running out. . . .So, I went to this school 12 weeks . . . .*

ROY. *Okay. What did you do after that?*

DENNIS. *After that I decided, you know, like I say the transportation was . . . jus' too much for me. Had to get up at 4:00 a.m. to be downtown to catch that bus, so I could be out there, and then I'd have to hustle me a ride. If I couldn't hustle me a ride, I'd have to walk five miles down, to where the nearest bus came, and then I wouldn't get home till 7:00 p.m.*

ROY. *For $120 every other week?*

DENNIS. *Uh huh. That's the only thing I could find at that time. I worked at Scripps from February to August. I guess that got too much for me. I hand in my resignation and give them two weeks notice, the whole ride. . . .(In September, Timbers got a job at a local factory until Christmas.) I was minus one week, and they come in here and chopped up everybody. And, like I said, I'd only been in there a little time, so my head flew first.*

ROY. *That put a hardship on you?*

DENNIS. *That's when I first went to the County (for welfare).*

Barbara Hill described her side of the unemployment experience:

DOC. *Well, you were on welfare for a while, that was when he was in honor camp.* (Referring to Bobby's 18-month sentence) *So then when he got out, then were you still on?*

BARBARA. *I was still on there until, I think, a week later. He got a job at the carwash, and I called them up to tell welfare. . . .*

DOC. *Did he go long periods without work?*

BARBARA. *Yeah, mostly because of his record. I lived with my grandmother for so long. You know, like he go look for a job—him and his sister's boy friend, and his sister's boy friend always get a job before him, because he don't have no record—he only been to jail one time. . . .And when he call on the phone to look for a job, the man said, "yeah, come on in, you can start workin' today," and when they find out he colored, they don't need him. He went a long time without a job.*

DOC. *Well, how did you manage then?*

BARBARA. *Uh, my grandmother, odds and ends. I'm tell you, it was bad.*

BOBBY. (Entering the conversation) *I'm gonna tell you how it goes—a lot of em is got a record, jus' like I do, and it ain't easy. Jus' like I tole you, if I was sittin' home on my butt and you had the record and was lookin' for the job, you'd see what I was talkin' about. To find a decent job, somethin' that I can put clothes on my back and on their back and get things we want, is hard to find. Carwashin', dishwashin'—that ain't my game. I'll sit on welfare before I do that, and that's the way a lot of the rest of us feel. They not gonna wash nobody's car for $1.25 an hour—all day for no nine hours or ten hours. And they ain't gonna wash no dishes for no $1.35 an hour for eight hours; for which I can't much blame em, cause I did both of em, and it's not easy. All those that can get away on the welfare, goody for em—that's the way I feel . . . . Like I was tellin' the guys at work today, "My hand don't fit no pushbroom too fuckin' good; it don't fit no carwash rags, and it don't fit no dishwashin' rags. I will not do that kind of work, period! There is not enough money in it!"*

WORK DEPRIVATION AND THE LARGER-THAN-LIFE JOB

What little employment the hard-core trainees had experienced had done little to prepare them for industry, because for the most part, the work had been intermittent and menial. Consequently, most of the men were shocked when they suddenly acquired job status in industry. Some were euphoric, especially when their first check reinforced the reality of their new status. Darrell Johns had insomnia for weeks—dreaming about the job, jumping up in the early hours of the morning to see if it was time to go to work. Lester Banks talked constantly about how lucky he was to have a decent job, and this sentiment was quickly transformed into a fixation not to lose it. He refused to miss work for any reason whatsoever. By the end of his first year, he had been late only four times and had not missed a single day. Lester's record is not typical, but his job anxiety is. What we see in both of these instances is a form of deprivation—work deprivation.

It would be incorrect to call work deprivation a void. A void implies a *lack* of experience. To desire something and continuously not get it, *is* experience, negative experience. This experience is vicious when the culture that reinforces the desire is the same system that withholds the status desired. Perhaps nowhere in the world is work, and the status and riches associated with work, more glorified than in the United States, and perhaps nowhere in the world is there a more rigorous system for classifying, rewarding, and penalizing people in terms of the relative financial returns from employing them. Career achievement is glorified in soap operas, magazines, and textbooks, and individual betterment through work is the basis of the mythology sometimes subtly and sometimes brutally drilled into every child in school—white, black, Indian, Caucasian, and Mexican alike. Hence, mental recognition of the importance of work and the emotional desire for a career are instilled into every citizen apart from his personal values, practices and capabilities, his family, and his culture, and, quite apart from the racial and cultural prejudices of American society. In the land of "equality," the work ethic is a model provided for everyone but the rewards of work are not, and efficiency becomes the cardinal rationalization for inequality. Thus the egalitarian experience of valuing work begins setting the stage for accomplishment for some and deprivation for others.

The hard-core unemployed are not simply people without work. They are people who have learned to *cope* without work. Their life styles and living strategies imply a permanent state of unemployment, a permanent lack of status in mainstream society, and permanent deprivation of the material benefits most Americans take for granted. When they are accorded occupational status, they bring with them the attitudes and behaviors which have helped them to cope with unemployment and use them to begin developing their work personalities. Using an analogy, occupational status is to work deprivation what an abundance of food is to food deprivation, or love is to love deprivation. How the deprived person reacts to the sudden availability of what he was deprived of depends upon the behavioral complexes he has developed to cope with his deprivation. The coveted good is not always enough to obviate the deprivation. In fact, availability may simply transform a person's deprivation into inadequacy.

In Chapter 2 we discussed some of the inadequacies of the plant system in relation to the hard-core. Here we discuss some of the inadequacies of the hard-core in relation to the plant and the job.

BECOMING VISIBLE IN THE PLANT—FOUR PATTERNS

Virtually all of the trainees lacked in common the ability to meet the job experience on a realistic basis. If unemployment was the cause of all problems, a good job was the solution to all problems, because it provided the job-deprived man with the means to fulfill his every aspiration and desire. If the men had an unrealistic view of the job's rewards, they also had an unrealistic view of its requirements. Such a distorted perspective required compensating mechanisms, and because the trainees lacked industrial work personalities, they compensated quite naturally by constructing new ones from the personalities they did have. But the behavior patterns which enabled them to adapt to the old situation of chronic unemployment and status deprivation were now maladaptive in their new situation. For this reason we use the term "inadequacy" when describing these patterns. This inappropriate juxtaposition of behavior and situation might also be called "dissonance," "deviancy," or simply "adjustment problems."

Without digressing into analyses of the function these behavior patterns may have had in the trainees' pre-job situation,[26] we describe and analyze them in the context of the social system of the factory. We observed four patterns of behavior, which in this setting we call occupational inadequacy: "bravado," "compartmental," "dependent," and "overperformer." There is a fifth pattern which might be termed "natural," but of the 28 hard-core there were only three that fit this category. Because the term hard-core implies people with work behavior problems, one would expect to find few "natural" workers among the trainees.

Although our criteria are subjective, they are based on intensive observations, extended over a period of a year or more, of behavioral interaction between plant personnel and the hard-core. Therefore the behavior pattern in question implies not only a set of habitual responses on the part of the hard-core, but also a set of responses on the part of plant personnel reacting to the hard-core and, to a certain extent, reinforcing their patterns.

Of the 28 men, we classified seven in the bravado, seven in the compartmental, eight in the dependent, three in the overperformer, and three in the natural category. While all of the men in a particular category exhibited the characteristics of that pattern to some degree, there was individual variation. Each pattern is examined separately. The order in which we discuss them is not random but corresponds to the natural sequence in which they developed. The bravados exhibited their traits almost immediately. It took about three months for the compartmentals to reveal their traits; dependents took from five to seven months to reveal theirs, and overperformers did not reveal some of their criterial traits for almost a year.

Because all of the men were placed in an alien environment and were trained via a common program, the development of their work personalities was bound to share a rough chronological similarity. The natural order of interactions between plant personnel and the hard-core was as follows: first, the classroom and DOT staff, including the teaching, counseling and administrative functions; next, interaction with the shop group—the lead men and other coworkers; then the interaction with the supervisory system and the system of plant regulations; and finally, the interaction of the trainees with their job assignments. In the final analysis, this was where the proof of the pudding lay. If the trainees could respond positively in this area of interaction, they would generally succeed.

Bravado Pattern

Two weeks after the first class had begun, teachers and foremen met informally and evaluated the trainees. Almost unanimously they ranked Bobby Hill at the bottom and Gary Nolan near the top of the class. A year later Bobby had joined Southwestern's permanent work force and had gone to Mississippi on the first paid vacation of his life. Nolan had disappeared in the quicksands of narcotics and had long since been terminated.

From the beginning Hill and the six other blacks in the bravado group caused the most controversy, but consistently produced on the job. All of these men were outwardly aggressive and hostile, and they were adept at verbalizing their hostility, particularly in the classroom. They interrupted, intimidated, and belittled. And when assigned to individual work, they used the time for more self-expression, usually at someone else's expense.

The following account of a class session in Social Problems illustrates this point. In an attempt to help the trainees find new ways of coping with their problems, the teacher frequently introduced lecturers to the class who from the hard-cores' point of view represented some type of threat. During one session, he brought in a group of policemen to speak to the class. Oddly, there was very little interaction or discussion between the police and the trainees. The moment the police left, however, a virtual volcano erupted.

Hill led the outburst saying, "... it was a bunch of bullshit! They were ... full of shit!," and "... it was a bunch of crap!"

Such verbal hostility was characteristic of the bravados, and in many cases bore little resemblance to the action they would take in a real situation. It was an almost automatic response to any constructive suggestion, particularly if it came from authority.

Perhaps most characteristic of the bravados' attitude was their difficulty in showing appreciation, a lack which never kept them from relying on people and using them to the utmost advantage. They would not hesitate to ask for the most outlandish favors, particularly from the DOT staff. Each time the favor was granted, bravados would take the occasion to ask for another one. They even tended to complain if the favor was not granted fast enough or in just the right manner. This behavior contrasted sharply with that of most other trainees.

Bailing them out of trouble did not stop them from continuing to do what got them into trouble in the first place. Manners was constantly in difficulty because of gambling, Timbers because of his drinking, and Leon Smith because of his hustling activities; and each time they got into trouble, they would appeal for help.

The most outstanding example of this type of behavior was Bobby Hill's activity with his automobile. Keeping in mind that Bobby was on eight years probation from honor camp and that he had a suspended license, one can see that handling an automobile could jeopardize his job, because an arrest and conviction would mean automatic referral back to honor camp, as well as automatic dismissal from his job. This risk never discouraged Bobby from driving. His '55 Buick was the center of his life, and because he knew people in "important places," he felt he could manipulate the system. One morning after receiving a traffic ticket while driving to work, Bobby appealed to the DOT staff and their relationships with the court to get him out of this difficulty. When they did, he was very nonchalant and flippant about the affair saying, "Oh, I knew you would get it fixed!"

To Bobby everything could be fixed. At one point in the program he had 57 unresolved traffic violations. He thought nothing of driving 80 miles an hour on the Freeway, drinking from an open can of beer, all the while explaining that there was nothing to worry about, because if he got another ticket, he knew who would get it fixed for him.

On the floor the bravados attracted immediate attention because of their refusal to follow shop etiquette. This refusal was reflected most obviously in their dress: Porter in his bright hustler suit; Manners in his Dick Gregory beard, stocking cap pulled down over his ears, sandals and sloppy sweatshirt; Smith with his Malcolm X beard and golf cap; Hughes with his $40 Stetson shoes; and Hill with his huge, snow-white

Phil Silvers "Top Banana" cap did little to inspire the confidence of their coworkers and supervisors.

Bravados asserted their egos in numerous other ways. They generally did not defer to either senior workers or their lead men because they felt they could do *any* job and do it better than their lead men. Furthermore the bravados saw any attempt to keep them from demonstrating their knowledge as evidence of racial prejudice. Very rarely could lead men instruct without some feedback, ranging from smart aleck comments like, "Any damn fool can do that!" to more subtle reactions including surly silence. The lead men resented this behavior, and the trainees resented the lead men's disapproval. Union restrictions on the use of tools further aggravated matters, because the bravados generally ignored these restrictions when they could, thus causing added friction.

In the social grammar of the shop it was important for the individual worker to demonstrate his status and, of course, the trainee had the lowest status. Acting in accordance with their low statuses was something the bravados resisted, and their resistance provoked a great deal of resentment. As a matter of fact, bravados prided themselves on their ability to outperform others. To accomplish this, they tended to work too fast and then to violate another unwritten rule of plant etiquette by sitting around obviously doing nothing, thus causing further resentment among their coworkers. From their point of view a job assignment was specific, and when it was done, it was done. They could see no reason why they should "look busy" picking up scraps of metal, sweeping, and so on. It was a common sight to see Andy sitting on a bench pointing out to the rest of the men how quickly he had done his work. To bravados it was more important to receive recognition for the job that had been done than to show a willingness to continue endless work, or to demonstrate such middle-class attitudes of wanting to improve one's self, as watching a senior man perform a task and asking questions. Thus, much of the foremen's and lead men's time was taken up in trying to find tasks that were comprehensive enough to keep these men busy throughout the day.

(Padfield). I remember one day in particular when Johnson felt confident in giving Bobby a sufficiently difficult assignment of

dismantling a stationary power plant. Bobby ostentatiously began the work demonstrating to everyone within earshot that this was an easy job.

He dismantled the heads in less than an hour, and then sat down, propped up his feet on the highest table he could find, pulled out a cigarette, and called out to people walking by with joking insults like, "Hey, Joe, how come you so slow!"

Traditional informal patterns of teaching etiquette did not work with the hard-core in general and the bravados in particular. Joking behavior was one method of signaling a novice that he was breaching the etiquette essential for smooth social relations between different status groups. With bravados a joke meant a challenge, a demonstration of masculinity, not a signal to be acknowledged. For example, Bobby Hill was literally cashiered out of Plant Maintenance because he outdid his coworkers in verbal abuse. If Jerry, one of the senior men, would brag about how he would go to Tijuana and ". . . get all that leg," Bobby would match him story for story. For every name he had for Bobby, Bobby had a better one for Jerry. If Jerry called Hill a "big mouth," Hill would call Jerry a "peter snatcher."

But the main etiquette problem with the bravados was their openness, the fact that they would readily declare their opinions on what the blue-collar worker considered sensitive issues. To these aggressive representatives of the black ghetto, their methods of coping with the police, racism, welfare, the drug scene, the streets, and the problem of eking out a living were *accomplishments* to be proud of, and they resisted adopting hypocritical behavior to hide them. Exploiting the welfare system was no different from the cotton or the wheat farmer exploiting the system of farm welfare subsidy payments. Just as blue-collar workers, the hard-core would brag about their friends in high places and their ability to beat the system. Such bragging increased the friction between the trainees and their coworkers.

Bobby Hill frequently boasted about his relationship with management with remarks like, "I don't deal with foremen anymore, they are only peons!" Leon Smith bragged about his pot-smoking experiences, and Andy Manners bragged about his gambling exploits. It wasn't unusual on Monday mornings for Andy to strut around the plant proudly displaying several hundred dollars in winnings in a huge roll.

Bravados not only wanted to outshine the regular workers; they seemed especially interested in demonstrating, verbally at least, that they were better than other trainees. Bragging was not the only method; downgrading and belittling was its complement. Also a good deal of oblique informing about rule infractions occurred. The bravados informed not to get the individual in trouble, but to demonstrate their own knowledge and the fact that they were not doing such things.

In the area of supervision and plant routine four characteristics of the bravados stood out—their propensity to test the rules, their pattern of conflict with authority, their tendency to have a racket going, and seemingly somewhat contradictory to this, their amenability to the right kind of pressure. However, this pressure had to be explicit, manageable, fair, and decisive.

Bravados tested practically every rule they encountered. They paid little attention to even the major rules—sleeping on the job, the use of drugs or alcohol on the job—the infraction of which justified immediate dismissal. Ghetto life and plant life differed vastly in this respect. Premises underlying rules in the ghetto are altogether different from those imposed upon the ghetto by outside agencies, such as police and social welfare. These men tended to view major rules in the plant as they viewed the rules of society imposed upon the ghetto. Violating rules had nothing to do with the man's wanting the job; it was simply that he had no way of appreciating the integrity of the rules in terms of the job.

In the area of minor rules, the bravados ranked higher than any of the other trainees in terms of latenesses and early departures. In contrast to compartmentals and dependents, who tended to be higher in absences, these men showed a willingness to appear on the job, and a great capacity to stand up under criticism for their behavior. In the latter respect they displayed remarkable ability and fantastic imagination. Bobby would claim that he had to leave work because his wife had had an epileptic fit. Leon Smith would have to check with his probation officer at midafternoon. Andy Manners would frequently have to see some obscure "brother" who was deeply involved in ghetto politics about helping to keep peace in the ghetto.

When faced with major or minor infractions, the bravados invariably preferred to defend themselves in terms of their proficiency in working. In most cases there was some validity in this. They would use this justification, especially in the area of lateness and early departures, because from their point of view there was little rationale for remaining on the job once the work was finished.

In conflicts with authority, frequencies ranked in this order: first senior workers and lead men, next foremen, and the least frequent but perhaps most explosive, Plant Security. In the shop authority structure, bravados were quick to find the highest chain of command and to look for some special sign of compensation from it. This compensation might be little more than a gesture, but it was important to them. Perhaps this behavior was rooted in the prejudice they had experienced all their lives. At any rate, it was a pattern.

Another important pattern was that of attempting to dominate the figure of authority in the shop. If one could belittle the strongest person in the shop, he thereby strengthened his own ego in the eyes of his coworkers.

The race issue was a dominant feature of the conflicts between bravados and supervisors. Sometimes it was vague and general, other times overt. Other blacks might tolerate racism, but the bravados would not. Dennis Timbers was keenly aware of racial attitudes. He delighted in baiting supervisors or other workers who showed any sign of racial prejudice. He had the knack of using subtly inflammatory expressions to surface these feelings. One of his favorites was, "He looks as though I have shit on my collar."

Bravados' contacts with Plant Security were especially sensitive. Plant Security officers dressed, looked, and acted like police. To the hard-core they *were* police. On one occasion Plant Security summoned Weldon Greer from the job to be taken to jail on a charge. A minor scuffle broke out, and he had to be handcuffed.

As a sign of his individuality, Andy Manners refused to wear his employment badge. One day a security guard stopped him in the plant, and asked Andy where his badge was. Andy retorted, "I've got it, but I don't have to show it to you!" The guard called the training office and Andy was told that he could be fired for not wearing the badge. Andy immediately put it on.

Much of the plant behavior of the bravados was explainable only in relation to their outside activities (see Part II). Most of them were engaged in some outside money-making activity that had to be juggled with the job, and that affected their attendance. But because they were highly motivated to keep the job, they tended to sandpaper their work time with latenesses and early departures rather than cut into it with absences. For example, Leon Smith was engaged in hustling that kept him active during the day. As a result, when he reported for the evening shift he was so tired he slept on the job. With the exception of Weldon Greer, all of the bravados were engaged in some illegal or quasi-legal activity and sooner or later would have to choose between this and the job.

In the final analysis, only when the meaning of the job took hold and penetrated the hard-core personality, was there leverage for behavioral change. This was especially true for the bravados. The job was important to their egos. In this arena of employment they could express themselves, and the job was a new means of gaining recognition. As the transfer of the means of gaining recognition began to shift from the streets to the plant, progress began. The bravados constantly said in one way or another, "Look at my work!" They said this to justify their latenesses, their early departures, and their absences. They said it to justify insubordination, flippness, ostentatious dress, bad language, or whatever they were criticized for. And sooner or later this very thing could be turned back on them and used against them—the desire to keep the *job*.

(Williams). One day about midway in Andy's year when his absences were frequent, I called at his house. I knocked for about four minutes. Finally, Andy came to the door in his shorts. He started making excuses almost as soon as he asked me in. He spent five minutes telling me what kind of work he did and how fast he was.

I argued, "We'd rather have a man who did less work, but one who could get to the job every day."

Andy snapped, "Well you're an old Uncle Tom!"

I countered, "I may be Uncle Tom's Daddy, but I still want you on the job!" I continued to pressure him. Suddenly he jumped up, rushed into the bedroom, and started pulling his work clothes on. It was too late then, but he showed up the next morning.

Challenge to perform was what the bravados responded to. If they were fired, they fought it, and if they were given ultimatums about a specific fault, they responded. If they were passed over in upgrades or pay raises, they complained.

Most of the foremen sensed the budding significance of the job to the bravados. They were quick to seize upon it as a means of recognizing the man in spite of his infractions of rules. With one exception, all bravados had received more than one citation for job efficiency. In fact, Andy's foreman criticized him because he injured himself trying to work too fast. But, first the job had to take hold. Until then it was useless as a leverage for change. In some cases it took months, but slowly and surely the taproots of recognition and rewards began to penetrate and transform the priorities of these men.

Compartmental Pattern

Seven trainees (six black and one Mexican American) exhibited the general characteristics of the compartmental pattern. Five were terminated short of the reference year—two within four months, two within six months, and one within seven months. During their employment, these men shared in common certain traits and stimulated similar reactions among plant personnel. Compartmentals were in constant trouble. In this respect, they shared with the bravados the distinction of being highly visible. A compartmental surprised no one when he was terminated. When a bravado was not terminated, it surprised practically everyone. Whereas the bravados tested the rules, the compartmentals ignored them. There is a vast difference between the two patterns. If a compartmental broke a rule, it was generally because he couldn't see the risk he was taking. Bravados generally knew the risks and broke the rules deliberately, balancing the risks against some desired gain. Although both patterns were dysfunctional, one was more deeply so then the other, because bravados at least recognized the realities of their situation.

Bravados were adept at verbal abuse and consistently projected hostility as a shield. In contrast, verbal abuse was not the compartmentals' style. They talked little and tried to hide their hostility. When they did talk, they tended to reveal their true feelings. Perhaps because they were more deeply hostile then the bravados, they withdrew to protect themselves from confrontation, the outcome of which they could not control. Bravados had many ways of fighting, short of serious conflict; the compartmentals had only one.

With supervisors, bravados were willful contenders, but compartmentals wanted as little to do with their foremen as possible. They simply wanted to be left alone. Instead of gravitating to people of rank, they tended to rely on familiar contacts, a "brother" or intermediary they could trust as a guide in an alien environment.

To the compartmentals, the job was a partial entity. It provided one set of satisfactions—status and money—but not the satisfaction of performance. Although physically at work, their minds were not on the job. This failure to see the relationship between performance and rewards was apparent from the beginning of their training. For example, Tim Carter slept through most of his classes, including Shop. Failure to respond in class was one thing, but failure to respond in Shop was more damaging, because here the teachers were the same foremen who were to supervise the men on the job. Carter's attitude affected his promotion and job assignments.

One day Ryan, the forman instructor for Shop, was demonstrating plumbing fixtures. At the end of the demonstration he turned to Carter and asked him to give the size of three specimens he had just explained.

Tim shrugged and said, "I don't know."

Ryan patiently responded, "This is a half, this is a three-quarter, and this an inch."

Carter repeated, half mimicking, "half, three-quarters, and inch," and laughed. Although angry, Ryan said nothing. As a result of his behavior during classroom instruction, Tim's first assignment was in gardening rather than in a more skilled classification. In addition, he was given a poor evaluation.

Tim was bitter about his first assignment. He could see no relationship between it and his performance in class.

(Williams). Shortly after Tim got his first assignment and his

evaluation letter, I went out to his house and talked to him and Angie, the girl he was living with, about Tim's reaction. I asked him how he felt about the evaluation.

"It's all right—except when they got to handing out the jobs."

"How did you feel when they gave you your job?"

"Felt cheated a little bit. I'm not mentionin' nobody's name, but here I am up here—I can read, I can write, I can do mathematics, and he (Lester Banks, who can't) still gets the best, and here I am out here diggin' in these damn people's (white) gardens, grass and shit!"

"Did you feel that that was gonna happen?"

"In a way, I guess. It sounded too good to be true, really."

Attempting to get him to see the brighter side I asked, "Now did he explain what was gonna happen, you know, how he was gonna rotate you?"

Tim answered, "Yeah, well he left my other two weeks open. He filled everybody else in, but he left mine open."

"Why do you feel he did that?"

Tim thought a little and responded, "Kick me out the gate, I guess—shit!"

I added, "Tim, if you show your interest—because I was a little surprised, even when you were late you gave me a call. That did let me know you were interested in the job."

Angie interjected, "He went all the time; he went everyday."

Bringing in the other topic I wanted to get him on, I said, "Now, by the same token when the guys saw Tim sleep, they thought he didn't want a job."

"Even though he was there?" Angie asked incredulously.

"Even though he was there."

There was a long pause, and I finally asked, "What did your letter say?"

Tim brought me the letter, and I began reading it aloud, "You are a good reader, and you understand mathematics very well. You have told us that you want a better job, and your fine attendance record, in part, proves it. If you continue to improve your attitude . . ."

I interrupted the reading, "Tim, that lets you know that your attitude must be improved, because it says, 'if you continue to improve your attitude and begin to pay more attention to your foremen and instructors'—that sounds true."

Tim sullenly predicted, "I be payin' attention to them, but not lookin' at em!"

The *them* Tim referred to were white. This antipathy showed time and again in Tim's withdrawal and was closely linked to the fact that most of his associations with whites had been with authority figures—school teachers, policemen, and wardens.

At another point in this conversation I asked him, "Do you think it would help if more 'soul brothers' were counselors?"

"Yeah, cause, you see, another brother know how it is. You can't get one of them old Uncle Toms now to do it."

Angie, explained, "You know, Tim looks at *you* like you really must have tried and worked hard to get up there, and, you know, like he looks at a white guy and say, 'Oh, he got it easy, he don't have to work, he can talk.'" She added, "I told him he got to take a *little* stuff, though."

Tim continued, "Yeah, but you know, there was a supervisor that was Jones . . ."

"Where was this?"

". . . I was in Preston (prison) then . . . . See, Jones, and most of them (white) counselors didn't want me to go home. He said if he had his way I'd stay there. Well, it was another—one white man there that helped me get out of there. He was over all of them. . . ."

I interrupted, "Now right there, Tim—there was *one* white man!"

Tim emphasized, "One!"

As far as work performance was concerned, most of the compartmentals lived in a fantasy world. Even when his job hung by a slender thread, it was not unusual for one to ask why he was passed over for a promotion. In making their decisions to miss work, compartmentals made choices which from an industrial-occupational point of view were irrational. Moreover, as long as these decisions made sense in their own private system of priorities, they could see no reason why their decisions should matter to people at the plant. For example, Darrell Johns would stay home to take his wife to see the doctor, because, as he explained, he didn't have enough money for bus fare, or he couldn't afford to pay someone else to take his wife. By doing this, he shortened his wages by more than the amount of money he saved.

Much of the compartmentals' "important business" involved pathetic efforts to buy cars or to get drivers' licenses. To most middle-class, blue-collar workers, an automobile is as common a possession as a pair of shoes. On the other hand, most of the hard-core had never owned cars. Of the 28 trainees at Southwestern, only three owned automobiles at the time they were hired. So, it was only natural that the purchase of a car became the chief concern of all the men the moment they were hired. Indeed, for most of them, a car was essential to keep the job. But the way the compartmentals approached the task was completely illogical. Darrell Johns was a case in point. On one occasion, he telephoned to say that he had important business and would not be coming to work. Since this was the latest in a series of absences, we investigated the reason for it.

We discovered that the first thing Darrell had done was to go to a used car lot. After selecting the car he wanted, he was told he needed credit for the purchase. He then drove around shopping for credit in a car borrowed from the car lot. At one of the more expensive credit companies in town, he was informed that he needed a license to obtain credit. At this point he arranged for a driver's test. The following interview with Darrell after the incident illustrates his inverted system of priorities:

> ROY. *Like you were sayin', you had some business to attend to. That can be once or twice, but if you look at your record, that's too many times, and I know that people aren't going to stand for it! I don't blame them. If you want that job, let us know....You are still on probation! I don't know how you feel about it, and I may be wrong. Maybe the people we are taking in don't want a job; but I don't believe that, because most of them are panning out. They've shown up, and they really want to work. We only have about three or four people, and you are one of them, who just keep it up.*
> DARRELL. *Who is this? Me and Andy Manners?*
> ROY. *Yes, but you're not in the same class with Andy Manners. Andy comes to work. He even left his kids this*

morning and showed up on the job, and his wife is in jail. You know the main thing, Darrell, is that the people went to bat for you. I'm not lying, they really went to bat for you!

DARRELL. . . . *It just seem like every time I'm off like it's a big thing.*

ROY. *It* is *a big thing. If you weren't in that spot* (a critical production area) *where you are . . . you are critical. The man felt you could do the job; he went and talked to the union for you. Told them he would promote you when he wanted to. He needed you today! . . . You want to talk about a driver's license—right now? You say they are giving you a lot of trouble about a driver's license? Did you get your license?*

DARRELL. *I took written tests, driver's tests, everythin'.*

ROY. *Then what is the problem?*

DARRELL. . . . *See what I did. . . the man was goin' to let me have the car; then he asked me for the number to my license, and I didn't have no license. . . .And then today they come talkin' about I got a bad credit record—I goes back out there, and he lets me use one of his cars to go to another bond company, and it's a different thing there. When I come back, I said forget it, and I left!*

ROY. *Now, the first thing is if you want a car, you have to have a job. . . . If you don't have a job, it's going to be hard to make a payment. What you will have to do is to protect your job in order to get your car.*

DARRELL. . . . *I was aware of what I was doin' this mornin' . . . I had some loan papers that I had to get.* (Pause) *And when I lose all this here* (the job) *I mean, I don't even need them!*

MRS. JOHNS. *He wasn't here that long, anyway.*

ROY. *Yeah, but the thing is he never called me or nothin'. He should have said something, because he had me in a bind. I told the man* (foreman) *just what you told me—twelve o'clock.*

DARRELL. (To wife) *You lied on me! I told you to tell that man that I won't be in today because I had some very important business to attend to.*

ROY. *As long as you* had *very important business!*

DARRELL. *That's what I told you.*

To the compartmentals, the job was the key to a world of material benefits they had been denied all their lives. Once they had the key, they wanted to get into this world as quickly as possible. But their fierce determination to enjoy the benefits the job would provide stood in the way of their keeping the job.

Compartmentals had to be fired; they did not quit. Their involvement in the responsibilities of the job never materialized. In fact, most of them were not in one shop long enough for any meaningful relationships to develop. In the case of two compartmentals, the job did tenuously begin to develop and take hold.

Dependent Pattern

There were eight trainees who were classified in the dependent pattern (six blacks, one Mexican American, and one white). From the beginning, the dependents were the favorites of the shop. Together with the overperformers, they showed the most promise. They were unobtrusive, attentive, malleable, and had the necessary basic skills for the job. In fact, their minority background was the only evidence that they were hard-core.

Each man had a honeymoon period preceding a crisis. Depending upon the man, the calm varied in length, from seven weeks to almost the entire year. But eventually the crisis came, usually without warning. It invariably took the form of a sudden rash of absences. Two trainees survived the crisis; six did not.

All of these men used alcohol or narcotics to the extent that it seriously interfered with their work. All had deep feelings of inadequacy—generally not visible to others, but all too visible to the individual himself. In contrast to the bragging of the bravados, dependents almost never bragged. In fact, the pattern was for their supervisors to brag for them. It was common for the man himself to protest that the lead man or foreman was bragging about him too much.

Anxiety about inadequacy was, perhaps, the chief characteristic of the dependent. Each man revealed it in his own way in a particular set of circumstances. For some, anxiety arose when they were given specific or exacting job assignments. For others, boredom increased anxiety, and some feared the close interpersonal relationships that began to develop between them and their coworkers—a solicitous lead man, for example.

These anxieties pointed to scars of the past, but they were rekindled by situations which developed within the job experience. All of the dependents found classroom training easy. However, the encounter with the job and the resulting anxiety did not really begin until a few weeks after floor assignments, at which point, almost to a man, the dependents resisted upgrade, some obliquely and some directly.

For example, the blueprint class was an *ad hoc* arrangement whereby the hard-core could be upgraded to jobs free from union pressure. While Carl Brown was preparing for an upgrade in this class he began to report sick, and to complain about a fear of heights.

He complained, "I tell you I haven't been in class for a long time, and it keeps me upset when I'm tryin' to keep up with the class. There are other people in the class that dig it; but I keep gettin' a headache, because it puts pressure on me."

(*Williams*). I explained how valuable machine training was in this day and time. I pointed out that in plumbing he would have to do some climbing and reminded him, "You're supposed to have acrophobia!"

He said dejectedly, "I wish sometimes that I could just pick up my bag and leave."

The compartmentals were also prone to conflict created by having to perform tasks associated with unpleasant experiences. For example, Brown had had a traumatic experience stemming from a false conviction for which he had served six months. During this time, he had been placed in a felony tank, a form of solitary confinement. One day while on the NAB job, his foreman gave him a broom and asked him to sweep up. Brown responded that the broom didn't fit his hand and said that he was sick and was going home. The next day we talked to him about this incident.

Brown said that during the screening interview for Southwestern, he had asked the interviewers if he would be given any sweeping or janitorial work to do, and they had assured him that he would not. We pursued this point:

DOC. (Padfield). *Let me ask you a question, this is hypothetical, suppose they had not made that commitment?*

CARL. *Knowin' me, I probably would have played it until the sweeping came along.*

ROY (Williams). *And then would you have quit?*

CARL. *No, I wouldn't a quit.*

ROY. *What would you have done?*

CARL. *I woulda did it like I did. I woulda told somebody about it. That's how sweepin' makes me feel, and if we couldn't a come to no understanding no more than I had to sweep, I still woulda quit.*

ROY. *Would you have, even if they had told you, "Well, Carl, right now we can't find you another job, and you'll have to sweep until we get something"? You would have told them to forget the job?*

CARL. *I told them I can't sweep! I know one time I was in jail. I was waiting to go to court, and they asked me, "You want to paint?" And I told em, "No, I don't want to paint because I don't like to paint. It makes me sick!" They say, "Either you paint or you get locked up; you go to the hole!" All right, I'm already locked up, so what's the need of gettin' locked up any further? I done been there one time before for two days. Six in the morning right before breakfast, they come in and take that little pad away, this is in the city jail, and your blanket, and all day long you're sitting there on this cold steel or on the cold cement. So I went on in there. I done very little paintin', but at least I faked it; and I still don't like it, but it was better than being locked up in that jail!*

ROY. *This is the same thing . . .*

CARL. *It's not the same thing. I'm not in jail, Mr. Williams. I am* free *out here. I can move around; I can make a decision of my own. They make decisions for me in jail . . . they make them; I didn't make them. So I coulda went to the hole, but what's the need of going in there, freezin' to death. But right now, for once I can get up and walk outta here, and it won't hurt nobody but me. But it's one thing you can be sure of, when I walk outta here, I'm free!*

With the dependents, an upgrade, rather than becoming a source of personal satisfaction, became a crisis. Carl Brown was eventually transferred into machine operating. His work was good but his feelings of inadequacy still persisted. He complained continually about nerves, anxiety, his inability to relax, and depression. A month later he quit.

Other experiences which would be considered normal or desirable by the average worker caused crises for the dependents. Pete Martinez and his wife describe Pete's reaction to his inactivity in the plant:

> WIFE. *When he first started workin' at Southwestern, he used to tell me that he liked the job and everything. And then after a couple of months he started tellin' me that he was tired. It was the job, because he didn't hardly do nothin', you know. He just sat at his desk . . . and he wanted to work more; he would ask his foreman if he would put him to work, and his foreman would tell him, "Yeah," but still he wouldn't.*
>
> PETE. *You know, uh, I think a lot to myself; I think more than anybody else. . . . I sit at that desk and think all day. Good things and bad things, you know. Whatever comes to my mind—you get tired of that. Want somethin' to do with my hands. Just wanna tell Freddie, uh, why don't he . . . teach me to alkaline clean? But I guess he couldn't because I don't think he know it himself. . . . And, he told me to draw little cartoons, you know; sit down or walk around, talk to everybody.*
>
> ROY. *Okay, you're a 23-year-old man, what's going through your mind when you're sitting down with nothing to do?*
>
> PETE. *I sit down and look at all the people. Try to think what they're thinkin'. . . . Maybe they're bored at this job, you know, like I am. Half of them are. They're more mature than I am. They can accept it. Either that or they're lazier than me, you know. People are getting paid for doin nothin', and I'm watchin' them gettin' paid. I think about . . . other things—like quittin', findin' somethin' else—you know, go home and get drunk or somethin'!*

Martinez had worked most of his teenage life as a seasonal farm worker, and his inactivity on the present job was a drastic change.

He would say, "Work out in the fields is not bad work. It's not the best either. It's hard work. I'd do that again if they paid a lot more. But they don't, so I have no choice. Cause most of the jobs they have down at Southwestern is an easy man's job."

The dependents seemed hounded by fundamental feelings of unworthiness. Excessive praise produced guilt feelings because it increased these feelings of unworthiness. The emptier their backgrounds in terms of human relationships, the stronger their guilt. Gary Nolan had been an orphan all of his life. He came into Southwestern with high expectations, and elicited high hopes from his coworkers, especially his foreman, Ken Johnson. He received upgrades, wage increases, and glowing evaluations for almost ten months. Then suddenly he regressed. The crisis came when Mary, the girl he was living with, started pressuring him to marry her. Gary had put her off many times before with the excuse that he didn't have a job and couldn't support her, but now that he was employed that reason was no longer viable. The pressure became intense, and finally when she made him agree to marry her, he developed a work crisis and was eventually terminated (see Chapter 7).

The responses of coworkers and supervisors to Gary's conflict probably had a negative effect. During his period of breakdown they stressed how much they thought of him, how well he was doing, how good a worker he was, and this increased his feelings of unworthiness and intensified his conflict.

The upgrade signified praise as well as new responsibilities. We have already discussed the effects of praise in Brown's instance. In the case of Henry Boice, as soon as he was transferred to North Plant and upgraded to machine tool operator, he simply stopped coming to work.

The dependent's pattern was rooted in an inner world that had meaning in past and ongoing relationships outside the plant. To them the struggle at work was only a dim reflection of the real struggles in their intimate lives, some of them active, some memories. All dependents were from hopelessly wrecked homes. Pete Martinez had no memory of a father, except that he had been jailed for nonsupport. Henry Boice had no father and had spent ten years in San Quentin.

Carl Brown's father left him when Carl was five years old. Another man married his mother, and as he put it, "took his mother away." He felt this deeply. Carl recalled experiencing a vivid nightmare when he was sick as a child:

. . . Weird thing, I even do it now when I start getting sick or get sick. It's something I ain't never heard of before. Remember, I told you about that dream I used to have about a ball of clay about the size of a marble would come out of my mother's room, go through the whole house and when it came back it would be just one *big* ball of clay? Remember, I told you about that? Well, that's what happens when I get sick; although it doesn't come out of my mother's room any more, it's still there. Maybe somewhere my mind got confused on what to believe in—what I really believe in—I don't know, but I wish it would straighten out. Things go good for a month, maybe two months, then bang!

I don't know where it started from, but I just remember it from when I was small. It would always come out of my mother's room and it would go through the house and then it would come back and we used to sleep on the couch in the front room and it would come back in there where I was. It never did get me but it was coming. But it also made some kind of noise or feeling . . . I can't actually pinpoint which one and even now it happen sometime like when I start feeling like I do now . . . the noise that it makes or the feelin' that it gives comes back. It comes back and I be all hung-up again.

It's small when it starts and then as it goes through the house and comes back, it's really big then. It's bigger than the door! It comes outta the door and things—you know, just like it's coverin' up half of this room. It's really big! You know how dreams is—they skip, you know, and leave out little pieces and things. I was just always afraid. Nowhere to run to—but I was always afraid.

Carl still dreams this dream.

Overperformers and Naturals

There were only three trainees who could be classified as overperformers. These men were still on the job at the end of the reference year, and they were everyone's favorite workers. Like the dependents, they received constant praise from their supervisors and coworkers. In spite of personal problems, they could find a release in the job. Unlike the compartmentals, they linked rewards and recognition with performance. The more they were upgraded the harder they worked. Unlike bravados, they never demanded recognition or upgrades, and usually had to be urged to accept such rewards. Also unlike the bravados, instead of bragging, they worried about losing the job in spite of their high performance.

All of these men (two black Americans and one Italian-American) had an overdeveloped sense of responsibility. They tended to be older than the other trainees, cowed and undereducated. Lester Banks was 33. He had an East Texas background, a fourth-grade education in segregated schools, and was illiterate. He migrated to California as an adult. Herman Cooper was 32, also born in the South, but his family migrated to Philadelphia when he was a child. There, he worked in nonunion shops for most of his life. Robert Barreca, 28, was born and raised in Italy. He worked as a poor fisherman and did not immigrate to the United States until he was an adult.

Overperformers were quiet and almost invisible except in contrast to the other hard-core. They tended to be disgusted with the other trainees, especially the compartmentals. The overperformers had learned to repress their resentments, but occasionally they did allow their feelings to surface. For example, on rare occasions, Lester Banks drank. At these times he might consume as much as a fifth of whiskey which released his repressed resentments. One time he blacked both his wife's eyes and literally knocked holes in the partitions in his house. Herman Cooper's resentment was also expressed at home where he and his wife fought continuously, intensely and physically. To Barreca the job was a means of getting away from his family which consisted of eight children, six preschool, a domineering wife, and a smothering family of in-laws.

The work patterns of the three naturals resembled the work patterns of the average non-hard-core worker. This does not mean that they had no serious difficulties in their private lives, as indeed many normal workers do. We simply comment at this point about their plant behavior. They did not overperform, worry about their job performance, or overreact. They had normal attendance records and were interested in upgrades. Moreover, the occupational experience of the naturals had an immediately beneficial effect on the problems they faced in their private lives. As did the overperformers, these men moved directly into their work patterns and were still on the job at the end of their respective reference years. We place the naturals last because their visibility was lowest.

WORK ATTENDANCE AS A FURTHER INDICATOR OF GROUP CHARACTERISTICS

To most supervisors job attendance is the critical index of a man's performance. Since other indices tend to be subjective, it is important to have this objective measurement as a final dimension of hard-core behavior in the plant.

In order to make a valid comparison between hard-core and non-hard-core attendance, we selected a control group of 28 non-hard-core employees who were hired at the same time as the NAB trainees. Thus, these employees conformed to the hard-core group with respect to two important variables having a possible causal role in absenteeism—being *new* to the company and being hired *at the same* time in the calendar year.

Each man in the control group was selected as a cohort for an individual in the hard-core group. We used employee numbers as the basis for this individual selection—the cohort number being that closest to his hard-core counterpart. There were never more than one or two numbers separating cohorts from counterparts.

The selection of the control group was random in that we knew nothing about the man whose employee number we chose. It was purposive in the sense that we were controlling for time of the plant year and also for employees who were new to Southwestern.

First we compared the hard-core group with the control group and then compared their aggregate figures for absences and lateness for the twelve-month reference period (see Table 2).

Table 2
COMPARISON OF ABSENCES AND LATENESS BETWEEN
HARD-CORE AND CONTROL GROUP
FOR 12-MONTH REFERENCE PERIOD

	Hard-Core (28 men) 5588 Work Days		Control Group (28 men) 6144 Work Days	
	Days	Percentage	Days	Percentage
Absent	478	8.55	295	4.80
Late	334	5.98	183	2.98
Total	812	14.53	478	7.78

NOTE: Reference period established for each individual beginning with his starting date and ending with his termination date or first anniversary if with the company more than one year.

Table 2 indicates the absence percentages of the hard-core group were slightly less than double those of the control group. The latenesses were almost exactly double the control group's. The absence and lateness percentages of both groups were higher than the figure for Southwestern's total work force for 1969, which was about one percent.

Table 3
MONTHLY TRENDS IN HARD-CORE
AND CONTROL GROUP ABSENTEEISM
USING CHRONOLOGICAL SEQUENCE

Calendar Month	Hard-Core			Control Group		
	Possible Man Days	Days Absent	Percentage	Possible Man Days	Days Absent	Percentage
August	100	4	4.00	100	0	0
September	180	10	5.56	180	4	2.22
October	120	17	14.17	340	8	2.35
November	420	38	9.05	440	14	3.18
December	500	44	8.80	560	56	10.00

TABLE 3 *(Continued)*

Calendar Month	Hard-Core			Control Group		
	Possible Man Days	Days Absent	Percentage	Possible Man Days	Days Absent	Percentage
January	500	80	16.00	500	60	12.00
February	490	63	12.86	480	14	2.92
March	440	39	8.86	480	32	6.67
April	380	35	9.21	460	16	3.48
May	380	40	10.53	450	27	6.00
June	360	31	8.61	430	22	5.12
July	340	31	9.12	410	19	4.63
August	280	20	7.14	320	5	1.56
September	240	15	6.25	270	6	2.22
October	140	6	4.29	140	12	8.57
November	60	5	8.33	80	0	0

NOTES: Chronological sequence listed by calendar month beginning August 1, 1968. Each employee is included in the month he was hired and removed in the month of his termination or first anniversary.

Man days are computed by multiplying the number of men on the payroll for the month indicated by 20. Fractions of months under halves are rounded off to half months; those over half are rounded off to next whole month.

Table 3 shows the work chronology of the two groups in terms of the calendar year. This scheme reflects plant events and other temporal and seasonal factors which could have affected work attendance. Since the social environment of the hard-core was different from that of the ordinary worker, we would expect to see some of these differences reflected in their work attendance. In October, the month when the union-management confrontation reached its peak, hard-core absences almost tripled. Of course there were no such experiences for the control group.

December's and January's high rates suggest seasonal factors, since the control group rate was also high during these months. In addition, job shuffling of the hard-core was going on during those months and reached its peak in January.

Table 4
MONTHLY TRENDS IN HARD-CORE AND
CONTROL GROUP ABSENTEEISM
USING PHASED-ORDINAL SEQUENCE

Month Sequence	Hard-Core			Control Group		
	Possible Man Days	Days Absent	Percentage	Possible Man Days	Days Absent	Percentage
First	560	28	5.00	560	21	3.75
Second	560	56	10.00	520	14	2.69
Third	510	62	12.16	520	26	5.00
Fourth	490	58	11.84	520	30	5.77
Fifth	460	58	12.61	480	41	8.54
Sixth	410	32	7.80	460	50	10.87
Seventh	400	37	9.25	460	25	5.43
Eighth	380	39	10.26	450	13	2.89
Ninth	380	25	6.58	440	20	4.55
Tenth	360	42	11.67	440	21	4.77
Eleventh	340	24	7.06	410	16	3.90
Twelfth	300	17	5.67	380	18	4.74

NOTE: In the phased-ordinal sequence all individuals were phased together according to their first month on the job regardless of the calendar denotation of that month. A terminated individual was removed according to the ordinal position of the month of his termination.

Two striking differences between the hard-core and control group appear in what we call the phased-ordinal sequence (see Table 4). This sequence brings into one common focus the temporal world of each individual employee.

The first difference is the enormous increase in percentage of absenteeism from the first to the second month among the hard-core. This reflects movement of the hard-core from the classroom to the plant proper.

There is another trend difference between the two—the tendency for major fluctuations of hard-core absenteeism through time. A check on possible man-days for the month indicated provides a partial explanation. These reductions indicate that a termination occurred. For instance, in the sixth month, the ninth month, the eleventh month and the twelfth month, there were hard-core terminations of individuals responsible for much of the absenteeism in the preceding months.

In the control group, absenteeism increased from the fourth through the sixth month at the very time that possible man-days were being decreased as a result of terminations. We do not have sufficient data to explain this, nor do we wish to speculate.

The five hard-core groups we have described throughout this chapter were made up of individuals grouped together on the basis of common characteristics and behavior in the plant. We now compare the attendance characteristics of these five groups (see Table 5).

Table 5
ABSENCES AND LATENESS OF HARD-CORE BY GROUPS
FOR 12-MONTH REFERENCE PERIOD

	Compartmental (7 men) 1082 Work Days		Bravado (7 men) 1576 Work Days		Dependent (8 men) 1385 Work Days	
	Days	Percentage	Days	Percentage	Days	Percentage
Absent	148	13.68	184	11.68	110	7.94
Late	66	6.10	145	9.20	81	5.85
Total	214	19.78	329	20.88	191	13.80

	Natural (3 men) 769 Work Days		Overperformer (3 men) 776 Work Days	
	Days	Percentage	Days	Percentage
	31	4.03	5	.64
	31	4.03	11	1.42
	62	8.06	16	2.06

The compartmental group ranked highest in absences. Bravados were second, dependents third, naturals fourth, and overperformers, last. This tends to support our more subjective observations.

The compartmentals were consistently the most naive about the effects of poor performance and absenteeism, in particular, on rewards. They hung onto their jobs until terminated; therefore, one would expect their absences to be the highest.

On the other hand, we would expect dependents to be lower than the bravados, because their absences accumulated abruptly as an indication of their quitting. Naturally, under these circumstances they would be kept a minimal length of time once the absence behavior began.

The absence percentages of the naturals compare closely to the absence percentages of the control group. And, of course, the absence percentages of the overperformers indicate the unrealistic performance aspect of these men, .64 is lower than the absence percentages for the plant as a whole.

The lateness profiles of the groups also support other differences. Bravados, as we've indicated, had the temerity to stand up to their supervisors and defend their lateness. Their 9.20 percentage is the highest of the five groupings. Latenesses of the compartmentals, dependents and naturals are roughly the same, and again the overperformer group is low.

Trend analyses of absenteeism reveal further contrasts (see Table 6). This is dramatically illustrated by the *first* month record of the compartmentals in contrast to the other four groups. They also ranked highest in eight out of twelve months. The ninth month drop reflects termination of an individual with excessively high absenteeism.

Among the bravados, the possible man-days are fairly constant and their above average absenteeism percentage continues generally throughout the year, but does begin to drop toward the twelfth month.

Absenteeism trends of the dependents reflect their pattern of abrupt withdrawal. Drops from the second to third, fifth to sixth, and tenth to eleventh months are due to the termination of individuals who had excessively high absenteeism.

Table 6
MONTHLY TRENDS IN HARD-CORE ABSENTEEISM BY GROUPS USING PHASED-ORDINAL SEQUENCE

Month Sequence	Compartmental (7 men)		Bravado (7 men)		Dependent (8 men)	
	Possible Man Days	Percentage of Absence	Possible Man Days	Percentage of Absence	Possible Man Days	Percentage of Absence
First	140	11.43	140	3.57	160	4.38
Second	140	10.00	140	16.43	160	11.25
Third	140	21.43	130	16.92	120	2.50
Fourth	130	19.23	120	17.50	120	4.17
Fifth	100	20.00	120	15.00	120	11.67
Sixth	70	14.29	120	9.17	100	9.00
Seventh	60	15.00	120	11.67	100	10.00
Eighth	40	12.50	120	14.17	100	14.00
Ninth	40	7.50	120	6.67	100	12.00
Tenth	40	20.00	120	19.17	80	13.75
Eleventh	40	10.00	120	10.00	60	6.67
Twelfth	40	10.00	100	9.00	40	5.00

Natural (3 men)		Overperformer (3 men)	
Possible Man Days	Percentage of Absence	Possible Man Days	Percentage of Absence
60	0	60	0
60	1.67	60	0
60	3.33	60	6.67
60	10.00	60	1.67
60	10.00	60	0
60	3.33	60	0
60	6.67	60	0
60	5.00	60	0
60	3.33	60	0
60	0	60	0
60	6.67	60	0
60	3.33	60	0

REASONS FOR WORK INTERRUPTIONS

More important than the simple enumeration of absenteeisms are the reasons for work interruptions, and the facts these reveal about the social system outside the factory. We kept exhaustive records for the first three months of Southwestern's hard-core program, during which time we enumerated 65 work interruptions for the first 18 trainees. The greatest number, 14, were for difficulties with the police and court system. Twelve resulted from self-indulgence—alcohol, narcotics, venereal disease. Another 12 interruptions were the result of simple illnesses of either the worker or his immediate family. Ten additional cases of sickness were catalogued separately from this because they were preceded by family strife—violent arguments, physical fights, temporary separations. In all but a few cases the families were reconciled during the period of sickness. Of the 17 remaining interruptions five were for therapy, one occurred as a result of confrontation with a supervisor, five resulted from mechanical causes—such as malfunctions of clocks, cars, and problems with bus schedules. We were unable to determine causes for six.

We kept less exhaustive records of these types of intervening factors for each worker throughout the rest of the reference year. We are able to say on the basis of a year's field notes, interviews, observation schedules and other records, that the profile described above is generally valid for the 28 men as a whole. Police and public agencies ranked first, self-indulgence second, simple illness third, and family strife fourth.

It is only natural that as the hard-core began to move from the ghetto and develop a more active and visible life in the industrial system, they would encounter difficulty with the legal system. The types of police and court problems they had are revealing. First in terms of frequency were traffic problems—driving violations, vehicle registration, licensing, minor accidents, and so on. The second most important problem was being held on suspicion. Although many of these arrests did not result in charges, they nevertheless caused the men to miss work. We discuss this more thoroughly in the next chapter. Court appearances ranked third in order of importance. Frequencies of charges were in this order: petty theft, drunk and disorderly conduct, burglary, narcotics, child support, and child custody problems last. Such causes for absenteeism in the factory reveal the importance of social systems external to the factory (see Part II).

BASIC ISSUES

The critical issue in Chapter 3 centered on the question of differential access to *good jobs*. The issue in Chapter 4 is this: Are the ghetto or hard-core unemployed people willing to change their lives and rearrange their priorities in order to work in industry, or do they want the best of two worlds—compensatory opportunity plus no change in their value system? We have described four dysfunctional patterns of occupational behavior—the aggressive, divisive patterns of the bravado, the occupational naivete of the compartmentals, the self-aggression of the dependents, and the repressed aggression of the overperformers. To what extent and in what numbers will these populations of hard-core unemployed be able to make the transition? Will such a transition open and obviate the ghetto?

There are no clear-cut, simple answers to these questions. Solutions will require complementary adjustments on the part of both industry and the hard-core unemployed. Complementary adjustment, especially in the case of black and other nonwhite Americans, implies a transition from a single, culturally dominant system to a culturally pluralistic system.

This poses another basic set of questions: Are we going to accord the full benefits of our society to culturally different ethnic groups? Can they participate fully in the overall social, economic and political system and still maintain their own cultural identity, or is the NAB program simply a device to obviate the ethnic systems of these culturally different people and force them all to think and act like white, middle-class Americans?

PART TWO

Stress in the Old Arena

4

Law and Order: The Ghetto Frontier

Must I concern myself, with such low-thinking class?
No! I shall get drunk, then break my empty glass
I shall crash the wall and make glitter upon the floor
Rip the lights out of the night, and remove my barricade from the
    door.
I shall caress the space that surrounds my tormenting place,
I shall call the law and let them look into my mirror at their
    hollow face
And laugh before them, singing a ghostly hymn
Tearing the thoughts out of their minds in a passionate whim,
Then slowly look down at them, with a pleasant smile
And hear them cry at my feet like a sinful child.
Indeed I shall be drunk, but not fooled for a moment by their
    devious minds
I shall curse their souls and break their hideous spines.
"Fool" I shall cry "Children of the Devil now you know your
    fate."
Then I shall laugh and collect their coins on a paper plate
Off I shall dance into the sparking night
Until my deeds are past, and my being is far from sight.

*("Must I Concern Myself," by Charles J. Butler, NAB trainee, written
December 8, 1969)*

Just as experiences with unemployment and the occupational system vary drastically by class and race, so do experiences with the law and the police.

To most property-owning, middle-class Americans, "strict" law enforcement poses no threat to anyone except those who break the laws or want to break them. But to most nonpropertied, nonwhite Americans, justice is a privilege of class and race. To them most laws are biased, justice is largely inaccessible, and prison is disabling. In short, the legal system is a political instrument protecting the social position and cultural values of predominantly one class and one race of U.S. citizens.

Experience with the law varies so sharply and is compartmentalized so completely that people from either of these two groups can sincerely and truthfully describe two different realities. From a cognitive standpoint, it is more logical to say that there is in fact a dual system of law and order—one for mainstream society and one for ghetto society. This dual system creates a barrier which those in the ghetto must break through in order to gain entrance to mainstream society. Too much has been written on this subject to dwell on it,[27] but this background is an important point of departure for discussing how police experiences affected the trainees' jobs and vice versa. The system of law and order described here is one which the hard-core's middle-class coworker seldom encounters firsthand and seldom believes secondhand.

To the hard-core unemployed, legal and occupational discrimination are mutually reinforcing institutions. The greatest obstacle to employment is a police record, and the greatest obstacle to obedience to the law is unemployment. Most hard-core have accumulated an imposing set of negative credentials before they have reached the legal age of adulthood. Among the 28 trainees all but 4 had police records at the time they were hired, and 16 had juvenile records, mostly petty theft.

THE DISHABILITATION* OF CLASS GUILT

To the hard-core, living in the ghetto is living in legal jeopardy. Some people refer to these low income residential areas as slums.

*This term is used as an antonym for rehabilitation.

Others, including the hard-core trainees, call them ghettos. In law enforcement semantics they are high crime areas. The implications of this pejorative for police procedures should be obvious: fringe area, fringe tactics.

Because a high crime area is a known location for nefarious activities, a collecting ground for "shady" and even "subversive" characters, people in the ghetto will see more policemen more often than people in suburban communities. In addition there are a variety of legal and quasi-legal options policemen can use as tactics to flush out "criminals" and "prevent" crime. Being poor and powerless members of a high crime population, the ghetto resident, young or old, male or female, is frequently exposed to these tactics, whereas the suburban resident experiences them rarely, if at all. We will discuss these police options from the hard-core point of view which contends that such tactics provoke and increase rather than prevent crime.

One strategic option is the individual policeman's right to make "field investigations", i.e., the right to stop and question any person, any place. Stopping a vehicle in a ghetto usually leads to some type of citation: expired license, faulty equipment, an empty liquor container, too many passengers, a concealed weapon in the glove box, and so on. However, field investigations are not limited to traffic situations. People can be questioned anywhere. If they refuse to answer, they can be booked on suspicion, taken to the police station, and questioned there. This provides a broad latitude for police action in the ghetto, because crimes are frequent and descriptions of suspects vague. In addition, investigations can usually provide suspicion charges for violating statutes which discriminate against the lower classes: loitering, vagrancy, prostitution, gambling, harboring criminals, and so on. An individual booked on suspicion may be held for 48 hours, or until bail is posted.

At best, field investigations and suspicion arrests are annoying. When they occur frequently, they are oppressive, especially when wages are forfeited from work time lost. Weekend arrests are equally frustrating because the suspect is usually detained until the following Monday. But the major threat of such tactics is the increased likelihood that the suspect will break a law in the course of these procedures.

Repeated interrogations and suspicion arrests will naturally provoke reactions. When the individual lacks legal knowledge and resources, his natural reaction will likely be emotional rather than rational, frequently resulting in such additional charges as eluding a police officer, disturbing the peace and disorderly conduct, resisting arrest, and occasionally, assaulting a police officer.

Publicly, privately and in group sessions, the trainees complained more about police harrassment than any other single problem. Half of the trainees had arrest records for suspicion charges which did not materialize. These records give an objective indication of police action in the ghetto. A list of minor infractions gives another. The following are arrest categories taken from the records of the 28 trainees:

1. Disturbing the peace (This includes disorderly parties, domestic squabbles, and so on.)
2. Traffic violations
3. Nonsupport
4. Child neglect
5. Concealed weapon
6. Prowling
7. Drinking
8. Accessory to those committing a crime
9. Marijuana
10. Petty theft

Regardless of police intentions, investigations and suspicion arrests have negative consequences. Here, Carl Brown talks about his experience with the police:

> ROY. *In other words, the first three times you got in jail did they book you for anything?*
>
> CARL. *Just for suspicion.*
>
> ROY. *How long did they keep you?*
>
> CARL. *They only keep you three days. Most of the time they kept me around two-and-a-half days.*
>
> ROY. *What happens when they book you like that?*
>
> CARL. *They put you in the felony tank, and you come out,*

and a detective talks to you. If the detective didn't talk to you the first day, you didn't come out the first day. And if one didn't talk to you the second day, you didn't come out the second day. Not at all. And then one had to talk to you the third day. Or else they just have to let you go. But they always fixed it so they always had one talk to you. . . .So after you talk, they put you back in the cell for another coupla hours or so, and then they let you go. I don't understand—I don't understand the reason for that. It's frustratin' to be arrested when you're not doing anything. It really is! It makes you feel unsafe. . . .

ROY. *What's it like in solitary in the city jail?*

CARL. *The city jail—it's cold, it stinks, and it's hard!*

The more extreme forms of police tactics extend the option of interrogation to arrest, conviction, and punishment all in one action. Such treatment is not limited to blacks. Gary Nolan describes one of his experiences in a California beach town. He was sitting in a bar when a friend came in and asked Gary to take a ride with him to see if they could pick up some girls:

GARY. *Anyway the guy who owns the bar came over. He says, "Come on, let's go find some broads." We go to this restaurant that I know, so we'll talk to them. And we're double parked. This cop was walking around the corner, and I don't know what his beef was or what he wanted but he said, "Wait a minute, I want to talk to you guys." And Jimmy Nelson—he did own the car; he had a couple of traffic warrants—panicked and took off.*

DOC. *Were you in the car?*

GARY. *Yeah, right. I was sitting there, and he goes around the corner; he hits right through a red light. The cop's sitting right there on the corner, and he chases us, and he's right on our tail.*

DOC. *I guess you ran a few red lights?*

GARY. *Yeah, we ran everything goin' 120-125 miles an hour. The cops just couldn't keep up. . . .We got into this residential area where we pulled over and parked, and there were sirens going everywhere. They didn't know what they wanted us for, but they knew we were doin' something, runnin'—all this stuff. So we stopped, and we got out, and he (driver) jumps over a fence. We just walk down the street, cause we ain't done nothing. . . . Well, we're crossing the center section, and there's a cop parked over there.*

He says, "Excuse me, bub, could I talk to you?"

So we say, "Sure," and walk over to the car; and he said, "Where're you going?" We said we were just ridin' around. . . .

So he says, "Where are you coming from?"

"Oh, we're down visitin' our girls just around the block."

So he called up on the radio and said, "How many were there in the car?" They said three, and there were four of us, but they said three.

He said, "I've got them here."

When he said that, I was getting ready to get in the wind (run) and he pulled out his gun, still sittin' in the car, and says, "Hold it!" Well, in about three seconds there were about 12 to 13 cop cars coming from every direction to the intersection, and they just stopped there in the street and blocked the whole place off.

They just grabbed us apart, and one cop said, "All I could think of was my family coming down that street, and you guys just hitting them!" They just beat the shit out of us! So they took us to jail, and the next day they cut everyone loose but me, because I had that ticket violation. Jimmy called up and said he had paid cash for the car—it was his car—and they got us for car theft.

DOC. *Did you tell them before you got beaten that you weren't driving?*

GARY. *Yeah, there was only one out of the three could drive anyway, so there's no need to beat all our asses. They know this—no three people can drive a car—they beat everyone of our asses!*

DOC. *Did you charge them with anything?*

GARY. *No.*

DOC. *Why not?*

GARY. *What could I do? I'm back on a violation; I still broke the law on a violation.*

DOC. *You could call an attorney.*

GARY. *Yeah, but I didn't think about what I could do.* (Pause) *I saw that same cop get a Hell's Angel. . . .These three guys were just walking down the sidewalk—one of them had "Hell's Angels" painted on the back of his jacket. Well, he's pretty drunk, but they're holding him up all right, and they aren't saying a word to nobody.*

This cop comes walking up and says, "Hey!" Then he starts ripping shit off their jackets as if he wants them to do something. So the drunk guy, he done something, and the cop just beat the hell out of him with the stick. So all these other cops came running over there, and they pound on his head a little too. So the guy is down on the ground, and he's out cold.

The cops drag him to the cop car and all the time this dog face cop who beat the hell out of us, is holding his arm up like this and is screaming his face off, "Don't make me mad, punk!" The cops handcuffed the guy and got him in the back seat, and there he (cop) *is in the seat beating the shit out of him, and he's handcuffed!*

Racial brutality is another equally dishabilitative aspect of police action in the ghetto. There is a personal intimacy about the interplay of brutality between the black ghetto and the police, and such brutality is nonrestrictive—men, women, and children are swept into the conflict. When women are involved the interplay assumes violent sexual overtones, because its primary aim is humiliation.

Three of the black hard-core trainees were married to or living with white women. All of them reported a peculiar pattern of police harrassment. Joan, Lester Banks' common law wife, talks about being arrested almost weekly for health-holds. (Police authority to place in legal custody a person suspected of having V.D. This authority has since been rescinded in San Diego):

JOAN. *I used to be in jail every weekend. I would call Lester and say, "Well, Lester, I'm down here again." Especially after I had Mary* (first child).

ROY. *Because of Lester?*

LESTER. *They just didn't want her in this neighborhood!*

JOAN. *The captain of the police department told me he was*

going to have me locked up, "... *so you can stay away from
here for a long time, and we can keep you away from colored
people."*

ROY. *Did they ever pick you up in the presence of Lester?*

JOAN. *Yeah, they stopped me one night; Lester was comin'
down the street—I think I was workin' down there—he walked
up and asked what was the matter.*

  They said, "Is it any of your business?"

  And he said, "Yeah, she's my wife."

  *They said, "Well, we're going to take her in for a
health-hold."*

ROY. (Incredulously) *Health-hold?*

JOAN. *Yeah, venereal disease. I couldn't hold a job hardly—
yankin' me out of there. One time we were sound asleep, and
they come and knock on our door . . .*

LESTER. . . . *fifteen of them.*

JOAN. (Mimicking) *"Can you people prove where you were at
such and such a time?" I said I was here—we were here—the
kids are in there. They said they had a report of a white
woman pregnant—I was pregnant with one of the kids—and a
colored man robbed this store . . . .*

ROY. *Joan, did they check you for health-hold?*

JOAN. *What they call it is "health-hold and grand theft,"
naturally.*

LESTER. *They book you for either one of them.*

JOAN. *The next day you have to go to the doctor and he
checks you, and the doctor is just as nasty as he can be. . . .He
will check you to see if you have a venereal disease.*

ROY. *Did you ever have it?*

JOAN. *No .*

ROY. *How many times did they arrest you?*

JOAN. *Just about every weekend; I mean just about every
Friday night, and they would hold me until Monday
morning. . . .*

ROY. *How about you Lester, when they picked up Joan what
would you do?*

LESTER. *Wasn't nothin' I could do but go to work. They fix it at the police station where you can't get them out. . . .*

ROY. *Was it any particular policeman that used to pick on you?*

JOAN. *Any police, all of them was on me. They would come up and knock on the door and say, "Hey, Joan!"*

They asked me why I hang on to colored people—"Do they have better things?" You know how—nasty-mouth . . . .

I say, "Yeah, they pretty good!"

ROY. *They ask you that?*

JOAN. *Yeah. I say, "Yeah they good. Better than you!"*

Racial brutality is not restricted to sexual insults. Periodically suspects may be stopped and searched. The search may include their car, their possessions, and their person. Barbara Hill described an incident which took place at a Jack-In-The-Box restaurant:

DOC. *Why did they stop you?*

BARBARA. *They thought me and Bobby had some dope or somethin'. I'd just come from the wash house, washin' my clothes—they looked all through my clothes—threw my clothes on the ground—got them all dirty. I had to do em all over again. I went downtown and pressed charges on em, but they didn't do anythin'.*

DOC. *Who did you see when you went down there?*

BARBARA. *The captain, the head man, because they tried to arrest Bobby.* (Referring to another incident)—*We was at the park one Sunday, and Bobby took off—you know how you make the rubber* (tires) *squeek? Bobby did that, and they pulled him over, and the man started calling Bobby a nigger, you know. So Bobby started callin' him an old dirty hunkie.*

It was goin' back and forth like that, so they got ready to hit Bobby with that billy club, and I tol them, "Uh uh, don't hit him! You'd better not hit him! You take him to jail before you hit him!"

So they threw him in the car and (one policeman) *said, "This is a white man's world. No niggers belong in it!" I think he was out of place for saying that.*

So I went to press charges, and the captain said, "Well, you are niggers!"

DOC. *You mean the* captain *said, "You* are *niggers.'"?*

BARBARA. *Uh huh, he said it to my face—he said, "Well, you are niggers!"*

DOC. *. . . Did you complain about that to anybody?*

BARBARA. *Who?*

DOC. *Like the Community Relations . . .*

BOBBY. *. . . Ya don't find out that stuff until ya get around people that already know about it.*

BARBARA. *They know about it.* (Referring to the police) *. . . I tol one police officer it didn't do no good when I complained.*

He said, "Yes, it would, but you just don't know about it."

I said, "Well, all they'll do is take you off the beat for three days and put you right back on." He started laughin', cause it's true!

Police tactics were not the only legal problems experienced by the hard-core. The nonsupport law was another legal tool that was often used to discriminate against them. This law, which is rooted in strict anglo-puritan attitudes, states quite simply that a man may be imprisoned for not supporting his legal dependents. However, it may be extended beyond the refusal of an employed person to support his children and used against a chronically unemployed man living with his family. Alienating a man from his family can be as socially destructive as any of the police actions described above. Jack Davis' case is particularly revealing.

Jack, a black trainee, was born and raised in a rural town in Arkansas. His family migrated to California when he was seven. He did not finish high school, because he made a girl pregnant. The girl had the baby and went on welfare. At that point Jack was put on probation for nonsupport. He then dropped out of school, married the girl, and faced the task of looking for work with no diploma and no skills. The welfare office and his probation officer assigned him to compulsory work—street cleaning four days a week—to justify the welfare. Jack was allowed one day a week to look for work. Lacking both education and skills, he was unable to find employment. In addition to these pressures, his probation officer repeatedly threatened to send Jack to honor camp if he didn't find work. In 1964 he was sentenced to six months in honor camp. At that time his wife, with the help of an attorney, gained his release after two-and-a-half months. Because his family was still on public assistance, and despite the fact the he was again on compulsory work detail, Jack's probation officer continued to pressure him with the ultimatum of finding work or returning to honor camp.

In March 1964, Jack requested release from probation, and the court informed him he would have to spend the probation time (one year) in honor camp. Because this was preferable to the constant harrassment of the probation officer, Jack took the year's sentence. He was released in 8 months and 20 days for "good time" to find his wife pregnant and living with a navy man. When the sailor went back to ship duty, Jack offered to accept the child, and he and his wife made another try at marriage. Five months later the sailor returned, and she left Jack again, taking the children, Jack's included.

Such laws and the attitudes underlying them amount to a prejudgment not only of the individual but of the family unit itself. In Jack's case, the "undesirable" man meant an "undesirable" family. This type of prejudgment reflects the basic injustice of such class treatment.

In some cases the family, if it *is* recognized, is merely a tool in achieving the ends of law enforcement. This judgment is based not only on the trainees' accounts of past experiences, but on events observed during the NAB training period.

Darrell Johns and his wife, Justine, fought continuously. The fighting was intense, intimate, and much of it was violent. More than once Justine called the police. On one occasion when the police arrested Darrell after he had bloodied his wife's head, they took Justine to the police station where she was interrogated by the vice squad.

JUSTINE. *They asked me do Darrell mess with marijuana and stuff like that. They were trying to pick me, because they say they want Darrell real bad. They asked me something about him s'posed to be sellin' some rifles or somethin'. I told em I didn't know nothin' about it. I told them I wasn't goin' to tell them nothin' noway. I was jus' jokin' with him* (the detective) *and said, "If ya give me about $50 I'll tell ya anything ya wanna know." And so he said, "If he is, you tell us, and then we can pick him up and have something planted on him."*

ROY. *Why do the police want to get Darrell so bad?*
JUSTINE. *Why do they? I don't know.* (Pause) *Darrell told me they goin' to get him or somethin'—I don' know. They told me an my cousin when we was down there* (pausing and imitating their determination) *they goin' ta get him* off *these streets!*

To both the police and the welfare agency, corrupting an already weak relationship in a family was a means to a laudable end. In the case of Jack Davis, the family was incidental to the punitive purpose of the welfare system and the court. Jack was jailed for over a total of 12 months solely because he could not find employment, despite the fact that he had willingly worked in a compulsory program. A strong family would find it difficult to withstand this pressure. A weak family finds it disastrous.

Prison further extends the dishabilitation of the law enforcement system. Here the wall of darkness separating the "decent people" from the "undesirables" is complete. If most Americans lack the desire to know what is really happening in the ghetto, they have even less desire to know what goes on behind the walls. The prison experiences of the hard-core unemployed sound like horror stories involving extortion, rackets, sexual brutality, and race-violence.

A man behind bars carries with him all of the needs that he has developed in society. The lack of opportunity to satisfy these needs, especially sex, forms the basis for most of the atrocities that occur in prison. Every hard-core with prison experience said homosexual blackmail was a fact of life. The men said that each time they entered prison their immediate concern was finding some type of protection. Otherwise, "You would have to submit to taking it in the mouth or the ass."

Prisons are oriented primarily toward punishment. Prison experience divests a man of dignity and makes him less able to function in society. In offguard and casual moments, the trainees described certain aspects of their existing situation at Southwestern that reminded them of their prison experiences.

For Tim Carter, assignment to gardening reminded him of forced work in prison. He also compared the small house he lived in to his cell.

One day Tim and Bobby Hill were leaving the plant, and the guard asked to look in Tim's lunch pail. This incident recalled memories of his months in Tracy (a prison). Both he and Bobby had been in Tracy, and both shared in the bitter recollection.

Tim said, "They got them kind of men, too—see, with them uniforms on—only they be up in the tower with machine guns or somethin' like that. When me an Bobby walked out the gate he say, 'Damdest thing, looked just like Tracy!'—And it did, see, cause I look-ud up and I seen the balcony—we had a balcony with doors an ya know, everythin' look-ud jus' like it!—An when they said, *guard*—well that did it!"

(*Williams*). I suggested, "That's what really set you off?"

"Yeah!"

"You related that back to when you were in the joint?"

"Yeah—it was comin' from them (whites) too, see!"

Tim's basic problem was his struggle to overcome his own bitterness. He was haunted by hate and death—feelings he connected with prison. The following conversation which took place six months after Tim had been terminated at Southwestern reveals this association. At the time he was facing trial on a felony charge and the threat of another five years in prison—this time in a federal penitentiary:

TIM. *I'm going crazy, man!*
ROY. *Why do you feel that way?*
TIM. *Because sometimes I look at people—and look at em—you know that hate . . .*
ROY. *. . . . That hate?*
TIM. *Yeah.*
ROY. *For white people? Or just anybody?*
TIM. *That hate.* (Pause) *I jus' wanna jump on em and hurt em!—That's the way I feel!*
ROY. *. . . . You know, Tim, that's one reason I want to talk to you—cause I see you're heading back to the joint—seem like you're goin' down hill and can't get yourself . . .*
TIM. *. . . Can't come back up—I know it! I know it! I know—I'm goin' to tell you the truth. Every time I go down—no job, no money, and no source of any kind like*

this—I jus' don't care.(Pause) *If I get shot, I'm shot.* (Pause) *If I shoot somebody else, I shot them.* (Pause) *That's the way I feel—I jus' don't care.* (Pause) *Jus' like me an my father—he stopped by this morning, and I told him, and he told me—he said, "You're not part a the family any more!" I said, "No, no I'm not."*

ROY. (Pause) *What do you do when you get out of prison.*

TIM. *Same thing, same thing—jus' get crueler—evil—that's all!* (Pause) *That's the way it goes, Roy—you don't change! They don't make you if you're doin' time. Ya know ya gotta do it, so ya do it, and all the time you're doin' it, hate's buildin' up!*

ROY. *Is that the feelin'?*

TIM. *They're goin' to tell ya what they want ya to do. And you've got to do it. You've* got to!*—if you want to get a decent meal or somethin'—if ya wanna get outside . . .*

ROY. *. . . Hate building up all this time . . .*

TIM. . . . *I'll bet you there's been hate in me ever since I started* (being institutionalized)*—and it's gettin' worse!*

ON THE JOB AND CONTINUING CONFLICT WITH THE LAW

Prior to full time employment in industry there was a system of interaction between the trainees and the law as illustrated by Figure 1.

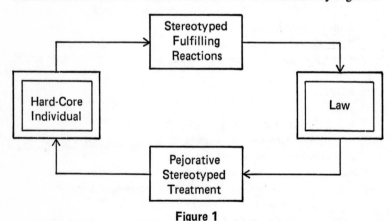

Figure 1
Pre-job Interaction Between the Hard-Core Unemployed and the Law Enforcement System

After employment, with the job and the status in the mainstream system it represented, the interaction system between the trainees and the law was elaborated (see Figure 2).

To demonstrate the continuing relationship between the police and the hard-core, a comparison between the trainees' pre-job and during-job arrest records was necessary. This formed a longitudinal comparison in terms of incidence of arrests in the aggregate and the arrest profile of the group as a whole.

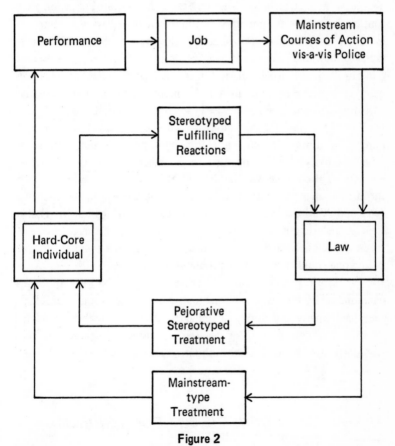

Figure 2
Interaction Between the Hard-Core and the Law Enforcement System
During Job Adjustment

The reference period for the pre-job arrest profiles varied with the individual. It began for each trainee with the date of his first recorded arrest, and ended with the date he was hired at Southwestern.

The reference period for the during-job profile was 12 months for those who were on the job for a year or longer. For those who were on the job less than a year, the reference period ended with the date of termination.

The incidence of arrests during the job (see Table 8) was nearly double what it was before the job (see Table 7), an indication that conflict with the law not only continued, it *increased* after employment. At first this may seem shocking. However, if one considers how radically new the experience of a job in industry is to the hard-core, one can see how, initially at least, this quantitative indication has some basis in logic. First, the men were more visible in the industrial environment, thus more exposed to legal sanction. Second, the requirement of getting to and from work every day plus increased purchasing power for buying automobiles meant a net increase in driving activity, leading in turn to a higher probability of traffic citations. Third, there was the indirect effect of stress stemming from the drastic changes required in household routine and in the changing roles and relationships both within the factory and within the ghetto society, including new relationships with welfare, public medicine, and credit agencies. New equilibrium had to develop in a number of areas before one could expect police problems to decrease.

The arrest profiles give qualitative evidence that the problems encountered by the trainees on the job were a continuation of problems they had experienced during unemployment. The same three problems lead the list on both profiles: traffic, suspicion, and drunk and disorderly arrests. However, the job introduced a new factor.

TRAFFIC VIOLATION: THE CITATION SYNDROME

Traffic violation exceeded all other forms of legal encounters combined. Not only was it the most frequent on-job problem, but it

Table 7
PRE-JOB ARREST RECORD

List of Arrests by Type in order of Frequency

Type	Frequency
Traffic violations	95
Suspicion arrests	20
(held but not charged)	
Drunk and disorderly conduct	15
Petty theft	11
Auto theft	6
Assault	5
Nonsupport	5
Burglary	4
Narcotics	4
Resisting arrest	4
Parole violations	4
Joy riding	3
Receiving stolen property	3
Disturbing the peace	3
Accessory to a crime	3
Concealed weapon	3
Strong arm robbery	2
Possession of alcohol	2
Malicious mischief	1
Restrained from family	1
Prowling	1
Welfare fraud	1
Total	197
Number of arrest records	24
Number without arrest records	4
Total number of man-months from date of first arrest to hire	2,004
Ratio man-months per arrest	10.17

Table 8
DURING-JOB ARREST RECORD

List of Arrests by Type in order of Frequency

Type	Frequency
Traffic violations	25
Suspicion arrests (held but not charged)	13*
Drunk and disorderly conduct	4
Nonsupport	2
Welfare fraud	2
Burglary	1
Gambling	1
Statutory rape	1
Assault	1
Total	50
Number with arrest records	21
Number without arrest records	7†
Total number of man-months of reference period	259
Ratio man-months per arrest	5.18

*5 of these cases are for suspicion of assault in connection with family fights.
†4 of the 7 without record got into immediate trouble with the law after job termination

was the problem with the highest increase. The increase is greater than that indicated in Tables 7 and 8 because over half of the pre-job traffic arrests were accounted for by one man.

For those few who owned cars prior to employment, the job reduced their activity because they had less time to drive around. But for most of the trainees, driving was intensified by employment. This is shown by the increase in car ownership. Prior to the job, only three of the men owned cars. After being hired, 21 of the 28 trainees owned cars.

To most of the hard-core, traffic was not *a* problem but a problem syndrome. If a trainee had one citation, he usually had several. In some cases, this resulted from the police making several charges simultaneously—a simple moving violation or a faulty equipment charge might be combined with a no license, open alcoholic container, or concealed weapon charge. Sometimes the emotional behavior of the trainee upon arrest led to successive citations—a simple moving violation might lead to a charge of eluding the police, disturbing the peace, or resisting arrest. In addition to multiple citations, there was the tendency for the trainee to compound charges by such coping patterns as ignoring tickets, mutilating out-of-date driver's licenses or forging new ones, or simply driving without a license.

There are numerous aspects of the hard-core situation which account for this mode of traffic behavior. One is their high exposure to traffic surveillance which comes from living in a high crime area. Another is their low economic standing. A hard-core is lucky if he can buy a car or keep one running. He cannot afford accidents, expensive repairs, traffic fines, or attorney's fees. Therefore, his responses to these events are appropriate to his selfish interest in the situation which tend to be shortcut, short-term-gain strategies for evading the formal rules. Although skilled in such strategies, the hard-core lack the necessary skills for dealing with traffic problems legally. This leads to bench warrants, suspended or revoked licenses, which lead in turn to forged licenses, ticket fixing, and so on. Such coping patterns create an additional barrier to the transition from ghetto to mainstream society that eventually must be removed.

The economic opportunity to make this transition put the hard-core trainee in an awkward situation. He needed a car for the job, but the methods he knew for acquiring and using a car brought him into conflict with the law, thus increasing the obstacles to keeping the job.

The automobile is like a number of other conveniences middle-class Americans take for granted. What is a medium for them is a frustration for the poor, and the poor's ways of coping with this frustration reinforce the boundary between them and the middle class. Thus, the trainees were caught between two societies, two subcultures, two systems of behavior, and in trying to move from one to the other there were stages when they enjoyed the advantages of neither and suffered the disadvantages of both.

We illustrate this situation with resumés from Williams' traffic diary:

Floyd Hunt

December 16, 1968: Floyd Hunt came into my office this morning to see if I could help him with a traffic ticket. I asked if this was the first or second one, and he said it was the second. He asked me if I could call the woman who had hit his car two days ago to see if I could get the name of the insurance company for him. When I inquired why he had not called, he said the woman wouldn't talk to him. He was worried, because he wanted to get his car fixed. I asked him if he was still driving, and he said no, because the mechanic who had fixed his car had left a bolt out of the oil pan.

February 7, 1969: Floyd came in this morning and said that *we* needed to do something about the driving school he was sentenced to attend (because of the two violations reported above).

I asked him what he meant, and he said, "Well, I'm supposed to report to a drivers' school on the thirty-first, and I thought that this was the month until I looked at the calendar and remembered February only had 28 days."

March 10, 1969: I went out to see Floyd at 5:00 p.m. I gave him back his traffic tickets and told him we could ˀo longer help him because he was not living up to the bargain we had agreed upon, i.e., going to drivers' education school.

Floyd showed no remorse and said, "I will take care of them myself."

When I asked him how, he replied, "I'll run until I get tired and then I'll turn myself in—spend my time out in jail."

Bobby Hill

Bobby Hill did not have two or three traffic citations; he had 57. In addition, he was on ten years' probation from a previous jail sentence and had a suspended license. Despite this, he drove to work. Shortly after starting at Southwestern, he received a minor citation for making a U-turn. Before he appeared in court for this citation, he had to do something about his license, because he knew that if it was checked in Sacramento he would be in trouble. He asked for help from the DOT staff. As we helped him, we became more deeply aware of the full implications of Hill's driving problems. At one point, we asked him to stop driving. He agreed to let his wife drive him to work, but later broke his promise. In September he was given another citation for equipment violation. Shortly thereafter he had a pre-trial hearing.

September 14, 1968: Again, I asked Bobby to stop driving and he told me he would. I asked his wife if she would be willing to drive him to and from work, and she said yes. But Hill had told the officer at the hearing that he wouldn't stop driving. Now it will be interesting to see what happens when this message gets passed to the judge. Bobby said that before he would go to jail, if he couldn't serve it on a weekend, he would split the scene.

September 18, 1969: At this point the DOT staff met with Bobby and laid it on the line. He was told that if he expected help from the court in straightening out his past tickets and his suspended license, he would have to promise to stop driving, which he reluctantly did.

September 23, 1968: As I was taking Lester Banks home, I stopped in the service station, and who drove by but Bobby Hill!

February 27, 1969: Bobby told me this morning he was going to take off work in order to get his driver's license. The license must be in effect when he has the ticket for equipment violation taken care of.

March 4, 1969: Bobby called me and informed me he had gotten his license Monday and described in detail what had happened. He said the first time he had failed the examination. He then went home, changed clothes, and came back but was recognized by the clerks at the license bureau and notified that he had already taken the test.

Bobby said, "I told the man that I was leaving town and needed my license tonight." This evidently persuaded the man to let him take the written test again. This time Hill scored 96. He now had a temporary license which was good for 60 days.

March 14, 1969: Bobby called me this morning. He had received a summons to appear in court for driving with a suspended license. He had asked Miller, the DOT director, to help him get it fixed, and Miller had agreed. Bobby was very frightened about the whole matter.

March 18, 1969: I was in Southeast San Diego at approximately 10:00 a.m. talking to a lady on the street. Bobby Hill, who should have been at work, drove by with a car full of people. He waved and kept going. Ten minutes later he returned. He said he wasn't at work because he had gotten another ticket that morning for equipment violation.

He promised, "I'm going straight home right now and fix my car."

I demanded angrily, "Are you really serious because it seems to me that you just don't want to play the game!" He got very defensive. At that moment his motor stopped, because the car had run out of gas. I took him to the gas station.

On the way home he started to mellow, "I realize I'm in trouble, and I don't want Barbara to know I'm away from work."

March 25, 1969: Today Bobby went to trial. Miller picked him up at noon, and drove him to court where I met them. Bobby was dressed in loud pink. Before the hearing both Miller and I spoke to the court attorney. While we were talking, Bobby was bargaining with a friend about buying a '69 Mercury.

The judge gave Bobby a suspended sentence on three tickets but sentenced him to spend four weeks in traffic school starting April 11.

March 26, 1969: This morning I spoke to Bobby alone and laid it on the line. I told him I didn't want any playing around, because we were taking a "hands off" attitude from now on regarding him and the courts. I noticed he wasn't bragging for a change. I told him I would be the first one to blow the whistle on him if he didn't improve, not only on the job, but in other things. I said that as far as we were concerned, he could go back to jail.

April 11, 1969: Bobby started driver's improvement school today and put his car up for sale. So far he has no buyers.

May 15, 1969: Bobby Hill sold his car today. He bought a late model car in its place.

SUSPICION

As stated earlier, a person arrested on suspicion of having committed a crime may be held up to 48 hours without being charged.

If he is released without being formally charged, the motives of the arresting officer must be questioned. Was the arrest: (a) a simple mistake; (b) a mistake resulting from prejudice against the person, his race, class, or possibly a combination of these; (c) not a mistake but a tactic based on a notion of probable guilt, i.e., several policemen arresting an individual they think might be guilty with the probability that one of them is right; (d) a deliberate act of harrassment? In all probability, the suspicion arrest in the ghetto is not a simple mistake. Certainly the experiences of the trainees support this view.

To mainstream society, suspicion arrests are a comforting sign of police vigilance; to the hard-core they are harrassment. Certainly one can see how the suspect's view would differ from that of the suburban housewife who fears rape and murder, but in the final analysis, one must consider not only the benefits but the consequences of such practices both for the individual directly involved and for society as a whole. Suspicion arrests run counter to hard-core rehabilitation. In view of the social objectives of the NAB program, this is an irony.

In addition to arrests related to family strife, there were eight suspicion arrests among the trainees. Six men were involved. In every case the transaction involved the loss of a day's pay and in one case two days' pay.

Floyd Hunt was arrested for suspicion of armed robbery one month after he started at Southwestern. He was arrested at home at 3:15 a.m. and taken to police headquarters for questioning. When we checked with the police department, they informed us that Floyd was being held for investigation, not suspicion. The difference, according to the sergeant in the robbery division, was that suspicion meant the police had no substantial evidence, whereas investigation implied that they did. In this case the police had arrested two men, one of them Floyd, and waited for a positive identification from a cab driver who had been robbed. Hunt was innocent, but he did miss a day's pay.

Leon Smith was held twice without being charged, once for theft and once for car theft and receiving stolen merchandise. On both occasions, he was released the following day without being questioned.

(Williams). I had occasion to observe firsthand how suspicion arrests develop while riding with the "chaplain's patrol," which was sponsored

by the San Diego police department to aid policeman-ghetto relationships. One of these rides took place on New Year's Day, 1970. My escort was an officer on his first tour of service after spending two years with the juvenile division. At approximately 10:00 p.m. we arrived at the corner of Euclid and Churchward in Southeast San Diego. In the summer of '69 this corner was the scene of numerous confrontations between young blacks and the police. We pulled into a vacant lot where two patrol cars were parked. A call was dispatched at that time concerning a possible robbery. The dispatch officer gave the description of a male Negro, possibly six feet tall weighing about 190 pounds. He included a description of his clothing and the getaway car. The patrol officers jumped into their units and began cruising in search of the suspect, despite the fact that the robbery had taken place in a different area, a white neighborhood.

The lieutenant and I also began to cruise the Southeast San Diego area. We were in a command unit which had a radio monitoring system. Thirty minutes after the original alert, the radio crackled with suspect reports from unit after unit.

The lieutenant looked at me and said, "Here we go again! Every time we get a report like this, every rookie cop figures he knows just who fits the description."

At this point I had visions of Barbara Hill complaining about the number of times Bobby had been picked up on suspicion.

The lieutenant said, "Although many consider this a good police tactic, it causes problems in the black neighborhood," and he added, "Those rookie patrolmen are always looking for action."

Field investigations, stopping people for questioning and search, also continued. Cases involving the 28 hard-core in the reference year on the job continued frequently as a matter of course.

On October 16, 1968, Paul Galvão reported that two narcotics agents had come to his house while he was at work and demanded to search the house because they suspected his boy of using narcotics. Despite the fact that they had no search warrant and that his wife refused entry, they kicked the door down, entered, ripped light switches off the walls, and took clothing out of drawers and threw it on the floor. They arrested the boy on suspicion, but did not hold him.

Incidents such as these were an integral part of the awkward transitional stage when the trainees were adjusting to the new identities associated with employment. They diminished somewhat as public agencies and the police became aware of the fact that the trainees were employed. Nevertheless, such tactics continued and were an obstacle to the trainees' transition.

OTHER ARRESTS

The job was a totally new experience because it forced the trainees into new roles requiring them to learn new rules and develop new capabilities and identities to a great extent incompatible with their old identities. The incentive of higher rewards weighed heavily. But if the rewards increased, so did the risks. In many cases the decisions as to which roles to assume were affected by the trainees' families. In some cases, other members of the family threatened the man's job by continuing old activities. In this respect the wife's role was critical, because if she became involved in court problems, her husband's job would be affected. A court sentence would remove the wife from the household, leaving the care of the children to the husband.

At one time Andy Manners had been involved in a stolen goods ring, but he no longer was. He was engaged in gambling which did not seriously interfere with his work, but Mildred, his wife, was a different story. Along with several other women in Southeast San Diego she operated a stolen goods ring, and she was on probation from a previous conviction. One week after Andy was hired at Southwestern, Mildred was arrested again and charged with three counts: petty theft, burglary, and assault with intent to kill. Mildred was big, and she was violent. Once she had almost killed Andy during one of their fights.

Although Andy's first reaction to her arrest was that it was a frameup, he changed his attitude after he saw the overwhelming evidence for the charges.

This incident was disastrous to Andy's new job, because the Manners had three preschool children. Throughout the rest of September, Andy was in a turmoil about what was going to happen to his children.

On October 4, Mildred was sentenced to 90 days in the county jail. Even though it was a comparatively light sentence in terms of what might have been expected, it still meant three months without a mother in the house to care for the children.

(*Williams*). At the suggestion of the judge and with my help, Andy wrote a letter asking the court for a reduced sentence. Later the probation officer, a woman, conveyed the court's decision that because of her previous arrests Mildred's sentence could not be reduced. She said that the court would try to obtain a babysitter from the county welfare agency. The welfare office agreed to pay $135 per month providing Andy accepted a welfare appointed babysitter. As Andy was deeply involved in black separatism, the welfare decision was to him an overt white intrusion into black affairs. He wanted someone of his own choosing, "someone he could trust." Of course, the welfare office and the probation department disagreed.

The probation officer said, "If Andy had taken the two people they had recommended, or even one, they might have been able to persuade the judge to modify the sentence; but since he was 'hard-headed', I don't feel that he really wants help."

Andy responded with a few revolutionary terms mixed with obscenities. The shocked probation lady retorted, "If you were really concerned about your kids, these demands wouldn't enter your mind!"

Andy's view was that his children were not individuals, but part of a family, and it was his family and ethnic identity he was guarding. He even threatened to quit his job to babysit. Mildred served the 90 days while Andy alternated with friends watching the children. He was often absent, but he kept his pride without losing his job.

There were other job related stresses, some of which spilled over into police problems. A prime example was family strife. Family conflict increased in 19 of the 28 households after the man's employment. The job brought new life to old tensions and in some cases introduced new tensions where none had existed before. Table 8, suspicion of assault, lists wife beating as one legal manifestation of domestic strife. These cases represent five different family households: Banks, Johns, Manners, Cooper and Greer. Another legal manifestation was child support. Jack Davis and Oscar Walters were sued by their ex-wives as soon as they went to work. Their new incomes were the obvious incentive for this legal action.

The job activated other dormant issues. Old debts suddenly became payable. Some financial burdens were so impossible as to be ridiculous. Lester Banks' paycheck was garnished. He had only the vaguest idea of the total amount he owed, and it took several evenings of sorting through dresser and kitchen drawers to get even an approximation. The total, not allowing for lost bills, came to over $3000. Eleven hundred of this was a bill from the juvenile detention home for keeping his three preschool children for one month, despite the fact that the children had been taken from him and his wife against their will after the welfare office had obtained a court order on child neglect charges.

Eventually, even the most obstinate trainees realized that the old ways of coping with legal problems were incompatible with their new roles. Problems with the law had to be resolved in a way consistent with their identities in the industrial economy. Tickets could no longer be ignored. Driver's licenses could no longer be forged. In both respects the job was an instrument of rehabilitation, a beachhead for both the man and society.

Rehabilitation implies two essential sets of *experiences,* each involving a distinct social network or role system. First, status in the mainstream economic system had to be granted, and the dignity and the material benefits of this status had to be experienced. Second, the ongoing dishabilitative experiences had to be diminished. Both processes imply developing new patterns of relationships, changing two sets of people, the hard-core and mainstream people as well. Thus, building new experience and liquidating old experience were mutually reinforcing.

However, experience, new or old, cannot be fully discussed without mentioning another social structural dimension: the peer group, community, neighborhood, or, to emphasize the negative aspects of the term, "gang," or "old crowd." All of these terms imply a concept of the person as more than an individual to be transformed and absorbed into new institutions. Minority groups are no longer willing to renounce their ethnic identity—*community.* We have attempted to show how the pejorative "high crime area" becomes a community pejorative. In turn community alienation in a kind of backlash effect can become a focus of community identity and a powerful stimulus for revitalization. The interrelationships of the man, the job, and the law must also be considered in the context of those ethnic and community institutions in which the hard-core find themselves and from which their new experiences must also derive meaning.

5

Crime as Revolution

... Memories of yesterday will not assuage the torrents of blood that flow today from my crotch. Yes, History could pass for a scarlet text, its jot and title graven red in human blood. More armies than shown in the books have planted flags on foreign soil leaving Castration in their wake. But no Slave should die a natural death. There is a point where Caution ends and Cowardice begins. Give me a bullet through the brain from the gun of the beleaguered oppressor on the night of siege. Why is there dancing and singing in the Slave Quarters? A Slave who dies of natural causes cannot balance two dead flies in the Scales of Eternity. Such a one deserves rather to be pitied than mourned.

Black woman, without asking how, just say that we survived our forced march and travail through the Valley of Slavery, Suffering, and Death—there, that Valley there beneath us hidden by that drifting mist. Ah, what sights and sounds and pain lie beneath that mist! And we had thought that our hard climb out of that cruel valley led to some cool, green and peaceful, sunlit place—but it's all jungle here, a wild and savage wilderness that's overrun with ruins.

But put on your crown, my Queen, and we will build a New City on these ruins.

(Eldridge Cleaver, Soul on Ice, *New York: Dell Publishing Co., 1968, p. 210)*

A racial minority cannot survive except in a democracy. In saving it, we save ourselves.

(Roy Wilkins, "Challenge to Black Militants," as quoted by CBS News, June 30, 1970)

A racial majority cannot preserve democracy exclusively for themselves. They must ultimately extend it or destroy it. But in destroying it, they destroy themselves.
(Author's antithesis to Roy Wilkins' quotation)

It would be both naive and dishonest to discuss the hard-core problems with the law solely in terms of his being an individual with bad habits and undesirable companions for whom the job is a therapeutic device. He is also a member of an intimate group on whom he depends and a consciously explicit class and race with whom he identifies, and collectively they have a distinctive perspective on life. To reject either the culture or the peer group of the man is to reject the man himself.

In Chapter 4 we discussed several reasons why the conflict between trainees and police continued on the job. Another explanation may be seen in the race, ethnic, and class relationships between ghetto and mainstream society. Thus, we are elaborating still further the context of our discussions of trainee-police interactions (see Figure 3).

ANTI-INSTITUTIONAL SYSTEMS

We conceptualize anti-institutional systems as social and cultural organizations which normalize, or sanction and reward, activities which conflict with or oppose social or cultural elements in the dominant sociocultural system. These activities may be legal, such as boycotts and peaceful demonstrations, or they may be illegal such as the willful destruction of property, kidnapping, and assassination. The activities may be explicitly sanctioned by highly organized groups such as the NAACP or the Black Panther Party, or implicitly sanctioned by the values and norms of a diffuse group such as an ethnic neighborhood or an entire class of people. The chief criterion of the activities is *opposition*, hence "anti." But before they can be termed "institutional," they must be more than socially random, e.i. idiosyncratic. They must have a conscious (to the actor), identifiable, *supportive*, social-organizational context.

When this context for individual behavior exists, the behavior becomes social activity. And, although the activity may be labeled and treated as "deviant" or "criminal" behavior by established institutions, it must be examined on the same analytical level as "socially approved" behavior to acquire an objective understanding of it. Anti-institutions generate the same basic social-psychological processes that "normal"

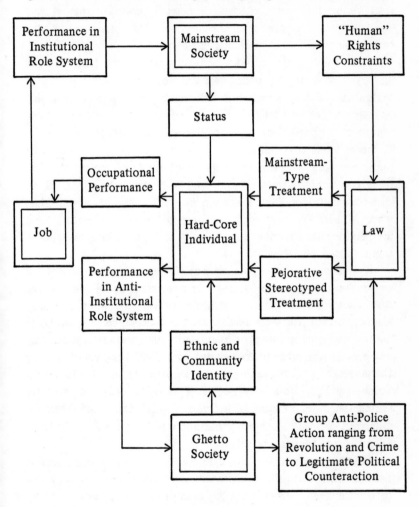

Figure 3

Interaction Between the Law Enforcement System and the Hard-Core
Unemployed as Members of Two Opposing Societies—
Mainstream and Ghetto

institutions generate. These processes include authorization and legitimization, identity formation, maintenance of self-worth and behavioral reinforcement. Moreover, anti-institutions do not depend solely upon their own internally generated processes; they receive significant reinforcement from the reactions of dominant institutions, such as law enforcement, to them (see Chapter 4).

Thus with many attitudes and activities of the hard-core unemployed vis-à-vis the police, we are not dealing with individual sentiments and acts as such, but with ongoing social systems, including mainstream society, which generate, support, and reinforce these sentiments and acts. This analytical framework, while applicable to the hard-core unemployed in general, is essential in the case of the racial minorities who comprise the majority of the hard-core unemployed (only two of the 28 trainees in this study were Anglo-American). In the case of a nonwhite ethnic American we are dealing with an individual who, in addition to having peer group and class identities and perspectives, has a racial-cultural identity and a racial-cultural explanation for his present situation.

As nonwhite ethnic groups are acquiring more education and global world views, they are producing increasing numbers of intelligentsia who interpret their ethnic experiences vis-à-vis the white American majority as an experience of colonized and exploited peoples. Quite naturally such perspectives are associated with appropriate heroes past and present who, more often than not, are regarded as revolutionary by the dominant society. Among the blacks there are such figures as Nat Turner, W.E.B. DuBois, Malcolm X, Eldridge Cleaver, Stokeley Carmichael, Huey Newton, Dick Gregory, Angela Davis, and others too numerous to mention. Among the Chicanos there are such figures as Cesar Chávez, Tijerina, and others.

Ethnic minorities also have their own networks of communication and their own culturally conditioned view of events regardless of how these events are reported by the established media. Just as white, middle-class Americans from coast to coast in hundreds of thousands of suburban communities, urban apartments, and rural towns are electrified by reports of a militant minority action on one college campus, so is a geographically scattered racial minority galvanized by news of a single police action in one shabby neighborhood.

Thus, nonwhite ethnic minorities oppose white ethnocentrism with their own ethnocentrism. To be sure, this process is but a part of the total process of cultural revitalization, but it is a vital part nevertheless. And although not all classes and age groups in an ethnic community may express it or profess agreement with it, the process is of inescapable significance to the entire ethnic community. Thus, not all Afro-Americans may participate in the "ethnic trip" or "black bag" as some call it, but they all benefit from the social changes anti-institutional sentiment and action help generate, such as the development of ethnic pride and the evolution of political and legal power and economic opportunity.

As stated previously, the criterial element of this sentiment and action is *opposition.* In the legal realm it ranges from overt ethnic emphasis in dress and language to legal and political action. In the illegal realm it ranges from hustling and drug use to individual and collective action against locii and symbols of established authority, such as schools, welfare agencies, courts, prisons, and police.

The hard-core unemployed members of racial minorities are very conscious of this contemporary racial-cultural image. They identify with their heroes and openly express this modern perspective. For example, among the trainees at Southwestern, police incidents in minority neighborhoods, whether local or national, were continuous topics of conversation. So were police raids on Panther headquarters, Panther ambushes of police, the trials of Huey Newton and Bobby Seale, the escape of Eldridge Cleaver. As a group they generally had one opinion on these events, the polar opposite of their blue-collar counterparts.

Black trainees in particular carried their ethnic identities to work in dress, speech, and philosophy, including a new intolerance for the unconscious, culturally imbedded racial slur. This was highly visible and, to a large percentage of white workers, objectionable. But the minorities' deliberate ethnocentrism simply accentuated the unconscious ethnocentrism of the whites. Some terms used by white workers in the factory when contrasted with terms used by the hard-core suggest some of the sharp differences in their respective viewpoints and behavior.

Majority Term	Minority Term
crime	the streets, revolutionary activity
your local police	the heat, fuzz, the Man, pig
white, Caucasian	white man, white boy, whitey, white devil, honkey, gringo
Negro, colored, boy, nigger	black, Afro-American, brother
Mexican, meskin, greaser, spik, chile-pecker, dirt nigger	Chicano, Mexican-American
law and order	harrassment, war on black people
patriotism	bigotry, white supremacy
standards, qualifications	prejudice
example of how a minority person ought to be (minority member of silent majority)	Uncle Tom, oreo
chip on shoulder, pushy, out of line, subversive	ethnic pride, black power, brown power, red power
decent people	do-rights, bigots
their own kind	soul

To a certain extent all hard-core unemployed, black, brown, or white, are members of class minorities and as such may participate in anti-institutional activities. But anti-institutional systems of the racial minority hard-core unemployed strike much deeper at the institutional fabric of white American mainstream society.

HUSTLING AS ANTI-INSTITUTIONAL ACTIVITY

The term hustling covers a spectrum of activities ranging from simply being aggressive and enterprising to stealing, pimping, and prostituting. In discussing hard-core hustling practices we limit our definition to such activities as stealing, gambling, soliciting, pimping, receiving and selling stolen goods, and such quasi-legal activities as exploiting welfare, exploiting women with incomes, engaging in unlicensed businesses, cheating on income tax, cheating on insurance, and so on. The majority of the 28 trainees were hustling when they started on the job.

To what extent individuals who engage in hustling develop a clearly defined anti-institutional ethos or rationale for their activity depends upon how much reading and thinking they have done about the social issues implicit in their total situation. We are convinced that most of the trainees in our study did rationalize hustling beyond simple pragmatism, i.e., that it was a rational thing to do under the circumstances. Most elaborated their rationale to the level of moral relativism. They defended themselves against the disapproval of the law and of their blue-collar coworkers by an aggressive moral indictment of "legal" practices they could see all around them, and by an indictment of the hypocrisy of the double moral standards of mainstream society.

We participated in numerous hard-core group discussions and observed and received accounts of verbal exchanges between hard-core trainees and coworkers on these issues. We summarize the anti-institutional rationale which emerged in these discussions as follows:

To the hard-core unemployed, locked out of the predominant economic system, survival is a matter of maximizing the available opportunities, a succession of short-term gains balanced against the risk of long-term losses. Instead of manipulating the stock market, government agencies, or natural resources, they exploit the tiny area of resources available to them. To mainstream society this is anarchy and crime. To the hard-core unemployed it is merely the application of the accepted policies of American capitalism to counteract their situation of permanent unemployment, chronic ill health, and persistent lack of access to justice. If this is anarchy, the seeds of it lie in the central institutions of American capitalist society, which stem from the anarchistic practices inherent in reconstructionist and segregationalist policies that create inequality in voting, housing, employment, education, union membership, justice, and so on.

Again, we emphasize the basic premise of this chapter, because we feel that it is frequently overlooked or minimized. And this oversight constitutes a glaring scientific bias in rehabilitation policy and practice. In the case of virtually every hard-core trainee, there was a deep ideological conviction based on firsthand contact with representatives of mainstream society—policemen, probation officers, judges, wardens, welfare caseworkers, and blue-collar workers—that the social order needed rehabilitating. The expression of this conviction was more than revolutionary rhetoric. It reflected a vital cultural-ideological dimension of their activity.

To the extent that hustling is a form of pragmatic adaptation to economic circumstances, employment should reduce this activity. In the case of the trainees, it did. In addition, observation showed that hustling declined as the trend in arrests increased, a view which supports the thesis that new, job-related factors were involved in the arrest trend. During unemployment, 12 trainees were actively involved in stealing, 10 in gambling, 10 in soliciting or receiving stolen goods, and 16 in one or more of these three activities. On the job, only eight of the 28 continued one or more of these forms of hustling, and this number decreased as time went on.

Those few who continued hustling sooner or later had to make a choice. Leon Smith was in charge of a prostitution ring. He received as much as $75 a week from the two women he employed. However, Leon's business soon began to interfere with his job, causing frequent absences. In addition, it interfered with his sleep, causing him to be tired when he did come to work. It also caused a crisis in his home. About five months after he had started work, Leon's wife threatened to divorce him.

In talking about it he said, "She doesn't understand the fact that I need the extra money!" Ultimately, Leon gave up hustling.

DRUG USE AS ANTI-INSTITUTIONAL ACTIVITY

"The first time it (LSD) was beautiful. You see, I went over to this guy's house about 2:00 a.m. There was a little party going—people all over the place . . . I got loaded and everything was groovy. Then we were going to take these broads home, and we got down to the car—I got on a panic trip; I could see cars coming out in front of us, and oh!

Then I got on a scare about the cops, because, you see, I just got out (of prison), and I hadn't been out too long, and I was on a panic. So, we were going down the street, and it was 3:00 or 4:00 a.m., and I'd keep on looking and cops were coming everywhere! ... Then I started looking at Jim, and he was just behind the wheel, and the wheel's above his head, and he's driving like this (mimicking a crouching demon). I guess he really wasn't, but it looked like he was, and I started screaming and yelling about this. (Pause) Once we got in the house everything was all right. But I was so loaded then I was begging to come down! I was praying to God that I'd come down! I was way out! ... But the loadest I've ever been was off Asthmador. That's a little bit different. Everyone tries it once, but never takes it a second time. Asthmador is for people who have asthma; they smoke it. It says, 'Dangerous—not to swallow,' but you can swallow it. It ain't dangerous, but you hallucinate. You go nuts! I mean everyone! ... Marijuana, LSD, pills—you always have your senses enough to know what you're doing; even when I was on a panic trip about the cars, I kept saying to myself, 'I'm just loaded.' I had that much sense that I knew I was just loaded, and it was just me."

(Padfield). "Well, isn't that what they mean when they say you need someone to talk you down, because this person can tell you that you're just loaded, don't pay any attention to them?"

"Yes, that's right, but on Asthmador you can't do that."

"You really are out?"

"You are *out!* (Pause) Now, I'm quiet—I'm myself; if I get loaded, nobody knows it. Well, I'm walking down the street, and I'm so completely out; I'm standing on the corner and here's someone I'm talking to, one of my old partners, and I glance at a car and there's no old partner there. You hallucinate—people are there who ain't there—you know. And it's so real, and then you look around and you see the people looking at you and then it catches you, but you're that far gone that you *know* he's *there.* And this happened, and my legs kept giving out. And I went up to the apartment, and there was bugs all over the bed. They were just completely everywhere—just everywhere— I remember some of them were glowing on and off. I had a green, real fluffy blanket, and they would go down under, like they were in water. They would come up to the top and glow, and it was really too much!

(Pause) Then I remember finally, when I was with the bugs for two hours, I got them all off the bed. I took the sheets and everything right off. First I was picking them off, and that didn't work because there were too many. So I just sat down and pulled everything off the bed and checked the whole mattress—so I'm sitting there, and all these people come in—all of a sudden there are three or four people besides me. So, I go in the bathroom and come back out, and there's not a soul in my room—nobody! I go check the door—the door's still locked."

"Did you talk to them?"

"Yes."

(Laughing incredulously) "Did they respond?"

"Yeah!—I *guess* they did—as far as I can remember they did."

"You talked to them, and they talked back?"

"Yes, I guess they did. This is what scares me, because this is where you could jump out a window. This is because you have no sense, no control. This is why I'll never take that again—never!"

This conversation with Gary Nolan was one of many we had with the trainees concerning the all-pervasive topic of drug use. All of the trainees were involved with drugs, either by personal experience or by direct association with friends on drugs. During unemployment 12 of the trainees used drugs continuously, eight marijuana and four both hard drugs and marijuana. During the job six men continued to use drugs, four marijuana, and two heroin. Three of the six were eventually terminated, and in the cases of two of them, heroin addiction was primarily responsible for the dismissal. The third trainee's use of drugs was not directly related to his termination. Of the 15 men still employed after the reference year, three were still using marijuana.

Drugs have long been an integral part of ghetto society and economy. But, if drug use is related to chronic unemployment and ghetto economics, why did the trainees continue to use drugs after they had been employed? An in-depth answer to this question would require a separate study. However, certain observations are suggested by the experiences of the trainees. First, like alcohol, drugs provide a method of relaxation, a habit, part of an individual's life style. Second, the trainees, although employed, lived in the ghetto with their associates and families, many of whom were unemployed and using drugs. Third, ghetto relationships with other institutions, primarily the law, continued regardless of employment, and as the following discussion will illustrate, drug use had a function in these relationships.

All of the trainees had reference groups within the ghetto with whom they related. There were two basic groups, the "park crowd" and the "street crowd." The younger trainees tended to relate to the park crowd and the older ones to the street crowd. Some moved between both groups, and a few individuals related to neither, preferring the company of relatives and nonkin groups that were peripheral to these two centers of activity.

The park crowd conducted its activities in the Ocean View Park in Southeast San Diego. Its membership was informal, but usually consisted of one basic group of people who met there every Sunday and in late summer evenings to jive, make love, listen to music, drink, smoke pot, and act out anti-law enforcement aggressions that occasionally flared into major confrontations with the police. The members ranged in age from 18 to 23 years, and tended to be dropouts with little or no occupational skills. Militant and rebellious, they had a distinctly different approach to their rejection and segregation by mainstream society as evidenced in their mode of dress and behavior. Natural hair styles and low slung cars were prevalent. The group was intensely ideological and angry, and much of their conversation centered on racism, repression, weapons, and guerrilla war. Male self-assertion was a part of their ideology and was expressed by verbal and physical displays of hostility toward mainstream society and by man-to-man competitiveness, especially in personal relations with women.

In contrast, the basic attitude of the street crowd was one of fatal acceptance of their rejection by mainstream society. This group was an amalgamation of hopeless individuals, disorganized and desperate, whose hate (anti-institutional ethos) had been turned inward. They tended to be older than the park crowd and were fathers of families or part-time husbands. Most of them had few skills but were willing to do spot work and take menial jobs. They also tended to be workers displaced by technology. They tended to be passive in their relationships with their wives, who were generally considered the head of the home and who received the welfare checks. Many were from the rural South or Southwest and in this environment had been exposed to rural religion, as opposed to the younger group, most of whom were reared in the secular environments of the urban West.

Narcotics were an integral part of the consumption pattern of both groups. The park people tended to be light users—pills, marijuana; the street group tended to be more deeply dependent on drugs. For the park crowd, using drugs, especially marijuana, was a multi-racial rebellion against what they felt to be the hypocrisy, discriminating laws, and institutionalized inequality of mainstream culture. The trainees' use of marijuana was also a form of anti-racism. For them pot-blowing was a means of democratic social interchange involving the young of all races, white, Mexican-American, black, Puerto Rican.

Needless to say, hard drug use conflicted with job performance more than marijuana did. The hard drug habit provided an escape from conflict and there was a tendency to revert to it when job-related stress developed. For example, Gary Nolan could not withstand the personal conflict that was precipitated by the transition in his economic role from dependent to breadwinner (see Chapters 3 and 7). His first drug relapse resulted in a temporary suspension. Three months later, another relapse led to final termination. By the end of Gary's reference year and after, his relapse was seemingly complete. But when we last spoke with Gary, we found that he was again receiving rehabilitative treatment.

Tim Carter was also unable to withstand the initial stress of the job, and he returned to heroin three months after he started to work at Southwestern. He described some of these stresses, most of which involved the family he had inherited from the woman he was living with:

"[Everything was] catching up with me—the kids hollering; they couldn't get what they needed and the rent was getting behind; the bills were getting behind; and I thought when I had an interview with the welfare worker, they were going to help Angie. (Continued her support because she had three school children, none of whom were Tim's) But it seemed they were putting all the responsibility back on me. I needed shoes, and I needed clothes. I wasn't getting anything for myself. I was just spending all my time and money on her and the kids. It was just too much."

Tim had always talked about the streets and the job as being mutually exclusive. In his case, they were. After his termination, he was back on the streets, literally, and as we followed him for the rest of the year, he was in and out of temporary employment, in and out of jail, and on and off hard drugs.

However, the use of marijuana did not interfere directly with the job, because most of the trainees who used marijuana did so as part of their regular, off-work pattern of life. Socially, of course, marijuana conflicted with the job at least as it is now conceived by the blue-collar worker and industry because of the larger set of activities it is generally identified with, such as police-baiting and the anti-establishment youth culture. But these attitudes are subject to change, and there are indications that as marijuana consumption among the labor force increases, it may come to be regarded as no greater a stigma than alcohol consumption.[28]

It is interesting to note in this regard that among the trainees, dependency on alcohol was greater than dependency on drugs. Twenty-five of the 28 men used alcohol. Of the 25, eight used it to the extent that it interfered with their work. Six of these eight men were eventually terminated for excessive absenteeism. Two were still on the job at the end of their reference years and showing improvement. In the cases of both the alcohol and drug users, the consumption patterns had one common feature—withdrawal and escape.

THE ANTI-POLICE COMMUNITY

What is a community? It is like any town. It has families where children are conceived, born, and raised, and where values and attitudes are engrained in accordance with the daily experiences of parents and children. It is a place in which those living have a feeling of belonging that transcends individual ownership of property. It extends to the streets, shops, and boundaries of the area. Members of communities are sensitive to threats to the integrity of the areas they identify with. If 40 policemen with riot guns and patrol cars descend on a ghetto neighborhood, shoot three blacks and arrest 20 more for not dispersing, the residents' sense of community is disturbed just as much as that of white suburban residents when hippies invade their parks.

Community identity extends to the schools where participants feel a sense of proprietary interest, despite not being on the board of education. In ghetto communities as in white suburbia there are local organizations. Instead of the Neighborhood Pool Association there may be the local office of the Urban League. Instead of the local Committee to Remove the Hippie Menace, there may be the local Committee of Responsible Citizens urging a Citizen's Police Review Board. When a proposed freeway threatens ghetto residents' property or living arrangements, they also organize. Moreover, the enforcement of sanitation, building, and housing codes is as important to them as to any suburban resident.

Ghetto residents, like suburban residents, have leisure and pursue pleasure. But, because they cannot afford to own as many cars or travel as far, or to patronize cocktail bars, go-go parlors, hotels, and golf courses, they must act out their aggressions and bawdiness in their own neighborhoods, in contrast to the middle-class suburbanites who can leave their neatly kept neighborhoods and go to another part of town or to another city to indulge themselves. Because of their pathetic resources and their blackness ghetto residents are not allowed the luxury of split-level living. Therefore they live in and among all their activities, and because of this they see human realities white suburban citizens generally do not see. Their children witness the whole community—the whole gamut of human experiences, privations, appetites and expressions, whereas the suburban child and the suburban woman can to a degree be insulated from reality and nurtured on mythical and ideal norms.

This luxury of being able to live compartmentalized lives influences the middle-class concept of law and order. White, suburban, mainstream society has always viewed the ghetto or the slum as an area of crime and danger. And it is to this unrealistic view of society—the partial, cleaned up, school-book view as opposed to the high crime area of the ghetto—that the police system is addressed to maintaining.

In short, there is the same zeal and identity associated with the ghetto community as with the suburban community—at least among the younger generation blacks. Even in the mind of a young alcoholic or heroin addict, a feeling exists that what happens to the least of them—even one black prostitute—happens to all. Is this community consciousness harmful? Its opposite would be apathy. In white suburbia this kind of identity is regarded as honorable. But because community identity in the ghetto is directed against what threatens residents the most—the police, an insensitive school system, and the patronizing welfare establishment—such spirit is regarded by middle-class America as subversive and threatening.

This concept of community is also alien and threatening to the police. To them the ghetto is an *area* of crime, confrontation and danger. It is a population boundary containing the city's highest concentration of known suspects and criminals. The concept of "high crime area" blends into a theory of action in which concepts like "command posts," "staging areas," "tactical units," and "riot squads," play a logical part. We have witnessed police activity in the Southeast San Diego community that confirms this view: surveillance teams with binoculars posted on hills overlooking Ocean View Park; emergency units kept in reserve with mace, tear gas, shotguns, and M-14s to be summoned at a second's notice. Such constant daily evidence tends to confirm what some ethnic nationalist groups are saying: This is war and the ghetto is an alien land—a place where the concept of "responsible citizen" is as illogical as it is at a hippie rock festival. The following discussion will illustrate this point.

Southeast San Diego is to San Diego what Watts is to Los Angeles. Both negatively, by those outside the community, and affirmatively, by those within the community, this comparison is often made. In the aftermath of the Watts riots in 1965, Southeast San Diego was the scene of frequent minor disturbances. One of our informants described his brother-in-law's experience as a black patrolman on the San Diego Police Department during one of these disturbances:

A police sergeant was walking patrol on Imperial Avenue. Some black teenagers who were standing on the corner made some smart remarks. The sergeant accused one of them of throwing a rock at him. He walked up to the group, singled out one of the teenagers, and said, "You threw a rock at me. You're under arrest!"

The teenager denied it and said that he could prove that he had been watching on the other side of the street. His friends supported his story, but the sergeant would not believe them and said, "I'm going to take you in!" The boy refused to go.

At this point, a crowd was beginning to gather, and the sergeant called in two patrol cars which arrived filled with patrolmen. By this time the crowd had grown. Several bystanders said they weren't going to allow the police to arrest the boy. Some adult members of the community intervened and told the sergeant that they had witnessed the incident and that the boy was innocent. They were willing to testify to this. However, the sergeant would not accept their word.

By this time tensions had reached the breaking point. Three of the policemen were cornered by one part of the crowd and three were cornered by another part. Someone put in a call to the informant's brother-in-law, and told him to come as quickly as he could. He raced to the scene and asked one of the bystanders what had happened. Then he approached the sergeant and told him that the best thing to do would be to take the word of the adult members of the community and withdraw. The sergeant still deliberated although it was obvious by now that his actions could provoke a major riot. Our informant said his brother-in-law, as one policeman to another, was finally able to talk the sergeant out of taking action.

The police issue was intensely relevant to the hard-core trainees. When they began work at Southwestern, this issue was uppermost in their minds, and only as the job began to take hold did it diminish in importance. But, occasionally, the issue would flare into prominence as incidents occurred which involved either the trainees or their friends in the community. In addition almost weekly minor incidents took place in which police shot "suspects." Although the San Diego paper had what seemed to be a news blackout on such incidents, most of the trainees knew the details, because they had access to local communications networks and were eager clients for ethnic media which they felt broadcast police incidents as effectively as the *American Legion Magazine* or the *San Diego Union* featured campus disturbances for white suburbia. Moreover, they were personally involved in these incidents. They witnessed them, participated in them, and occasionally when major crises erupted, they were engulfed by them. We could not follow the lives of these men even in the plant without inquiring into events which involved them directly or indirectly with the police, and regardless of whom we were observing or interviewing, whether the men, members of the community, or the police themselves, it became clear that our trainees and the police would converge at some point.

A major crisis for the trainees and the ghetto community occurred with the shooting of a man called "The Preacher," which took place two and a half months after the NAB program started at Southwestern.

Timothy Thompson, or "The Preacher" as Andy Manners called him, was a small man—about 5'5" and 150 lbs. He lived alone in the Southeast San Diego community. Before the shooting, he had never been arrested, but he empathized with the men who were in jail, and used what little money he had earned from odd jobs to help them. There was no limit to the time and help he gave to other black people. In addition, he preached a type of black religious revivalism, about the Second Coming and the day when the world was going to be burned and the black people exalted.

To Andy Manners, Timothy Thompson was an apocalyptic prophet. In conversations, bull sessions, and interviews, Andy spoke of him as the final authority for the disconnected dreams, visions, and mystical meanings that Andy seemed to see in every black experience.

There are two versions of the shooting. The *San Diego Union* version is as follows:[29]

MAN SHOT FIVE TIMES ASSAULTING DEPUTIES
2 LAWMEN HIT BY HOE IN EVICTION

A steelworker facing eviction for failing to pay rent was shot five times yesterday after he attacked sheriff's deputies trying to enforce a court order.

Two of the deputies suffered injuries when struck by a hand hoe wielded by the man, Timothy D. Thompson, 27, of 3282 Steele St.

Thompson was taken to Paradise Valley Hospital first for treatment of five wounds and later transferred to University Hospital, where he was placed under guard as a suspect for assault with a deadly weapon on police officers.

Deputies Slashed

The injured deputies, Ronald Ahlgren and Benny McLaughlin, were taken to Mercy Hospital for treatment of cuts on the arm and face. Ahlgren reportedly suffered a severe cut on his right arm while McLaughlin suffered a cut on the right side of the face.

Sheriff Joe O'Connor gave the following account of the incident which occurred around 2:15 p.m. at the Steel [sic] Street address:

Sgt. Walter Kenrick and Deputies Ahlgren, McLaughlin, Dennis Parrott and Thomas Staninger went to enforce a court-ordered eviction notice which was served on Thompson Friday.

Eviction Notice

Thompson's landlord obtained the eviction notice when he failed to pay rent for some months.

When the deputies arrived at Thompson's home to evict him by force, Thompson ran out of the home with a hoe and began swinging it at the deputies and throwing large rocks.

Ahlgren attempted to ward off the blows and was struck on his right arm, falling to the ground. When the attack on him continued, Ahlgren drew his service revolver and fired at Thompson.

Others Fire

Thompson continued his attack on Ahlgren and the deputies despite being struck by bullet [sic] and other deputies and city Patrolman John Hartman, sent to assist, fired more shots.

Thompson suffered wounds in his left thigh, left forearm, left bicep, left shoulder, and left side of his neck, O'Connor said.

Chief Sheriff's Deputy Warren H. Kanagy and Lt. Robert S. Newsom investigated the matter for the Sheriff's Department.

Kanagy said the Police Department would conduct the investigation to seek a complaint in the matter but that his office would investigate it as a matter of routine.

A different version was provided by witnesses:

Timothy Thompson had almost no income and was in constant debt. Because he was two months behind in his rent, his landlady, a black woman, had him evicted. When the county deputy sheriff served the eviction notice Thompson was watering his garden. He accepted the notice calmly, but when the deputy demanded that Thompson move out immediately, Timothy became belligerent and refused.

The deputy then walked into the house and started removing

Thompson's things. Thompson threatened to stop him. The deputy said, "We'll see about that!" and called in additional deputies and San Diego policemen. When they arrived, Thompson lost his temper and threatened to protect his belongings. He brandished a hoe, the only weapon he had, and hit one of the officers. The officer pulled his gun and shot Thompson pointblank. Thompson tried to run away and was shot four more times in the back and side. He was taken to the hospital and handcuffed to the bed. An armed guard was posted at the door of his room. He was later charged with attempted murder and resisting arrest.[30]

To the San Diego community at large, an article on the first page of the B Section of the *San Diego Union* was perhaps an appropriate indicator of their interest in the shooting. To the Southeast community of 90,000, the incident should have made the headlines. The entire black community as well as the Black Panther organization, The Citizen's Interracial Committee, the Urban League, and the NAACP were angered by the shooting. They were aroused not only because five policemen shot a poor, unarmed black man, but also because Thompson had been charged with murder and had no money for a defense lawyer. The tragic irony of this incident was that Thompson preached nonviolence, and as Andy Manners put it, "They tried to kill him!"

Twelve days later, the *San Diego Union* reported that Stokeley Carmichael had spoken to a group in Southeast San Diego. This speech was reported on the fourth page of the B section as follows:[31]

CARMICHAEL CALLS FOR MORE VIOLENCE

The non-violent civil rights movement was rapped by a former leader of the Student Non-Violent Coordinating Committee yesterday because "it is unsuited to a very violet [sic] world."

Stokely [sic] Carmichael, former chairman of SNCC and now prime minister of the Black Panther Party, said the world faced by black people is violent and they need to respond the same way.

Speaking to approximately 500 persons at a rally in Oceanview Park in Southeast San Diego. Carmichael said America has legitimized blacks' killing of yellow people in Vietnam, but sends other blacks to the electric chair if they kill a white here.

Carmichael said, "We are the most violent people in the U.S.A.— Against each other," he said. "It's time we turned to our enemy and let him know where we stand."

Carmichael said the black vote "doesn't mean a thing. The vote has never and will not ever meet the needs of the black people; we have got to back up our demands with guns."

He urged the growth of undying love among blacks. He said the love must be so pervasive that if "they touch one of us, they touch us all."

Black [sic] should stop loving this country and white people more than themselves, he said.

Between this and the previous *Union* article lies an enormous information gap. As in most local communities where such incidents as the shooting of Timothy Thompson occur, biased and incomplete news coverage rather than subduing the tempers of the minority community, probably serve more to perpetuate the ignorance of the white community. No information was given as to *why* Carmichael spoke or *why* the Black Panthers held a rally on the lawn of the Memorial High School Park in Logan Heights. Many of the trainees were present at this rally, and those who were not there knew about it. An account of the preparations for the rally by a participant follows:

Three days after the shooting, the Black Panther Party in Southeast San Diego organized a meeting closed to whites, at which they planned the Stokeley Carmichael Rally for the Timothy Thompson Defense Fund. At this meeting the local Black Panther Minister of Defense gave a report that two lawyers had been secured who were willing to take the case without fee, if necessary, and that Timothy's mother had been flown from Chicago to see him in the hospital. The rally was to be held in late October with Stokeley Carmichael as the featured speaker. It was to be open to *"anyone* who desires to come." The reason for this was that the Panthers did not have the money in their organization to pay for the defense, and they wanted to use whatever means were available to secure funds for this purpose.

During the meeting, one man jumped up and said, "If a pig mess with you, just be prepared to kill him and go ahead and get it over with!" At this a Panther official rose to state that this was not the purpose of the rally, and that if any brothers got out of line, they would be taken care of because the one thing they did not want was any violence at the rally.

(Williams). After the meeting I walked outside and listened to the conversation of some of the people who had attended the meeting. The feeling was that Thompson would get some time. I don't know why this feeling prevailed, but it was there. No one denied the fact that Thompson was wrong for not paying his rent, but they were very disturbed that there were no blacks on the sheriff's warrant serving committee and no blacks in any position to deal with the population of Southeast San Diego as a whole. It was the consensus that the white establishment was not geared to deal with the problems of the black community.

The Defense Fund rally was held on a balmy Saturday afternoon, October 26, 1968. Over 500 people, mostly young blacks, attended. Their speakers included the local chapter officials, a Brown Beret representative, Timothy's mother, and of course, Stokeley Carmichael. The speaker's stand was flanked by black guards wearing black jackets, gloves, and berets. Some of them appeared no older than 12 years. All struck a steady pose of somber hostility. Stokeley delivered a speech powerful in its logic, detail and style.

The speech developed three basic concepts which he contended the black people must understand. The first concept was: "We are a *colonized* people, and as a colonized people we have no respect." There is no self-respect, only self-hate. He pointed to the violence that black people show toward one another—fighting in their homes and on the streets. He said it was time that this violence was directed outward toward the white establishment.

To accomplish this, he said, black people have to love themselves, and he added, " . . . love of oneself should be greater than your love for the white man or your love of America, and this comes first!"

He dwelt at some length on the effects of the school system—the fact that as soon as a black child enters school he is exposed to a subtle form of racism. He gave numerous examples. One was the teaching that Columbus discovered America. As he put it, "They say Columbus discovered America because he was a honky." And, he added sardonically, "He was a dumb honky at that, because he thought he was in the East Indies and all the time he was in the United States!" This statement was loudly applauded.

The second concept was "Every Negro is a potential black man." Here Carmichael dwelt on the difference between being Negro and black. He said that black people should be kind toward Negroes who identify with the middle class and try to win them to the black cause instead of making fun of them.

The third concept was the difference between a black revolutionary and a black militant. Carmichael said that he, himself, was a revolutionary.

He said, "A militant is a person who makes a lot of noise, who keeps running back and forth to the mayor and power structure threatening to riot and burn until they get a $20,000 job in a poverty program! Then they turn around and go back to the black community and tell them, 'cool it, everything's all right!'"

He added, "There is far more business black people should be engaged in, and that is revolution—complete, fundamental, absolute change! Revolution in the economic system. Capitalism has to go, and a complete turnover for all institutions in America, and if this takes violence then violence will be given!"

He emphasized, "When the pig touches one of us, he touches all of us! And if they shoot one of us, shoot one of them!"

He developed the view that the state wants to control violence and put it to its use. "The state only believes in nonviolence as far as they're concerned, but then when they want to do something against another country, then the state wants the black man to go out and kill and be as violent as he can under orders from the Army!"

The shots fired at Timothy Thompson were not the last police shots to be heard in the trainees' community. On July 13, 1969, another riot took place.

A number of trainees and other black workers at Southwestern witnessed this riot. One trainee, not among the 28 in our study group, lost his closest friend who was killed two steps behind him. All he knew was that his friend fell, gurgling, and died. The trainee did not come to work the next day because he did not want to hear the whites at the plant discussing their version of the riot.

By not recognizing the integrity and autonomy of the ghetto community, the law enforcement institution reinforces the identity of racial minorities. The revolutionary welcomes this reinforcement. Just as many of the white blue-collar workers identify strongly with the police community, many hard-core blacks identify just as strongly with the anti-police community. To them, being black and anti-police are hyphenated concepts. But the job tended to confuse this identity, and the trainees had to resolve this confusion.

IDENTITIES IN CONFLICT

After the incident with the Preacher, Andy Manners became deeply involved in black nationalism. He even hired teachers for his children to teach them "who they were."

(Williams). One night I joined one of Andy's sessions: there were about eight men at the meeting, all young, all angry. We talked about how Brother Timothy was being treated at the mental hospital and how we could get help for him. The conversation then turned to a discussion of how the things we had heard the white man was going to do to the blacks were coming true and how the incident of Timothy Thompson proved it. All profoundly believed that a plan to eliminate all black people was being put into operation, and they talked extensively of how black people had to mobilize to save themselves from this fate.

Someone said, "The white man is nothing. He would kill his own mother!"

Religion was another recurring topic of the conversation, especially the kind of spiritual teaching they were getting in the various groups to which they belonged.

Someone said, "We wonder about Christ at times, whether he was black or white."

On the whole, Andy's nationalism was defensive rather than subversive. He was determined to preserve his racial pride and integrity and to guard against the machinations of white racism. Rather than being an agent of revolution, he was an emissary of the black community within the factory community, and he talked constantly about his nationalism as he had talked about the shooting of Timothy Thompson. His talk alarmed some of his coworkers, but others agreed with him. However, Andy seemed able to keep both identities, the job and his blackness, in perspective.

In contrast, Tim Carter was never able to bring the two identities together. He wanted status in the mainstream, but not the identity. For Tim, hate of mainstream institutions was more than rhetoric and more than ideology. It was part of his emotional makeup.

Tim spoke of the anti-police defenses of the community with pride—"You know, I never been caught in action—I been finked on. That's the only way to catch me! I study—this last time, matter of fact I got caught at the spot, but they wasn't going to take me in on no 'ready-to-go'! (as a docile suspect) I got a little arrow on my name downtown—see, when they stick them arrows on there (indicating a dangerous suspect) they have to approach you in a manner that . . . "

(Williams). "What do you mean, arrow?"

"See, if they know you—if you resist arrest, they know who resists arrest."

"They're ready to hit you (on guard), huh?"

"Yeah, They got a picture, and they . . . like my cousin, he live in L.A. now. Get so that every weekend him and the policemen would get into it, and they still pick at him now. He's married and everything—they—you know—one police told him, 'I'm going to kick your ass! I'm going to get you one night, and I'm going to beat your ass!'—right there on 30th. Remember Hugh Gordon before he got killed? He used to run with my cousin. I used to see them on the weekend, give them police trouble, and they be just—they used to just get it. I see them strike out—they go they way, the police be just getting off the ground. *[Pause]* They didn't wear them helmets then. . . . And after I learned how to make the helmets come off—that wasn't nothing for me. . . . Right there on 32nd, that's where we first got into it. I hit that man's helmet—I went to hit him on the head, and I hit his helmet—his helmet snapped off—fell off on the ground, and it was just me and him then!"

"Who won?"

"Well, they won, you know, because they had reinforcements! I think it was about seven police we jumped on. The only way they got me in the car was they hit me across the head. I fell and hit the tail end of their car!"

Tim went on, "You know as much as them policemen set up there, they don't come in that park when they get to fighting. They set up there on that hill and look—the last riot they had in that park, they beat the mailman up—it was on Sunday!"

Tim added, "Taxicabs wouldn't come around unless they were Negro. They were scared. You call a cab at night, it's always a brother."

Among the trainees there were numerous examples of conflict in cultural identity. Bobby Hill's struggle is particularly revealing.

Bobby was born in Lincoln, Arkansas, June 3, 1943, during the war years when employment was at its height. His father moved the family to San Diego that same year. They moved for the same reason most blacks came from the South, to get away from the caste system and to find the "promised land"—a place that existed largely in their imaginations. His father got a job at North Island.

Like so many other blacks, Bobby's father came West too late. He had contracted tuberculosis prior to the move and died three years later, in 1947. Bobby was four and his young sister was an infant, born the year their father died.

In remembering, Bobby said, "He had to support my mother and me and my brother and my little sister. He was too far gone before we knowed it—when he did find out he had it, then it was too late. When he did start getting real sick and went and got a checkup, that was it. He came home, told my mother—this is what my mother told me—he say, 'I'm pretty sick—I got to go to the hospital.' He never came back. He said he *knew* he wasn't coming back."

Bobby's stepfather, a man he learned to hate almost from the time he first met him, entered the picture. His mother was young, 25, and had three babies to support, so she remarried. Her second husband was a rigid Baptist churchman who was twice her age. Bobby insisted that his stepfather was not religious, that "He just held a spot in the church." Kendall, as they called him, made Bobby, his brother and sister go to church three times every Sunday of the year. Kendall and the Hill children's mother had one natural daughter whom the stepfather favored over the three step-children. He punished the Hill children, especially Bobby, for every infraction of the rules, for picking a flower, for sitting on the furniture—Bobby claimed they were made to sit on the floor because Kendall wanted to keep the furniture from being worn. Also, the Hill children and their mother were made to walk to church, while the stepfather and his daughter rode. He never bought them toys, even at Christmas. The daughter got everything; they got nothing. Even today Bobby, Arthur, and his sister hate this girl. During this period Bobby began to steal.

School reinforced Bobby's rebellion. Kindergarten and first grade he remembered fondly. But, from the second grade on, he began to experience failure. His second grade teacher was a young Mexican-American girl on her first job. There were three black pupils in the class, and she flunked all of them.

Bobby recalled, "I did what I wanted to—if I didn't want to read, I didn't read. If I didn't want to spell, I didn't spell. If I wanted to do arithmetic, I'd do it."

From that point on Bobby was assigned to special classes. Some of them were called "Step-up Classes," for people, as he put it, "That didn't read good, didn't spell good, or do anything good."

He went from elementary school to Memorial Junior High where the experience of failure was intensified. His most vivid memory was of a social studies teacher, a black, who did hand spanking. He also remembered the principal and the system of what they called "case cards." The only individual attention that students received was for rule infractions, such as talking. Every time they talked, they got a mark on their case card. For every mark they were sent to the principal, who whipped them. More case cards led to more whippings, more case cards, and so on. Bobby said that he got a case card, "Damn near every class." And when the case cards and the whippings didn't work, he was suspended for a week.

The police system of behavior—punishment for nonconforming—begins at school. In Bobby's case, it began even earlier with his stepfather's cruelty. Teacher rejection, pupil rebellion, and punishment, lead directly into the law enforcement system of behavior control—first, juvenile detention, then honor camp, then prison, unless at some point a lucky break occurs—an uncommonly sensitive teacher, probation officer, judge, or policeman, or perhaps a good job.

Bobby met his wife, Barbara, when she was 14. Barbara's family was from Chula, Mississippi. They later moved to San Diego where Barbara was born in 1948. Her mother stayed in San Diego a short while but later separated from her husband and returned to Mississippi where she is now living with Barbara's brother and two youngest sisters. Barbara and the two oldest sisters stayed with her father and his mother in San Diego, but still maintained contact with their real mother in Mississippi.

To Barbara, Mississippi was a place to dread. Her mother still experiences night riders and shots at her house in the dead of night.

As Barbara explained: "See, she was working for this elderly white woman, and she willed her sixteen thousand dollars when she died, and since my mother don't work anymore, she don't say 'Yes sir,' 'No sir' to the white people down there. I guess they didn't like it, because they shot through her window twice with a shotgun and just missed—she say once it just missed her head. She say the second time, they went in the house and stole the furniture, the television, and everything—kids' beds. They didn't have a bed to sleep on! My mother once said they tried to set her house on fire."

For two years Bobby had planned to go back to Mississippi for a vacation, but Barbara, as she put it, "chickened out", because she still had dreams that something would happen to them back there. (Eventually, at the end of Bobby's first full year of employment at Southwestern, Barbara did vacation in Mississippi with Bobby.)

Barbara did well in school, until the ninth grade, when she started ditching, going to friends' houses where they played records and danced. She met Bobby during one of these escapades. Bobby wanted to marry her, but her father refused his permission. Barbara recalled, "So Bobby said, 'Well, I'm going to marry her some way, if I have to get her pregnant—I'm going to marry her!' And so, I'd say about four months after that, I got pregnant. My daddy still didn't want me to marry him, because he thought that Bobby was the kind of man that's a bully, you know, beat you up half to death and everything like that. So I told him that I wanted to be married, and July 11, 1964, we got married."

They were married before the first baby was born, and at the time Bobby came to work they had two boys.

The older boy, Bobby Jr., they called "little Bobby," the younger one Billy. Both boys called their father "big Bobby." Barbara said that

Bobby bought everything for his children because he never had anything. However, Bobby was a strict disciplinarian, and the boys were afraid of him. He hid his affection, and at times he told them that they would not amount to anything, and that they would end up in jail. Nevertheless, the Hill family was a tight-knit unit. Bobby played with the boys and took them on drives. On Sundays, they fished on the pier.

The police were a focal point in Bobby Hill's life, and because of that, they were an inescapable issue in the Hill household. The boys had seen Bobby taken to jail on numerous occasions, and they had been with him in the car when he had eluded the police. After the July 1969 riot, Bobby drove around the park, and as the boys became aware of the community's viewpoint of the riot, they hid in the back seat in order "not to be shot by the police."

Almost daily, in one way or another, the Hill sons shared in the focal experiences of the young black community of Southeast San Diego. There was much hot activism in this experience, but there was poignance as well.

(Padfield). One day I stopped at Bobby's house and spent an evening with the family when they were in a quiet, relaxed mood. Bobby had just gotten a hi-fi and a library of records from a friend of his. We listened to music for over two hours. Bobby selected the songs he thought I should hear—songs of "quiet" protest sung by Aretha Franklin. Running throughout this music were two concepts of the black experience: the old concept of patience and identification of their experience in biblical terms, and the new concept of impatience for change to correct these historic ills.

Bobby was also fond of "I've never loved a man the way I've loved you." As he interpreted the lyrics, all men and women have special moments to remember in their sometimes temporary relationships— something that brings them together, something they can always think about, even when the relationships are broken by events and situations which they cannot control. The memories of these relationships are permanent.

Tenderness and hostility make a strange combination. But with Bobby Hill rebellion was deeply embedded in his personality, and the fact that he shared this feeling and experience not just with a segment of misfits but with a complete ethnic community gave it depth and meaning. Rebellion was thus transformed from a personality problem to a criterion of identity. The police were the willing focus of this rebellion, and the automobile was the prime means of its expression.

Hill's first sentence at the age of 15 was for car theft. He had been in trouble before this, but had had no record.

His last and most serious sentence was in February 1965, for possession of stolen goods. Although Bobby was not actively involved in the robbery, he did agree to go with his friends when they tried to sell the goods they had stolen. The first stop they made was at a stake out, and they were arrested. Bobby was convicted and sentenced to one year in Barret Honor Camp, while his friends were paroled. Bobby considers this honor camp the worst he's been in.

As he explained, "I lost all my good time there." It was a camp for older men, and Bobby was in fights constantly and never got along with anybody. And, the other inmates used to report him to the superintendent for playing his radio at night.

"Over the squawk-box the man would say, 'Bobby Hill, would you come down to the office?' I'd go trippin' off down there, and Old Man Die—drinking on the job—old Southerner—drinkin' on the job—drunk damn near every day he's there—every day, he never comes to work without a fifth!"

(Padfield). "Couldn't you report his drinking?"

"Yep, I could've reported his drinking, but the letter would've to go out through them, and that would have went right to the shit can. Everybody else know he drunk—all the rest of those damn officers know he drunk!"

"Is Barret prejudiced as a whole?"

"As a whole, it is prejudiced. The superintendent, himself, said he didn't want over 10 Negroes over 115. San Jose has damn near all Negroes."

Bobby said he couldn't request transfer from Barret, but when he continued to rebel, they sent him to San Jose, another camp. For Bobby this was fortunate. There he was appointed head of a barracks and got his "good time" back again. He was released in March 1966, with 10 years probation. This was the last sentence that Bobby has had to date.

Despite the fact that Bobby was out of jail and had received no more convictions, police contact continued, as we noted in Chapter 4.

No doubt, some of Bobby's hostility was a front, because, as Barbara has stated, "Underneath that, he is just a tender baby, because he's nothing but a big bully on the outside." Bobby was intensely afraid of going back to prison and he has often stated that he would run away if faced with another sentence.

Barbara has said, "Bobby has been there (in prison) so many times, he's afraid he'll go back. He said he never wants to go back. That's why—he's been there, and he knows how it is. The last time they sent him up for 10 months; he was sittin' in the court room cryin'; he looked so pitiful!—He didn't do nothin', but he was kinda guilty because he let them boys use his car. I think that's the first time I've seen him cry. (Pause) I started crying myself."

After his last jail sentence, Bobby began to use the police system against itself, i.e., one police system as protection against another, and against his community by informing for the FBI. This might explain some of the ticket fixing in Hill's behalf.

(Williams). I had heard the rumors about his informing, and I confronted Bobby. He was defensive and vague, and said that it was possible before the job, but "no one is able to prove it is going on now." He wanted to know whether my information came from black or white sources. He said, "The only thing that anyone can prove is that I am talking to the Man, and no one knows what I am talking to the Man about."

Two weeks later, on his own initiative, Bobby came to talk to me. He wanted to clear up the matter of his activities with the FBI. He told me that he knew it hurt me to know that he was involved. He said he wished he could show me that the information he had given the FBI was not harmful to anyone. I asked Bobby how recent his activities were, and he stated emphatically that since the job at Southwestern, he had had no further dealings with the FBI.

I asked why he had become involved in the first place, and he said that at the time they contacted him he had had no job and that informing was just a good way to get money.

I asked him why he stopped, and he said, "Well, I think after I gave them so many lies and told them stuff that they already knew—they finally figured out what I was doing, and quit askin' me."

He was deadly serious this day. He kept saying, "I know how this hurts you, because I know that it would hurt me to know that one of the brothers would be finking on the others."

As the job and the status it involved began to affect Bobby's personality, he developed a new way of dealing with the police. Instead of blind conflict and fighting, instead of trying to manipulate the police at the expense of his friends, he was beginning to lodge formal complaints at the police department for what he considered harassing activities.

Other trainees, as well, experienced similar transitions as they acquired more status and economic power; anti-institutional ethos continued, and anti-institutional action, to the extent that it continued, evolved into more progressive forms.

6

Family

... The history of the Negro family since the time of slavery indicates that the most important single program is the elimination of unemployment. If Negro men can obtain decent and stable jobs, then many—and far more than we think—can at once assume a viable role in the family and can raise children who will put an end to the long tradition of male marginality and inferiority.

(Herbert J. Gans, "The Negro Family" in The Moynihan Report and the Politics of Controversy, *pp. 445-456.)*

... We do not have to see the problem in terms of breaking into a puncture proof circle, of trying to change values, of disrupting the lines of communication between parent and child so that parents cannot make children in their own image, thereby transmitting their culture inexorably, ad infinitum. No doubt, each generation does provide role models for each succeeding one. Of much greater importance for the possibilities of change, however, is the fact that many similarities between the lower-class Negro father and son (or mother and daughter) do not result from "cultural transmission" but from the fact that the son goes out and *independently* experiences the same failures, in the same areas, and for much the same reasons as his father. What appears as a dynamic, self-sustaining cultural process is, in part at least, a relatively simple piece of social machinery which turns out in rather mechanical fashion, independently produced look-alikes. The problem is how to change the *conditions* which, by guaranteeing failure, cause the son to be made in the image of the father ... If there is to be a change in this way of life, this central fact must be changed; the Negro man, along with everyone else, must be given the skills to earn a living and an *opportunity* to put these skills to work.

No one pretends that this is an easy matter, to be accomplished at one fell stroke. For many Negro men, jobs alone are no longer enough. Before he can earn a living, he must believe that he can do so, and his women and children must learn to believe this along with him. But he finds it difficult to begin without their support, and they find it difficult to give their support until he begins. The beginning, then, will doubtless be a slow one, but once started, success will feed on itself just as failure has done. (Italics added)

(Elliot Liebow, Tally's Corner, *pp. 223-224.)*

Just as job status had an impact on group and community identity vis-à-vis the law, it also had an impact on the family life of the hard-core unemployed. It required readjustments in interpersonal relationships, rearrangements of economic affairs, and reevaluation of household responsibilities. In short, the adjustment of the permanently unemployed person to permanent employment implies the evolution of new roles in the family for both men and women.

That stress should develop as these new family roles evolved is axiomatic. In fact the reverse is true—new family roles developed in response to stress. Thus stress could be regarded as a link in the causal chain of events that change in economic status set in motion.

Stress developed in almost every family and worsened every family member's situation for at least a time. It was worse for some families than it was for others, and for some it was insurmountable. One such family was the Johns, whom we will discuss at length to give a greater understanding of the evolving relationships between new job status and family life among the hard-core.

DARRELL AND JUSTINE

Darrell and Justine Johns were married in 1965. He was 22 and she was 16. When Darrell was hired at Southwestern in August, 1968, there were three children in their household. Two were theirs; one was

Justine's by another man. Although Darrell boasted from time to time about his girlfriends, he recognized only one child from his affairs, and his identification with this one varied with his mood.

To Darrell the job at Southwestern was all important. For days he was so excited that he couldn't sleep. The job had immediate consequences for him in all spheres of his activity, including increased conflict at home. The Johns' new status quite naturally resulted in new expectations from society and from one another. To Darrell the job meant Justine getting up to fix breakfast, making him a lunch, and attending to the house and children. To Justine, it meant a stereo, color TV, new furniture, Darrell staying home at night, and her controlling the money as she had done on welfare.

The first weekend after he was hired, Darrell was arrested for fighting with his wife and neighbors. He was released on bail shortly thereafter.

Following is a portion of the interview we had with Darrell and Justine immediately after his release. Darrell's voice was soft, almost inaudible, but his words trailed out in a distinctive, high-pitched monotone. The angrier he got, the higher the pitch. His primary concern was getting Justine to act like a working man's wife. Justine listened pouting and silent:

> DARRELL. *I try to explain this to Justine—I tell her the night before, "Justine go fix my lunch!"—you know. I got to be there to this bus at ten minutes after six. And I tell her sometime, "Look here Justine, why don't you get up and make me some coffee and fry me a couple of eggs or somethin'!" You know, cause I'm hungry. Like I tell her, if she get up she be up 15 or 20 minutes and back to bed—she can lay up all day if she want to!*
>
> ROY (Williams). *Will she get up and fix your breakfast?*
>
> DARRELL. *She won't do it! She gets mad! So I leaves for work every morning angry.*
>
> ROY. (Trying to baby Justine) *You realize that Justine? I sure hope you feed him cause I'm down there with him eight hours a day, and I don't like those grouchy fellows.*
>
> JUSTINE. *Uh huh.*

During this interview, we discussed Darrell's girlfriends. One woman in particular, Millie Jo, and her child, caused the most trouble, because Darrell had continued seeing them after his marriage to Justine. Sometimes Darrell defends his involvement with Millie Jo. Sometimes he flaunts it. When he flaunts it, the baby is his. When he defends it, the baby could have had any one of a dozen fathers. On this occasion he was defending it, because Justine had seen him with the child and Millie Jo. This meeting had caused the fight which led to Darrell's arrest.

> DARRELL. *Like I been tryin' to tell Justine, there's some kind of jealousy in this girl.* (Referring to Justine) *I don't know what it is, but I know she don't dig Christine.* (Darrell's child by Millie Jo) *Because me and Christine go walkin' at night, and she look at Christine real funny. The way that I take it, she be sayin' within herself, why can't I be walkin' with her and her baby, you know.*
>
> ROY. *All right, you don't give this girl any support do you?*
>
> DARRELL. *Naw, you know what man? I don't have to—see when this girl had this baby, it was a big ole confusion bout this, man. She was selling her body and this and that. And she tole me my cousin raped her . . . . The first time I met her, she was in the bed with somebody, and she split with me . . .* (Pause) *I just got myself wired up in a predicament, man, you know—two young ladies both pregnant by me.* (Referring to Justine and Millie Jo) *I love one and the other one I don't care nothin' about, because I know she ain't no good. This is why I get mad at Justine the other night. She come around here, and I wake up and the girl is in my face!*

The Johns argued continuously about Darrell's women. Justine got even with Darrell by neglecting the children, refusing to cook or clean, and constantly running home to her mother who kept telling her to leave Darrell. Darrell reacted by staying away from home, picking up old girlfriends, and propositioning new ones. He went home only when he wanted to see his children. When he did, the house was usually dirty, the children sick and hungry, and Justine absent.

During the interview, Justine cried in anger numerous times and seldom uttered more than a phrase at a time:

ROY. *Will you tell Darrell how you feel he's treating you?*

JUSTINE. (Blurting) *Like a child! I sit up and tell him all the time; he tells me, too, "You're not my mother!" and then I say, "You're not my Daddy!" . . .*

DARRELL. (Interrupting) *. . . Naw, man—let me explain somethin'—okay? When me and Justine be talkin', you know—she have a little ole temper and she get to runnin' off at the mouth—see. Well, this here was somethin' that I went through during my life. I'm lookin' at my father and mother, fights and arguments—this is the only mother I know, but she's really my stepmother, see—I've never seen my real mother. As I grew up it was jus' arguments and then as I got older—I guess this must have affected me or somethin', me never knowin' who my mother were.*

ROY. *Does Justine know this? Have you told her?*

DARRELL. *Yes, I have tole Justine this.*

JUSTINE. *Yes he tell me that all the time!*

DARRELL. (Ignoring Justine) *See what I be tellin' her, I say, "Justine you know about comin' up, you know." I used to tell her, "Justine don't do me like this; you my wife not my mamma!" But she would make me feel like I'm still livin' in the sa-ame tha-ang!*

ROY. *By the same token, Justine, have you told him of the problem of how you feel since you came up without a father—did you tell him just like him telling you?*

JUSTINE. *Yeah, I told him.*

ROY. *All right what did you tell him?*

JUSTINE. (Again avoiding herself) *He tells me . . .*

ROY. (Persisting) *I mean what did you tell him about how you feel?*

JUSTINE. *I tell him—he be tellin' me to do this and to do that, and then he tells me hisself he's gonna be my father!*

DARRELL. (Objecting) *Naw, you know what I tell her?*

JUSTINE. (Persisting) *. . . He gets jealous and he makes me—*(Pausing) *you know, seriously—I'm not tellin' no lie—you know what Darrell do?*

ROY. *What?*

JUSTINE. *He gets mad, and he makes me go in the closet and get on my knees, and he takes a belt and make me get on the floor in front of him, and then he pop me like a baby or somethin'—seriously, I'm not kidding!*

DARRELL. *Naw—she tellin' the truth bout that.* (Laughing in embarrassment) *I have did it.*

ROY. (Looking at Justine) *How do you feel about that?*

JUSTINE. *That make me feel bad and make me want to do anything!*

ROY. *In other words, you feel like a child?*

JUSTINE. *Yeah.*

ROY. *Did you ever tell him that?*

JUSTINE. (Looking at Darrell laughing) *He knows!*

ROY. *No—no, here you go again. You're taking it for granted—Justine tell Darrell!*

JUSTINE. (Mechanically turning to Darrell) *That make me feel like a child!*

ROY. (Turning to Darrell) *Did you know she felt like that?*

DARRELL. *No—I didn't—I know that she probably was feeling pretty bad—but not exactly like that—man—I have did because Justine done made me so mad.* (Lying) *I won't hit her or nothin'—I jus' make her do somethin' stupid—like she said, I have made her stand in the closet.*

Darrell was born in Louisiana, and when he was three, his parents moved to California. His father deserted the family shortly thereafter, but later returned and took Darrell away with him. As a result, Darrell has very few memories of his real mother, and he emphatically denies that he ever knew her. The person he refers to as his mother is actually his stepmother.

Darrell's involvement with Millie Jo, Justine, and the law occurred almost simultaneously. Here he recalls his life with his father and stepmother and gives some of the reasons why he started living alternately with Millie Jo and Justine, and why he began to steal:

DARRELL. *One night me and my mother was comin' from my grandmother's house and was ridin' down Market, and we seen my father, right there at the graveyard on Market, and it was a woman with him. My mother, she turns around and went in her purse to pull a knife out, so I grabbed the woman. And my father—I jus' told him why didn't he take his business home, you know, like that; so he got in his car, and he split. He went home. So me and my mother, we followed him. When I got there, my father went to hit my mother, and I grabbed him. He got to talkin' about, "What you grab me for, and she don't even want you in the house! You doin' this with your momma, and you do that, and you don't even know how she feels bout you." And he ran it down to me right in front of her face, and all she was doin' was cryin'—I say, "Well I'm a go!"*

ROY. *That's when you went with Millie Jo?*

DARRELL. *Yeah, to me she was just a good thang . . . When this came up, I jus' split. I went over to my cousin's . . . . Anyway this girl (referring to Millie Jo) comes along—it was an accident the way it happened man; I went with her a long time ago.*

Darrell also described his early childhood and the fact that his stepmother was unable to handle him. When Darrell was 12, his father threw him out of the house, saying that if he was a big enough man to smoke, he was big enough to get a job. Darrell calls his father a playboy and blames him for setting a bad example for his children:

DARRELL. . . . *He would never stay home. He was doing construction—come home—take a bath—get a good check, and he was gone. And my mother, this is the truth man, she was workin' at Dodge's washin' off cars an makin' about forty some dollars a week. She was tryin' to take care of me and my sister, and they was buyin' they house at the time—she was studyin' tryin' to pay for this house and send me and my sister to school, feed us, pay our bills on a little ole forty some dollars! My father, he jus' be runnin' out there in the streets throwin' his money away. And, you know, I jus' didn't have everything that my friends had. This makes me feel bad. I jus' couldn't go to my mother and say I want this and want that. She couldn't get it. She say, "Well Darrell wait till next week."—Next week it's the same thang—but I understood, man. And I kinda developed a grudge against my father behind this. But anyway, all of a sudden I was out of there stealin'—man, like I was tryin' to keep up, but I was jus' doin' it wrong.*

A few days after this interview Darrell appeared in court, and because Justine did not press charges, his case was dismissed.

On September 23, 1968, Darrell began his on-job training. His fighting with Justine continued and during the month of October became chronic, with Justine calling the police and Darrell staying out entire nights, night after night. By now the conflicts were affecting his job, causing a critical increase in his absences. As a result on October 24, 1968, Darrell received the first of many verbal warnings about his attendance.

(Williams). At this point I had a counseling session with Darrell to find out why he had been staying out at night.

He said, "I left because I jus' can't take Justine talking about if I leave, her momma will help her, and if I stay, she won't help her." He added, "I can't even live with Justine because of the confusion that I have with her family, so I jus' split the scene!"

I asked him why he stayed with Justine, and he replied, "I feel obligated to her and the kids." He spoke repeatedly of the children, and also mentioned that on several occasions Justine had tried to stab him and that he had beaten her. But he said he didn't do that anymore; he just walked off. He spoke repeatedly about the other women who liked him and how he couldn't stay away from them or turn them down, and kept interspersing these comments with statements about how much he and Justine loved each other.

On November 11, another major fight erupted. Justine called about 7:00 a.m. to say that Darrell could not come to work because he had to go to the doctor. From the tone of her voice I (Williams) could sense that something was wrong. She began to tell me that Darrell had beaten her. I told her to tell Darrell to come to work if at all possible, and then I drove out to their house. When I arrived, Justine was outside.

She said fiercely, "He's inside!" I went in and found the house torn apart. It was obvious that they had been fighting. Darrell had scratches on his face, and Justine was holding her side. Nevertheless they tried to minimize the battle. I took Darrell back to the plant, and he punched in at 8:10 a.m. The following night, Darrell, Justine, and I had a long counseling session. Portions of this follow:

DARRELL. *It seems that in so many ways I'm on my way back to the joint.*

ROY. *I'm sure that's not where you want to go.*

DARRELL. *I don't know, man; the joint ain't so bad—I mean it is, but if it's bad, it's just bad—Ain't no big thing . . . .*

ROY. *Can you remember telling me how much you and Justine loved each other? Have you changed that statement? Do you think you still love each other?*

DARRELL. *I dig Justine so much deep down in my heart, but Sunday* (the previous night) *I almost killed her! Her mother stopped me—I just didn't care.*

ROY. *Those are pretty strong words. You are going to have to come to a point where . . .*

DARRELL. *This is what I'm speaking of. I'm under tension; things have built up so that I don't know how to let it come out right. I jus' don't know what to do. I don't know whether to leave or not . . . .*

ROY. *Well Justine cares.*

DARRELL. *But when Justine gets to goin' off and leavin' them kids in this house by theyself . . . . I come here, and it may be two or three hours before she come. Now Justine thinks I'm jivin' about this, but I'm serious. I'm goin' to get Justine about leavin' them kids; Justine should know better!*

ROY. (Persisting) *Justine, aren't you afraid of him hurting you? When I came over yesterday you hadn't been exactly playing.*

DARRELL. (Continuing to pour out his feelings) *Her mother for the first time . . . I didn't hear it all—I was listening at the door, and her mother talks pretty loud . . . she was trying to explain to Justine that—Justine is less than a woman, man. Like I always tell Justine, if she would stop drinking that beer and acting a fool, start cleaning the house and cook, then I think I could be a better man. I go out there and work all day, and when I get off I don't want to come home, man, because I don't want to hear all that bullshit. Something has changed my mind; I don't care about my work . . . . I've got to the point that this is the way I feel. I'm going to say word for word just how I feel. I look at the job down there, and I have a real good chance to make it. Them people down there likes* me, I mean in department 30, not just the men but all them that work around there. You know I like the job, I really do. I guess it's the changes I be going through; like today when I didn't come to work, I thought about it all day. Down on the job I think—"What kind of fool I must be! Why don't I go to work and just split, but I can't do that because of my kids; I feel that my kids need me!" (Bitterly) And then I come home, and my wife didn't work a bit! The woman out there in the street (referring to his girl friend) don't mean a thing; this is where I lay my head....

ROY. Have you put your hand on any real cause of your problems?

DARRELL. I can understand this, Justine is young and going through them changes....I was down on Imperial and here she come, an old wig on her head, nasty clothes...and she's drunk. This made me mad, because this is my wife. I don't want Justine down on Imperial drinking just like everything else I look at on the street on the weekend, dropping pills and getting drunk. The way I look at it is they ain't nothing. I want something nice and decent that I can love.... This here is drawing a lot of feeling from me.

ROY. Do you think she's getting drunk and dropping pills?

DARRELL. You know, Mr. Williams, what she did? She done fell out there in the backyard; me and her mother tried to pick her up, and she's out there just hollerin' real loud, "He's going to kill me!" It's about 2:00 a.m., and it's real foggy, and I tell her somebody is going to call the police.... So we get her in the house, and she still do that all night, man. Beating on the wall, saying he's going to kill me. Even her mother told her she was going to call the police.

JUSTINE. You tell me someone beatin' my ass, and I ain't going to be hollerin'?

DARRELL. Wasn't nobody beating on you for you to be hollerin' like that!

JUSTINE. You was!

DARRELL. (Shifting) Well, like I say, you deserved it!

ROY.... Justine I notice you aren't defending yourself. Why? Did he almost kill you? This is the first fight in quite a while.

DARRELL. (Persisting) Because I've been taking it....I say,

"Justine stop doing me like you are. I'm a man; I'm supposed to rule!"

ROY. (To Justine) *You and Darrell talk any?*

JUSTINE. *Just fight!*

ROY. *Do you think there's some hope?*

JUSTINE. *It don't make me no difference!*

ROY. *What do you mean, "It don't make you no difference"? If it didn't make no difference, you wouldn't be here.*

JUSTINE. *I got to stay here.*

ROY. *He make you stay?*

JUSTINE. *I was going to leave the other night.*

DARRELL. *You were so damn drunk.*

JUSTINE. *You a damn lie! . . . He come home with motel tickets in his pocket, woman's phone number. I just called Mary Sunday and talked to her.*

DARRELL. *She goes in my pocket, so I pulls it out and shows it to her—that woman ain't no woman of mine!*

JUSTINE. *You lying!*

ROY. *That's the first time you tried to defend yourself.*

JUSTINE. *You lying! You lying! You even show me the phone numbers . . . .*

ROY. *Do you love him? Tell me, why do you stay here? Darrell makes you stay? You couldn't take off while he was at work?*

JUSTINE. *I am afraid to.*

ROY. *In other words you are afraid of him.*

DARRELL. *She couldn't be too scared because if she was, she would split, and it won't be nowhere I could find her.* (Hatefully) *I won't leave no town to find you . . . .*

ROY. . . . *Darrell, you said Justine tried to treat you like a boy.*

DARRELL. *She tried. I have to explain to her where I'm going and where I've been. I come home and change clothes, and Justine be gone.*

JUSTINE. *No I don't. Sometimes he go to work, and I don't see him all night. Then he have the nerve enough to come home the next morning to change clothes and leave again. Don't be here 10 minutes . . . .*

DARRELL. . . . *Like I say, Justine done went through them*

changes so much that I don't want to come home anymore.

JUSTINE. *All you do is sit up and lie!*

DARRELL. *All those times you have threatened me.* (Mimicking) *"When you go to sleep, I'm going to get your ass!" And throwing hot water on me....Justine is keeping a pipe behind the door. Sometimes we be talking, and I stand up, and Justine grab that pipe!*

JUSTINE. *So what do you expect? My ribs all sore and cut up!*

DARRELL. (Purring a threat) *I tole Justine she going to keep on, and she was going to lose me one of these days. A sweet little lady is going to come up and . . . so long Justine.*

ROY. (To Justine) *Do you want him to go?*

DARRELL. (Interrupting) *Mr. Williams, you know, it's something I try to tell Justine. You see Justine have been on that welfare so long until she depends on it. She have this feeling in her that, "Darrell, you ain't doing nothing for me"—This have kind of spoiled Justine. She feel that if I split, she ain't going to do nothing but go back on the welfare.*

ROY. (To Justine) *Do you want to go back on the welfare?*

DARRELL. (Interrupting) *If it wasn't for the welfare and her people next door, if we was way out somewhere else, we could make it. Things would be a whole lot different.*

JUSTINE. *That's what he want to do. Like when I say something back to him, he can hit me in my mouth!*

ROY. *Why won't he do it now? Because your mother lives next door?*

JUSTINE. *That's what he must be talking about, he keeps saying it.*

DARRELL.... *It's not because of them people. It's because, when Justine be hollerin' through the wall like that, I know what she be doing. Every time we get in an argument she be hollerin', "My mother's going to blow your head off!" And it's getting sickening to me!*

JUSTINE. *You sit up and talk about your women and what they want to do for you; if they want to do so much for him, why don't he be with them?*

DARRELL. *Justine make me so mad and disgusted with all we go through.... And like all the downfalls me and her family*

*done had. "Justine is right and I am wrong." That's the way
they look at it, you know.*

Throughout the session the same themes recurred: intense jealousy, hate, and violence; Darrell's jealous regard for his children and his image of himself as a father; his longing for an escape, even prison; Justine's rejection of her supporting role for the job; her being more a child than a mother; her family's rejection of Darrell; and finally her dependence on welfare as a means of keeping financially independent of her husband and using it as a weapon against him.

Although less violent, their fighting continued throughout the year. At one point, Darrell even insisted that things were improving, and as he put it, he was changing.

However, shortly after New Year's, the Johns' household experienced another crisis. On January 6, I stopped by the shop where Darrell worked and asked him about the family.

He laughed and said, "You know I've split the scene—my woman come down from Los Angeles." He added, "My wife is crazy, and I think she's scared she's going to lose her good man." Four days later Darrell was in jail charged with the attempted stabbing of his wife. He was released two days later, at which time I went out to the house to talk alone with Justine:

ROY. *What brought it on? Darrell had left?*
JUSTINE. *Yeah, he did. I went out last Friday, and I stayed out all night. When I come home Saturday morning, he jumped on me and said I had been with some man . . . . He got his things and called hisself leaving, so I went over to Pat's house. When I got* (back) *to the house, I went to bed. He came in and asked me why did I leave the house. We started fussing, and he started telling me he was going to move to L.A. or something and that he was going to take his clothes, because a lady was going to meet him here . . . . He said something, and I said something smart, and that's when he jumped on me and started hitting me, and I didn't know that I was cut, cause I didn't feel it. He said, "You're bleeding; why don't you get up and go in the bathroom and wipe all that blood off your face?" I didn't believe him, cause I was crying and tears was*

running out of my eyes. I thought he wanted to get me in the bathroom to jump on me. My mother wasn't here. I laid back down, and he said, "I'm not playing, look at that sheet." That's when I saw the blood. When he was hitting me, the baby was in the bed. The baby started crying, and I went in the bathroom, and he followed me in there. I said, "Why don't you go in there and give the baby her bottle?" When he was giving the baby the bottle, I ran out and told my mother to take me to the doctor, you know, get my head sewed up. He left and called me up on the phone saying he was sorry and everything. By that time the police was here, and they saw him passing by; they snagged him. When we come from the hospital, the police took us down to the police station.

ROY. *Who called the police?*

JUSTINE. *I did.*

ROY. *You do that very often?*

JUSTINE. *No, I had stopped that. But he did it for nothing! . . .*

ROY. *. . . I have heard you say so often that you love Darrell and don't want him to leave. Do you still feel you love him, even though you have had fights, seen him with other girls, and so forth?*

JUSTINE. *Yes.*

ROY. *Do you want him back?*

JUSTINE. *Yeah, but I'm not going to be running up and down the street looking for Darrell; if that's what he wants, he can have that!*

ROY. *. . . What are you going to do if Darrell doesn't come back? This morning you said you would kill yourself; you sure don't want to do that. Do you love him that much?*

JUSTINE. *Yeah.*

ROY. *That you would kill yourself if he didn't come back to you?*

JUSTINE. (Pause—almost inaudibly) *I don't know what I would do.*

ROY. *This is a mystery to me, but . . . is that the way you express your love?*

JUSTINE. (Quickly) *It's not me; the whole thing is Darrell want to have his way, you know, and then expect me to take all that stuff off of him!*

ROY. *Does he ever throw it at you about the kids?*

JUSTINE. *What about them?*

ROY. *That one of them is not his, and he takes care of them.*

JUSTINE. *Yeah, he say he's going to call the welfare people and tell them he ain't going to take care of no kids.*

ROY. *What will you do now that he's gone?*

JUSTINE. (Bewildered—hopeless) *I don't know.*

ROY. *You have to take care of your family somehow.*

JUSTINE. (Softly) *I know it . . .*

ROY. *. . . . Did the kids see you fighting the other night?*

JUSTINE. *Yeah. They always see; he don't care!*

ROY. *Do you care?*

JUSTINE. *Yeah, I care. I always tell him when he do be fighting.*

ROY. *What kind of effect do you think it's going to have on the kids? . . . Did you ever see your mother and dad fight?*

JUSTINE. *No.*

ROY. *Well, it's not good, I'll tell you that.*

JUSTINE. (Softly) *I know it's not.*

Although he had been warned repeatedly about his attendance, Darrell's absences continued, and by mid-March, in the midst of chronic family conflict, he was approaching another crisis, the loss of his job. The Johns family was now on the verge of total collapse. On the eve of his termination, I had another long session with Darrell and Justine. Their problems were still the same—jealousy, hate, Darrell's women, Justine's lack of support, chronic fighting, and welfare. During this interview, Justine was depressed and worried about a nervous breakdown. She complained about blood clots and ill health.

Finally on March 25, 1969, Darrell was terminated. Both he and Justine were hopeless, despondent, disorganized, and increasingly violent. It was obvious that they were heading toward an even greater crisis, the inevitable loss of their children.

The welfare office had become increasingly interested in the abuse of the Johns children, and although Darrell and Justine knew this, they were powerless, too caught up in their own intense, intimate problems to face the needs of the children.

(Williams). Two weeks after Darrell was fired, Andy Manners came to work and told me that the police had chased Darrell out the back window of his house. Later that morning, we learned that Darrell had hospitalized Justine in another fight, that the police had been called in with a doctor, and that after the doctor had examined the children, a court order had been issued to make them wards of the court. The same day, Darrell's father and stepmother bailed him out of jail.

Ironically, the separation from their children posed an even greater crisis for Darrell and Justine than their chronic interpersonal problems. Now they were faced with the task of regaining custody of their children. The welfare office, the police, and even Justine's mother were common enemies during the weeks the Johns' were preparing for the custody hearing. Justine's mother was preparing to testify in support of the probation department's recommendation that the children be permanently taken from their parents. She was doing this to get custody of the oldest boy. She was also trying to find someone else to take the other children.

Both Justine and Darrell complained that her mother was only interested in the money she would get for child support. Justine said that her mother had collected welfare when she (Justine) was a child and had used it for herself and her boyfriends while neglecting Justine. They insisted that the mother had called the probation department and that her reports were the reason such harsh measures were being used against them.

They protested that Darrell never beat the children, despite the fact that Justine herself complained of just the opposite many times before. Both felt humiliated by the probation officer.

Justine snapped, "White people are always like that!"

(Williams). "Like what?"

She said, "Well, she talked to us so bad, until it just lowered us down; it made us feel less than human. She talked to Darrell like he was a small child."

The probation officer had insisted that Justine file for divorce before probation would recommend to the court that the children be returned to her. Justine wavered, but on April 21 she decided to file. In view of the fact that Darrell had threatened to kill Justine if she divorced him, the probation officer's tactics were questionable, to say the least.

In addition to the probation department, the social welfare office was also involved in the Johns' case. The attitudes of these two offices concerning Darrell and Justine are revealed by both the case records and the oral comments of the case workers.

When we examined Darrell's file at the welfare office, we discovered that it consisted of a "complete" report compiled from police department and correctional institution records. The report described Darrell as a marginal person, a very confused, but likeable man, and a "nuisance to society." It quoted a psychiatrist who described his father as being a "negative role model," and who emphasized the "frequency and ease with which Darrell described his sexual encounters with women." The report failed to mention many of the things about Darrell, both favorable and unfavorable, that we knew from our relatively short association with him. In short, it was all too familiar and repetitious of many similar reports put out by welfare and correctional agencies—it was superficial and biased.

We then checked with the probation office, and learned that not only were they advising Justine to file for a divorce with a restraining order, but were also advising her to bring criminal charges against Darrell. The probation supervisor defended this action by citing the department's report. It described the house as being unfit to live in, with no lights, gas, or running water, and it stated that Justine was an immature girl who had neglected her home and children. It also referred to her as someone "Darrell had picked up and married." The supervisor then called the probation officer who had written the report. Her recommendation to the department was that under no circumstances were the children to be placed back in the home until it was made suitable for them to live in. The supervisor's main concern was for the children and Justine. In his opinion Darrell was a nuisance to society and belonged in jail. Although he had arranged for the divorce, not once did the supervisor suggest marital counseling as a possible solution to the Johns' problems.

(Williams). Shortly after my conversation with the probation supervisor, I received a call from Justine. When I told her of the

department's recommendation, she broke into hysterical crying and asked if I would come out to the house so she could explain her side of the situation. I met her at 4:00 p.m., and we drove over to Darrell's mother's house, where Darrell was living at that time. Justine was still in conflict about what to do, because of the children. When we arrived, Darrell came over to the car and immediately began to tell me of his trying to make a deal with the police to be picked up. In this way, he felt that everyone would be better off. As we talked, Justine expressed a great fear that the children would forget her.

Darrell said, "You know, I feel that I'm going through this thing all over again."

I asked what he meant and he said, "My mother used to beat me with a switch. She would make me stand on one foot and hold out my hand while she beat me."

I asked him why she beat him, and he answered, "Well, if I would go in the icebox and get some fruit or maybe a sandwich or anything like this, she would beat me. I had no key to the house, and I would climb in the window. I would also get beatings for this . . . ."

He kept repeating, "Look like I'm going through this all over again!"

I pressed them as to what they could offer the children and why they were so persistent about regaining custody of them. After a while they agreed, "We don't really offer them anything, but we are afraid they will forget us."

I asked how they felt about the children staying with either of their parents. Justine said, "My mother would keep the children, but I'm not happy because that would mean I have to stay there." She said she would agree with that, "Just to get the kids back."

Justine's real father had been a complete stranger to her. She described in detail how her mother had had illegitimate children by different men and had hidden them from welfare, because she was afraid of being cut off. She stated, "The reason I'm not at home today is because of my mother's boyfriend. He used to come in at night and try to feel between my legs." Justine insisted that even now the same man was also sleeping with her 16-year-old sister.

I asked Darrell about the children staying with his family. He said,

"I talked to my father about it, and he could make my mother do it. But I don't want my children growing up under the same thing I had to take."

I asked what was wrong with a foster home. Justine said she knew many girls who were products of foster homes and had heard what they said about them. After spending 20 minutes on the subject, Justine began to relax. I asked them to try and make up their minds, because they were to see the children the following day. I suggested that if they were going to stay together they should get professional help. I also told them that if they felt they really wanted the children, one of the surest ways of getting them back was for Darrell to get a job, and make their home a worthwhile place to live in. I said, "You can always appeal to the judge, because he does not like to take children away from their parents."

It was at this point that they both began to brighten. They said, "Well, we can try that."

Darrell had wanted to try again for quite a while, but Justine was the one who felt at a loss. She kept repeating, "I've never been in trouble, and it's all because of Darrell's record that we are in such a mess now."

Three days before the trial, Darrell got another job, this time with General Training, a private nation-wide program which specialized in training the hard-core unemployed *prior* to being hired in industry. At the same time he secured a lawyer to represent him in court. Both of these factors weighed heavily in the judge's decision in the Johns' favor.

Darrell's appearance with an attorney caught the probation officer completely by surprise. The following interview immediately after the trial reveals some of the pretrial manipulation that took place. It also suggests that this reunion between children and parents was merely a pathetic interlude in a deeply disturbed, fundamentally unchanged household:

> ROY. *So the lawyer was a surprise to her?*
> DARRELL. *Yes, it was a surprise to her. Well, they didn't have anything against Justine about taking these kids. But they were holding the kids behind my record. This is what the whole thing was about—my record . . . .*

ROY. *Was your mother there?*

JUSTINE. *Uh huh.*

ROY. *What did she have to say?*

DARRELL. *First they asked me, they say, "Mr. Johns you have anything to say?" And I say, "No." They asked Justine, and she say, "No." They ask her mother, and she say, "Yes, I would like to get Sherman* (oldest boy). *Just like that. I had told the lawyer that Miss Daisy Ann* (Justine's mother) *is doing all this here for money. I really believe this. You know, she was doing this here for money and to try to hurt me in some kind of way. The whole thing is a personal grudge against me....Well I told Justine. I say, "Justine if I was to come up with that job, I do believe we can get them kids back."—By me having this paper* (letter from General Training) . . .

ROY. *. . . . They let you off?*

DARRELL. *Yeah.*

ROY. *. . . . So having a job, and having held a job really helped you?*

DARRELL. *Right....Because it was definitely against me. It was just the lawyer on my side, and I guess the judge at the end turn against them and got on my side . . .*

ROY. *. . . . Have you talked to your mother, Justine?*

JUSTINE. *Yeah, she didn't want to talk to me . . . .*

DARRELL. (Persisting) *Oh, what happen out there, the lawyer asked Sherman, "Do you want to go with your grandmother, or stepfather, or Mr. Johns?" And he say, "Well I want to go with him," speaking about me. This hurted her real bad, man, because while we were sitting up there I overheard Miss Daisy Ann, my mother-in-law, talking to Sherman, telling him to tell the people that he didn't want to come home with me, that he wanted to go home with his grandmother, you know.*

ROY. *She told him that before they went to court?*

DARRELL. *Right, right.*

JUSTINE. *Right.*

DARRELL. *So Sherman kept on saying, "I wanna go home with Darrell," you know. You can believe this boy; this boy is crazy about me, man. He is, cause I don't spank him or do him any kind of way.*

ROY.... *Well, you got the family back intact now. Justine how do you feel? What's the big smile for?*

JUSTINE. *Nothin'.*

DARRELL. *She was bout ready to let me go down the drain, man, even last night—oowhee!*

JUSTINE. *What?... What you tell me? When you came outta that court room?*

DARRELL. *What did I tell you?*

JUSTINE. *Uh huh. If I didn't get the kids back what you were gonna do.* (Referring to Darrell's threats to harm her)

DARRELL. *Naw, I just told her, Mr. Williams, that Justine been really threatening me, you know what I mean about this filing a complaint. Like she had me over some kind of barrel. You know, telling me she wanted to go to her mother's house and spend the night all last night.*

JUSTINE. *No, that wasn't it, because, see, yesterday after you came out there, he tried all his best to get rid of me, and then when he left last night he went and got with his ole girlfriend!*

DARRELL. *Ha ha ha ha! What you talking about?*

ROY. *You* know *that?*

JUSTINE. *Yeah, cause I saw em. He didn't know that I did.*

DARRELL. *I was talking to some girls ....*

ROY. *Huh? Well, how's it going to affect the two of you now that you got the children back? Do you think you will make it now?*

JUSTINE. *I hope so.*

ROY.... *This is really the beginning of, you might say, kind of a new start for the two of you.*

JUSTINE. *Uh huh.*

ROY.... *I guess what happens to the kids now will have to depend on what happens to you and Justine.* (Referring to their 90 day probation)

DARRELL. *Yeah, this is true. But that lawyer recommend that the kids come home for 90 days, and then the woman probation officer, she turn around and she holla, "Well, I think it should go the other way round; I think they should remain here at Hillcrest Receiving Home for 90 days and then we'll see if they can go home!" And like I told Justine, if they woulda did anything like that, Mr. Williams, you know, I*

*believe that they woulda kept them. I would just feel that I be
done lost everything, you know.*

The tactics of dividing the family by trying to remove the children
had succeeded in temporarily fusing the family. As the children were
the focus of the welfare agency's intrusion, they were also the hub of
the Johns' emotional identification. Darrell and Justine quickly became
sensitive to the fact that they hadn't really won the case, they had only
succeeded in postponing it. And now they were faced with an
additional emotional burden. The 90-day probation had made a vague
question an explicit one which they hung accusingly over each other's
head almost daily: Did they have faith in each other as parents?

A week after the trial another violent fight took place. On May 8
when Andy came to work, he said that Justine had been on the streets
the night before looking for Darrell and the baby. She had been crying
and asking people if they could help find him.

(Williams). That night I had my last interview with the Johns.
Darrell had finally come home with the baby. For the entire weekend
before he had been at a "hippie party" at Oceanside. He had been
arrested and was facing trial again—this time for petty theft. When he
did return home, he and Justine began fighting. In anger, Darrell took
off in his car with their youngest child and stayed out all night.

Throughout the interview they both seemed resigned and fatalistic
about the outcome of their 90-day probation. They had no faith in
themselves or each other. Darrell said that General Training was not
really serious about training the hard-core and that many men came to
work under the influence of alcohol or drugs. He made repeated
references about longing for jail, saying that this was the best place for
him, that Justine was an unfit mother, and that losing the children was
punishment for both of them. There was a constant interplay of
familiar accusations. Darrell spoke of the filthy house and neglected
children he had never seen clean. "Even now," he said, "they look like
little hoboes!" And he insisted, "They probably will be better off in a
foster home." Only when Justine began to cry did Darrell soften and
grant that she hadn't always been that way, saying that when he
married her, she was a nice sweet girl.

Justine's festering resentment was summed up in an unusually articulate outburst. With the baby crying on her lap she complained, "It's like his friend told me. Last night I asked had they seen Darrell, and they say, 'you not gon' find Darrell; he's probably laying up with some bitch and got your baby right there with em.' And they told me how Darrell went and got a job and talked about me like a dog, and how much I bitch and run around, and I'm a good thing for him and stuff like that. Just like yesterday we was together, and he told me, 'Oh you know what, I'm not gon' leave because look like you the only person I have to turn to.' He's trying in a way to use me, you know, because I do things for him wouldn't nobody else do; cause he could be out there, and I see Darrell with some woman, and then he come home, and ask me, 'Let me have a dollar,' you know."

The probation became a period during which the expectation of failure was intensified. In his own way, each spouse prepared for the inevitable. Both began regressing more consistently to familiar, mutually incompatible situations and identities. To Justine, this meant welfare and her mother who, living entirely on welfare had managed to secure a $15,000 home with French provincial furniture, wall to wall carpet, stereo, and color TV. To Darrell it meant mastery over women, including Justine, in increasingly degrading and violent ways. What made the vicious circle complete was that each seemed to be the other's most important audience. At any rate, they could not make a decisive break, perhaps because of the children. Although Justine moved in with her mother, she frequented the same places and saw the same people that Darrell did. In June, Darrell was arrested again for fighting with Justine's family and for stabbing her brother. Before the end of the probation, the children were placed back in the juvenile home until Justine could demonstrate that she could take adequate care of them, which by then clearly meant leaving Darrell. By the end of July, one year after Darrell had first been hired at Southwestern, the Johns had been billed for $573 by the detention home for the "care" of their children. Thus the Johns family seemed to be dissolving to the status of welfare-administered family with Darrell legally bound to the periphery and Justine firmly ensconced in the center.

FAMILY STRUCTURE OF THE HARD-CORE UNEMPLOYED

The representativeness of the Johns family in terms of the hard-core unemployed becomes apparent as we discuss some of the important structural characteristics of the 28 hard-core households.

Composition of Family Households

At the time of employment, the family households of the 28 trainees were as follows: 15 consisted of a man and woman legally married. All but one of these families had children; all but three were receiving welfare assistance.

Married	Welfare	Joint Children	Female's Children	Male's Children	Male's Children Not In House
Barreca	Yes	7	0	0	0
Manners	Yes	6	0	0	0
Jewell	Yes	6	0	0	0
Sanchez	Yes	6	0	0	0
Boice	Yes	4	0	0	0
Galvão	Yes	3	1	0	0
Wolf	Yes	3	0	0	0
Greer	Yes	3	0	0	0
Timbers	Yes	3	0	0	0
Hill	Yes	2	0	0	0
Johns	Yes	2	1	0	1
Cooper	Yes	2	4	0	0
Marcus	Yes	0	0	0	0
Hunt	No	2	0	0	0
Smith	No	1	0	0	0

There were seven households consisting of a man and woman cohabiting but not legally married. All but one woman received welfare.

Cohabiting	Welfare	Joint Children	Female's Children	Male's Children	Male's Children Not In House
Walters	Yes	0	3	1	0
Banks	Yes	3	0	0	0
Carter	Yes	0	3	0	2
Nolan	Yes	0	0	0	0
Hughes	Yes	0	0	0	0
Little	Yes	0	0	0	0
Till	No	2	0	0	0

Porter, Fry, Brown, and Cox lived with their mothers, two of whom were on welfare. Although all four men were sexually active and sometimes emotionally involved with women, they continued to interact emotionally with their mothers. We call these households "single with mother." Porter and Fry each had one child living with him in the mother's house.

Davis and Martinez were separated from their wives. Both lived alone but were emotionally oriented toward their estranged wives and children. In fact, the Martinez's were reconciled one month after he was hired at Southwestern. For this reason, we define these pre-job households as inclusive of the wife and children. Both wives were on welfare. The Martinez's had one child living with the mother. Davis' wife had five children living with her. Four were Davis' and one was fathered by another man while Jack was serving time for nonsupport (see Chapter 4).

Family Role Differentiation

One means of determining the structure of the trainees' families is a comparison of the male and female roles in the pre-job household. In Table 9 we list four domains of dominance assigning each to male or female or to male or female role modified by conflict. Our judgments are based on intensive and extensive retroactive case records accumulated over a year's period.

Definitions of the domains of control of finances, authority over

Table 9
ROLE DIFFERENTIATION IN HARD-CORE FAMILY
HOUSEHOLDS, PRE-JOB

Domains of Dominance

Family	Interpersonal Dominance	Control of Finances	Authority over Children	House- work
Barreca	F	F	F	F
Cooper	F	F	F	F
Boice	F	F	F	F
Banks	F	F	F	F
Fry	F	F	F	F
Brown	F	F	F	F
Cox	F	F	F	F
Wolf	F	F	F	FC
Timbers	F	F	F	FC
Walters	F	F	F	O
Hunt	F	F	F	O
Carter	F	F	F	M
Nolan	F	F	O	M
Jewell	F	FC	F	M
Till	F	FC	M	F
Marcus	F	J	O	M
Porter	F	O	O	O
Johns	FC	FC	F	FC
Galvão	FC	FC	FC	FC
Smith	FC	M	F	M

children, and housework are self-evident. We define interpersonal dominance in the household context as the domain of the person who tends to initiate and direct action, and pass judgment on action. It connotes a posture of having control of and assuming proprietary interest over functions of the household, a posture of moral or judgmental superiority which tends to put the other person in a defensive or dependent position. With the women it often takes the

Table 9 *(Continued)*

Domains of Dominance

Family	Interpersonal Dominance	Control of Finances	Authority over Children	House- work
Little	J	M	O	M
Manners	MC	MC	MC	FC
Greer	MC	M	F	M
Martinez	M	MC	F	O
Hughes	M	M	O	O
Davis	M	M	M	O
Sanchez	M	M	M	O
Hill	M	M	M	M

NOTES   In the domains of Interpersonal Dominance, Control of Finances, and Authority over Children: F=Female assumes responsibility, no open conflict; FC=Female assumes responsibility, open conflict; J=Joint or shared responsibility; M=Male assumes responsibility, no open conflict; MC=Male assumes responsibility, open conflict; O=Domain not applicable. In the domain of Housework: F=Female assigns or supervises work or male does work by default, no open conflict; FC=Male does work by default or no one does work, open conflict; M=Male assigns or supervises work or female assumes responsibility, no open conflict; MC=Male supervises work or female assumes responsibility, open conflict; J=Joint or shared responsibility; O=Not applicable, i.e., one principal ill or absent most of the time.

form of chronic nagging of the husbands about not being able to get a job, hold a job, or make more money. With the men it takes the form of ordering wives around and in some cases abusing them frequently.

Looking at the families before hire, we discern four general structural characteristics: the tendency to have children without marrying, dependence on welfare, matrifocality (female centeredness), and weak or stressful male/female relationships.

Childhood Family Households

There are significant similarities between the trainees' adulthood families and their childhood families. More than one-third of the trainees came from welfare-supported households, and 21 of the 28 came from broken homes. A breakdown of the rearing units is as follows:

Two men were reared in foster homes.

Seven men were reared by their mothers only.

Three men were reared by mothers and part-time fathers.

Four men were reared by their mothers and stepfathers.

Two men were reared by part-time mothers and stepfathers.

One man was reared by part-time father and stepmother.

Two men were reared by stepfather and stepmother.

Seven men were reared by one continuous set of natural parents.

Clearly, weak or stressful male/female relationships and matrifocality predominate in the background of this population. A more useful concept for our analysis of family structure is male marginality. By means of this we can compare households in terms of the male's position in it, i.e., the men as fathers to their fathers as fathers (see Table 10).

How do we define male marginality in the family? Nine of the trainees lacked fathers of *any kind* for most or all of their childhood; seven were raised with stepfathers; and five were raised with natural fathers who were absent from the household a significant part of the time. Thus, 21 of the 28 trainees were deprived of natural fathers for all or a significant part of their childhood. It is this discontinuity of male participation as father in the household that we define as the chief criterion for male marginality. Other criteria are patterns of interpersonal relationships between the man and woman which further indicate a peripheral role for the man, such as having no authority over the children or finances and being dominated by the woman (see above discussion of Table 9). However, in the cases of the trainees' fathers' roles in their families, these patterns can only be inferred since we have no descriptive data beyond discontinuity of male participation in these families. On the basis of the latter criterion, we can say that male marginality was a structural feature of 21 of the 28 childhood homes.

Table 10
INDEX OF MALE MARGINALITY IN CHILDHOOD FAMILIES

Name	Father	Step-father	Mother	Step-mother	Summary of Home Situation
Nolan	0	0	0	0	Abondoned by parents; lived in 21 foster homes; mother alcoholic
Marcus	0	0	0/+	0	Parents fought violently; father deserted when son was five; mother died when son was seven; son lived in numerous foster homes
Cox	0	0	+		Mother had several husbands; dominated son who had two breakdowns
Fry	0	0	+		Mother has many boyfriends and dominated son
Brown	0	0	+		Father deserted when son was five; mother had many boyfriends who alienated her from son
Porter	0	0	+		Mother had many boyfriends and pampered son
Boice	0	0	+		
Martinez	0	0	+		Father in jail; mother completely dependent on welfare
Cooper	0	0	+		Father deserted when son was two; mother had many boyfriends
Johns	0/-	0	0	-	Father alcoholic and beat wife; stepmother rejected son but supported him financially
Carter	0/-	0	-		Father alcoholic; mother passive; both rejected son in teens
Till	0/-	0	0	+	Mother deserted family; father rejected son who was raised by paternal grandmother
Timbers	0/-	0	+		Father alcoholic; mother on welfare; good mother-son rapport
Greer	0/+	0	-		Father alcoholic; mother had many boyfriends; son admired father and hated mother
Manners	0	-	0/-		Stepfather rejected son; then mother rejected and deserted son

TABLE 10 *(Continued)*

Name	Father	Step-father	Mother	Step-mother	Summary of Home Situation
Hill	0	-	+		Father died; stepfather rejected and beat son
Walters	0	-	+		No rapport with stepfather; average mother-son rapport
Hughes	0	-	+		Had stepfather from the age of four; mother's brother helped mother relate to son
Hunt	-		+		Working father nagged son constantly; mother indulged son
Galvão	0	+	0/-		Mother deserted father and took sons; uncle assumed role of father
Little	0	+	0	+	Both parents deserted; son raised by grandparents
Jewell	0	+	+		Average rapport with stepfather and good rapport with mother
Davis	+		+		
Banks	+		+		Rural South background; parents lax with low expectations for son
Smith	+		+		Both parents worked and indulged s
Wolf	+		+		Father's heart attack caused son's speech trauma
Sanchez	+		+		Background of extreme poverty in urban Mexican slum, nine siblings
Barreca	+		+		Background of poverty in rural Italy; 10 siblings

NOTES: Stepfather and stepmother = the mate of a natural parent or a parental substitute who is a member of the parental family

0 = Parent unknown, i.e., died or deserted when child was young

0/- = Parent absent for a significant part of childhood and rejected child when present

0/+ = Parent absent for a significant part of childhood but had support relationship with child when present

- = Parent present all or most of the time but rejected child

+ = Parent present all or most of the time and had supportive relationship with child

It is interesting to note that 13 of the 14 men from homes with no fathers or marginal fathers (Nolan, through Greer, Table 10) are found as adults in predominantly matrifocal households (Table 9). In fact, this group accounts for two-thirds of the matrifocal households. In most cases both the childhood families and the adulthood families have identical structural features: poverty or welfare dependency, matrifocality, and stressful interfamilial relationships, with male marginality as the key feature.

In reality what we have described is a family structure that is common to more than the hard-core unemployed—it is the family structure of the lower class.[32] And, although we do not rely upon socialization theories of the lower-class family to explain the stress which developed in the family systems of the hard-core trainees, it is necessary to put the lower-class family in proper perspective in order to establish a valid framework for analysis.

THE ISSUE OF THE LOWER-CLASS FAMILY

From being sons with marginal fathers to becoming marginal fathers is a family cycle distinctive of the lower class. The pattern of male marginality, as do other patterns of the lower-class family, exhibits an obvious continuity which easily leads analysts to the method of closed-system analysis, i.e., observing the traits of the families of one generation and comparing these traits to those of families of another generation. This method leads to the inevitable conclusion that lower-class family structure is self-perpetuating. But this method is based implicitly on the theory of the family as a socialization unit.

This definition provides an appropriate theoretical framework for the study of personality, but when the subject of interest remains the family, this theoretical system is redundant—family is the consequence of family, is the consequence of family, ad infinitum. Family one and family two are in reality two manifestations of the same system, and hypothesizing one as a consequence of the other may be comforting to certain classes and interest groups in the society at large, it does not offer much of theoretical or practical value from the standpoint of public policy. Sociologically, family cannot be the consequence of family. Family is a continuous, longitudinal intergenerational system more properly seen as one sociological entity—an institution. The question then becomes: What is this institution a consequence of?

First, the institution of the lower-class family must *not* be conceptualized solely in terms of its characteristics or structure but in terms of its *relationships* to the society at large. Any treatment of the lower-class family which focuses attention away from this is bound to yield closed-system propositions. This kind of treatment includes debating the issue of the pathology or disintegration of the lower-class family, Negro or otherwise. Debating such issues is not simply a waste of time, it is pernicious because it addresses analyst and practitioner alike to the *internal* dynamics of the ghetto system and excludes the *external* dynamics of the larger socio-cultural system of which the ghetto is an integral part. Even scientific defenses of the lower-class family that seek to prove its adaptability, resiliency, and so on reinforce the closed-system approach, thereby neutralizing ghetto people's power and effective courses of action.

What are the relationships between the lower-class family and mainstream society? All relationships can be characterized by economic and social powerlessness. The lower-class family vis-à-vis mainstream institutions is marginal and its individual members are marginal. But the family is the chief and frequently the only mechanism for providing the adult personality emotional compensation for its mainstream marginality, and this struggle for emotional compensation underlies the stress which pervades the family.

The institution of the poor family is an interpersonal refuge unit of economic and social outcasts. This lack of resources heightens the emotional intensity of poor families and makes the bits and shreds they possess more desperately important. The Johns family is a case in point, with husband and wife clinging competitively to children they admittedly were destroying and to one another even in hate.

To Justine the alternative to the family unit was her domineering, welfare-conniving mother and lecherous boyfriends. To Darrell it was his playboy father and pathetic stepmother. To the children it was the foster home with no parents or a welfare mother and no father.

The Johns family was to its members the social unit of first and last recourse, and as such, it assumed an importance magnified beyond reason. But this did not make the unit function. Instead the family was a refuge unit where even the children were treated as meager funds of human capital to be drawn on rather than invested in.

Is the lower-class family responsible for its own state? From a public policy point of view, i.e., from the standpoint of viable courses of action available, the answer is no.

We contend that the family system of the poor, the lower class and the hard-core unemployed, all of whom the Johns represent, is a consequence of the society at large. It is the consequence of inequality of opportunity in the educational and employment systems, and the lower status reinforcement of the welfare and the law enforcement systems. We have documented the effects of these systems on the hard-core family in this study.

The view that the lower-class family system is the consequence of inequality of opportunity has effective policy implications which have been demonstrated by the 1968 Jobs-in-Industry Program. One measure of this program's effectiveness is its 66 percent rate of retention of hard-core in the labor force.[33] Another is the impact the policy of changing the external system—the labor market—has had on the family structure of the hard-core unemployed. And, as this study demonstrates, this structure did begin to change.

FAMILY AS A CONSEQUENCE OF OPPORTUNITY

What happens to family structure when male heads obtain meaningful job status? As in the case of Darrell and Justine, the general rule was that rather than easing tension, the job intensified old tensions and created new ones. Like the Johns, some families could not resolve these tensions. In some families, tensions were resolved by the man's quitting the job and reverting to his marginal status. Others made role adjustments consistent with their new economic and social status (see Table 11).

Conflict in role differentiation increased in at least one area in all but six households. In the four domains defined in Table 10, conflict

TABLE 11
ROLE CONFLICT IN FAMILY HOUSEHOLDS AFTER THE JOB

Development of Stress in Pre-Job Domains

Family	Interpersonal Dominance		Control of Finances		Authority over Children		Housework	
Barreca	F	No	F	No	F	No	F	No
Cooper	F	Yes	F	Yes	F	No	F	Yes
Boice	F	Yes	F	Yes	F	Yes	F	No
Banks	F	Yes	F	Yes	F	Yes	F	Yes
Fry	F	No	F	No	F	No	F	No
Brown	F	Yes	F	No	F	No	F	No
Cox	F	No	F	No	F	No	F	No
Wolf	F	Yes	F	Yes	F	No	FC	Yes
Timbers	F	Yes	F	Yes	F	Yes	FC	Yes
Walters	F	Yes	F	Yes	F	No	O	—
Hunt	F	No	F	Yes	F	Yes	O	—
Carter	F	Yes	F	Yes	F	Yes	M	No
Nolan	F	Yes	F	?	O	—	M	No
Jewell	F	Yes	FC	Yes	F	No	M	No
Till	F	Yes	FC	Yes	M	No	F	No
Marcus	F	No	J	No	O	—	M	No
Porter	F	No	O	—	O	—	O	—
Johns	FC	Yes	FC	Yes	F	Yes	FC	Yes
Galvão	FC	Yes	FC	Yes	FC	Yes	FC	Yes
Smith	FC	Yes	M	No	F	No	M	No
Little	J	No	M	No	O	—	M	No
Manners	MC	Yes	MC	Yes	MC	Yes	FC	Yes
Greer	MC	Yes	M	Yes	F	No	M	No
Martinez	M	No	MC	Yes	F	No	O	—
Hughes	M	Yes	M	No	O	—	O	—
Davis	M	No	M	No	M	Yes	O	—
Sanchez	M	No	M	No	M	No	O	—
Hill	M	No	M	No	M	No	M	No

Table 11 *(Continued)*

Development of Stress in Other Areas

Wife began opposing job verbally and by not driving husband to work

Wife refusing to help husband off to work
Wife refusing to help husband off to work

Conflict over husband going out with his friends
Conflict over girlfriend pressuring man to marry her
Conflict over husband's drinking
Conflict over girlfriend pressuring man to marry her
Stress over husband feeling inferior to wife

Wife refusing to help husband off to work, husband philandering
Wife refusing to assume her responsibilities
Husband philandering

Wife refusing to help husband off to work; conflict over use of car
Intense jealousy; husband possessive
Conflict over husband having to support his in-laws
Conflict over girlfriend pressuring man to marry her
Separated but fought over wife's neglect of children

Fought over wife refusing to drive illegally customized car

increased in 38 percent of the cases where applicable, with interpersonal dominance and control of finances each showing a 60 percent increase in incidence.

Taking the matrifocal households as a subgroup distinct from the patrifocal households the incidence of stress increase was as follows:

Interpersonal Dominance	14 out of 20 cases
Control of Finances	12 out of 17 cases
Authority over Children	7 out of 18 cases
Housework	7 out of 13 cases

Thus, the aggregate increase was 40 out of 68 cases or 59 percent.

In the patrifocal subgroup the incidence of stress increase was lower in all domains:

Interpersonal Dominance	3 out of 7 cases
Control of Finances	3 out of 9 cases
Authority over Children	2 out of 5 cases
Housework	0 out of 8 cases

This indicates a much lower aggregate increase of eight out of a total of 29 cases or a 27 percent increase.

Having no objective measure of intensity nor comprehensive record of duration of conflict, these comparisons are rough and impressionistic. But they are firsthand impressions made over a relatively long period of intimate contact with the families. Combined with more descriptive data, they help illustrate that the incidence of stress was greater in the matrifocal households.

The major conflict in matrifocal, and to an extent in patrifocal households, centered on the issue of female centrality. In most cases, before employment it was a buried issue, but the job tended to force it to the surface.

The modern economic basis of female centrality and male marginality in poor families is well known—joblessness and the welfare system. In the welfare system, the children are the economic commodity, the mother the executor of the subsidy system. The welfare case workers, mostly middle-class and frequently naive women, are unwitting accomplices in an institutional system whose social structure and cultural orientation favors the woman of the household. The welfare check is most likely in her name if for no other reason than the high frequency of unmarried or divorced mothers. The pattern is reinforced by the fact that welfare generally makes legal fugitives of the men for fathering illegitimate children, and for not having steady jobs to support them. The money belongs to the woman, and she uses it as a weapon. We observed it used time and again as a naked threat in a conflict situation, as in the Johns' household.

To the man being economically rehabilitated, the paycheck is the symbol of his respectability and the natural weapon against the welfare check. This is a general rule and not an invariable one. Whether the man opposes the welfare check depends partly on how it is administered vis-à-vis the family structure. If done divisively, it is a threat to the integrity of the man in the family and he is well aware of it, if not before his job, certainly after. There were numerous cases of this type of conflict among the hard-core families. Perhaps the best example was Oscar Walters, who was living with a 50-year-old welfare mother. Four children lived in the household, three hers and one his. Although she was receiving $400 a month from welfare, the woman demanded support from Walters for herself and her children. When he refused, she took him to court for nonsupport. Because she filed the charges without telling him, Walters was in a state of shock. He started drinking again, had a car accident, and rather than stay on the job, face the accident, and fight the nonsupport charge, he quit work and left the city. This occurred after 10 months of successful work.

In addition to the welfare problem, marginal male/central female role conflict centered on issues that were much harder to define and which conflicted implicitly with job status in the industrial system. One of the most pervasive of these was the underlying family assumption of the man's unreliability. The important point is not the obvious fact that the dislocation of this premise is fundamental to job rehabilitation, but that there is a large investment in the validity of this premise, both in the home and among outside institutions relating to the family.

Interviews with the men and their families when they were hired disclosed a unanimity of enthusiasm. "Now things will be different." "This is the opportunity we've been waiting for." "Now Henry or Herman or Tim, etc., can take over the responsibility I've had to carry on my own." Yet within a matter of months, weeks in some cases, it became apparent that one of the consequences of permanent job status was an imbalance in the mutually reinforcing roles of long-suffering (dependable) wife or mother and unreliable (dependent) husband or son.

In almost every female-centered household, the woman began to shift from support to varying degrees of opposition to the man's new role. Sometimes the opposition was aimed at new behavior ancillary to the job, such as the man's taking over the finances or the woman's having to get up early to drive the man to work. Some of the opposition was directed at the job itself with the woman continually reminding the man that he wouldn't be able to keep the job.

In most cases conflict developed, but in some cases there was hardly a skirmish. Henry Boice was a case in point. Having been in a federal penitentiary for car theft and parole violation, as a trainee he was on parole and prohibited from driving. Since the Boice's lived out of the city, this meant that his wife had to drive him to work. Henry was hired at the end of September. By mid-November he had received an upgrade to machine-tool operator-learner. Henry was nervous about the upgrade, and his wife was beginning to resist having to drive him to work. The result was a sudden incidence of absenteeism. With his wife's counseling, Henry agreed he would be better off working in a dairy close to home doing "what he knew best." He quit his job, started milking cows, and two months later began drinking again, broke parole, and disappeared. Throughout the training experience, Henry's wife maintained a subtle attitude of condescension. He had been in confinement nine years during which time she became firmly established on welfare. When he was released, she announced that she was immediately shifting the entire burden of running the house to him—including the support of their four children. Throughout the interviews she did most of the talking, speaking for him as well as for herself. She said that Henry was shy and insecure, and that he felt the job was one means of gaining security. However, during the breakdown in his attendance in November, there were times when she had no reasons at all for not driving him to work.

With Herman Cooper the conflict over the same issue was quite a different story.

To his wife's friends and counselors it was obvious that Herman, with an eighth grade education and a string of arrests, was inferior to his wife, Jean.

Legally married, the Coopers had two children of their own, and the wife had four from a previous marriage. Jean was a respectable welfare mother and a devout Jehovah's Witness with a high school diploma and two jobs—one as a night waitress, the other as a teacher's aid in a ghetto school. She considered refinement, gentleness, and deference to the ministers of the church as the hallmarks of good character. Her belief system provided an explanation for everything. There was a place in it for herself, a place for her sinful, crude husband, and the way to redeem him, one of the reasons she married him, was the transformation of his character through the narrow religious passage presided over by her minister and herself. There were important externals to be sure, like welfare assistance, which was her due, work, and even occasional recognition of the need for a psychiatrist for Herman. An occupational career such as Cooper was attempting to build was strange, and if anything, a threat to her value system.

Cooper found this situation suffocating, but he loved his wife intensely, and he alternated between emotional acceptance and violent, guilt-ridden outbursts of rebellion. The children were disapproving witnesses of his pathetic attempts to master his wife with his fists and by threatening her with knives and guns. These irrational acts were seen by his wife as further proof of his low I.Q., and she suspected they cast doubt on his sanity. Always before on previous jobs, Cooper's jealous, resentful reactions culminated in his quitting and leaving town "to keep from killing her."

However, this time it was different. Cooper was receiving an unusual amount of recognition on the job—unusual in terms of his experience and unusual compared to other trainees. This base of support was the decisive factor in his staying "to face the music," as he put it.

The crisis erupted over a 20-cent pie. Herman went to a Jack-in-the-Box to buy an apple turnover that he said Jean had asked him to bring her. When he returned with the turnover, she denied asking for it. He lost his temper, they argued, and he started beating her. One of the children called the police. No charges were filed, but the next day at lunch when Herman opened his lunchbox, he found a note from his wife telling him that she was filing for divorce and that she would put his clothes on the front porch where he could pick them up after work.

Herman seemed resigned to the divorce saying that he wasn't made for marriage, that his wife was a good woman and, " . . . could probably find someone better than me."

(Williams). In an interview with Mrs. Cooper the next day, she said that Herman had called her that morning, but, "I wished he had not called because all he had to say was nasty things."

She told me how ignorant he was. "If he had not been so ignorant, he wouldn't have gotten so mad about the pie. He would have been able to do better in life."

She then turned and asked me the question: "What do you think of him? Don't you agree? Can you see these things in him?" I told her I was not capable of saying because I had not seen Herman as she saw him, and the only association that I had with him was in his work. I told her how highly people thought of Herman—so much so that they voluntarily went out to seek him better jobs.

She cut me off saying, "I am going through with the divorce because I have found nothing changed about him, even though," she added, "I still love him."

She considered the agencies to be on her side and stated that the social worker and the district attorney were looking for Herman because he had broken a restraining order, had forced his way into his home, and had stolen some of her things.

Herman was ambivalent. First he retained a lawyer to fight the divorce. Then he let him go because he was "just going to face the music." He said he still loved his wife and believed she still loved him. When the alternative of court of conciliation was mentioned, he said he was willing to get professional marriage counseling for himself and his wife.

On the eve of the court hearing, Mrs. Cooper expressed a different opinion: She told of his almost pleading with her to allow him the chance to prove that he was a man and to call off the court action. She said they both loved each other, but she knew that this was the only way she could protect herself. She talked of not being able to trust him because of things that she had found out about him. She also mentioned a cousin telling her that Herman had once told his mother that he had smoked so much marijuana he believed it had affected his mind.

She stated that she believed this was true. She talked of his not being himself whenever they were having a fight. She said, "I can see him holding himself back, not wanting to do any physical violence, but I can also see something within him, urging him on!"

She almost stated that she believed Herman was mentally ill, "I tried to get him to see a psychiatrist, but he would have no part of it."

The divorce proceedings were held on January 11. Jean and her lawyer met Herman in the corridor where he agreed to all they requested.

Herman said he did not want to see his children, but the attorney urged him to make the legal agreement (that he could see them on Fridays only) a matter of record in case he changed his mind. Regarding their bills of $1,200, Jean told the attorney she would pay them out of her welfare money and what she received from Herman.

With welfare, Jean's income was considerably higher than Herman's salary of $480 per month. She was getting $354 per month from welfare, $160 from her waitress job and $40 from her teacher's aid job. This made a total of $554 per month which would add up to $674 with Herman's support payments.

After the hearing, Mrs. Cooper's first words were how hurt she was about "having to do this."

When asked why she didn't withdraw the charges she replied that it was easy to start things and very hard to stop them, and added, "I'll just have to depend upon Jehovah."

In the coming months, Cooper stuck to his job, received more upgrades, paid his support payments, and lived apart from his wife. Although the issue of reconciliation came up as soon as the hearing was over, Herman kept his distance. Marriage counseling was acceptable to him, but his wife resisted it. She wanted him to come back "to the same old thing" as he put it, and he refused.

In April, Cooper spoke of how good it felt to take his daughters out to dinner on the weekends, "It sure makes me feel like a man again!" He also mentioned that Jean was always calling him and asking him to "come back out there." He added, "You know I've got too much pride—I'm not gonna let any woman pull me that low."

When asked why he took this stand, he argued, "You can't let a woman rule you, and you be the man at your house."

(Williams): I asked, "How does that tie in with the job?"

"A job gives you a chance," he said, "and this job is important to me." And he went into detail about his coming to work when he was sick.

He said, "Did you know she came to see me while I was sick?"

I told him, "Yes, she told me that."

He said, "You know, I didn't let the sickness keep me from working."

It was months before Jean was willing to meet Herman on even ground. The hardest thing for her to change was her religious orientation. For a time the only person she agreed to go to for joint counseling was her spiritual advisor, Brother Wilson, whose saint and sinner approach to the problem did not lend itself to any social reality. Even Mrs. Cooper could see that this approach was inappropriate for another reason: When Herman broke away this time, he did not run and then come back a penniless, repentant sinner. To Herman, the job made a financial and moral difference in his position, and he took advantage of this difference, which was something he had never done before.

Herman had told his wife repeatedly, "You are destroying me!" By the end of the year, they were not reconciled, but they were trying to work out their problems with a professional third party.

Of all the family adaptations to male marginality, the tendency of central females to be mothers and marginal males to be children was the most profound. In the five cases we have on record, this adjustment seemed to be irreversably stable. There was stress. There was an attempt to adjust, but the stress was finally resolved by quitting the job. The five families include Fry, Cox, Porter, Brown and Nolan. All except Nolan, an orphan, were actually living with their mothers.

Male compensation for male marginality was the basis for another structure of relationship. To a certain extent this was visible in the Johns' household by Darrell's continuous extramarital affairs. Invariably Darrell would make sure that Justine knew about his conquests, even though in the midst of fighting about a particular instance of it he would deny it.

Even in the male dominated households (Table 9), compensation for male marginality can be seen. Possessive of their prerogatives, resentful of women, these men tended to play their roles with a vengeance. The Manners', Greer's and Hughes' households illustrate this point. Expressions like "It's not going to be like my home!", "The mother of my kids is going to stay put!" are typical of their reasoning. In addition, as economically alienated men, they made the home the focal point of their competitiveness and self-expression. The domination of its affairs, the management of its finances, and the development of the children became the all-consuming goals of these men.

In Andy Manners' case, the home activities included gambling and black militant meetings. The latter increased the importance of Andy's role in the home, because militant doctrine demanded that he tutor his children to compensate for the brainwashing they were getting in the schools and that he safeguard them from being put in concentration camps by the police and the white power structure. These statements were no mere clichés in Andy's case. His belief in them was profound.

To Andy, his status at the center of the household organization was all important, and the job caused an immediate role conflict for him. He couldn't be in two places at once, and he couldn't assume two mutually contradictory roles. He partially resolved the identity conflict by bringing the message of the black people to his white coworkers in the plant. But being both housemother and wage earner was a more difficult problem to solve. Andy felt that Mildred, his wife, should carry out his dictums at home while he assumed his new role as wage earner. But Mildred would not cooperate. She had her own ideas and her own friends and activities which centered outside the home. Andy would call home repeatedly during the work day, and when he found that Mildred wasn't there, he would become angry and frequently left work to check on her.

Conflicts were frequent and intense. Andy and Mildred fought like men, with fists and clubs. Although Mildred was a large woman and could usually hold her own, she still took the brunt of the beatings. But she vowed she would never give in. Their fighting became so violent that more than once Andy was literally afraid to go to sleep for fear that Mildred would kill him. This was not hysterical fantasy, since Andy bore a huge scar from his chest to his navel where two years before Mildred had cut him open with a bayonet.

The violence abated when Mildred was given 90 days for grand theft (see Chapter 4) and a year's probation with court stipulation of psychiatric treatment. In the interim Andy began to identify more with the job and less with the home activities so that when the choice of either letting Mildred go her own way or facing unemployment developed, it appeared that he would choose the job.

THE EQUILIBRIUM OF FAILURE

The marginal male is determined first by being born in a marginal family which is a consequence of unequal economic opportunity. His experience of failure is reinforced by a class-biased school system and by reformatories, honor camps, and prisons. His final and permanent alienation is maintained by a profit maximizing, highly efficient, increasingly scientific occupational selection system. In negative terms, this means both an expanding definition of the labor surplus and an increasingly efficient means of culling out the labor surplus. Moreover, there is a natural tendency among those enjoying the class benefits of a system of unequal employment opportunity to preserve their economic and social investment in it.

The consequence is a subcultural system of adaptation. At the center of this system is the marginal family, which provides some type of economic and emotional solution to the permanently unemployed man at the price of reinforcing his marginality. Numerous factors tend to maintain the family system. Husbands become accustomed to being supported economically and emotionally. Wives and mothers learn to expect husbands to fail and are constantly assuming roles in their place. The children and the mothers become the natural clientele of welfare agencies and institutions dedicated to protecting and helping the poor, and these agencies reinforce male marginality further by their natural tendency to become overseers of their clientele who comprise only a part of a family.

What happens when a hard-core unemployed man assumes a viable role in industry? The entire marginal family system is thrown out of balance, and becomes maladaptive. Dominating wives must relinquish or share their position as family executor with husbands, who from their point of view are still marginal. Over-compensating males are torn between establishing themselves as wage earners and guarding their position at home. A reallocation of old tasks and the assumption of new tasks is required raising the issue of whose time, hence position, is more important.

Faith is necessary for all involved, but difficult to come by. The wives and children and their advisors, including welfare caseworkers, evangelical preachers, and mothers and mothers-in-law, who tend to consider the marginal male at worst a troublesome interloper and at best a high risk patient, must be convinced. Convincing the foreman on the job is the easiest first step. The hard-core unemployed worker frequently has as many as four or more sets of people to convince including himself.

Finally, the suddenly employed worker is forced to move by conflicting social pressures either into mainstream status or back into marginal status. His family emerges as the most significant institution implicated in this transition, because it is the most critical matrix of his self-identity. If his family does not change, he has the choice of either leaving them or quitting the job and regressing to his marginal role.

In the context of occupational rehabilitation of the hard-core unemployed, family stress is inevitable and must be considered a sign of progress to the extent that it signals a change in the social equilibrium of failure.

PART THREE

Change

7
Patterns of Hard-Core Adjustments

In analyzing the set of social transitions involved in transferring the hard-core from a permanent position outside of the labor force to a viable, stable position within, we begin with the fundamental assumption, based upon empirical evidence, that the hard-core unemployed desires an integral rather than a marginal role in society, and that a meaningful job is the first step toward achieving this goal. The labor market represents a major component of mainstream society in which the hard-core can be placed in a central position. As a result, conflict develops for the hard-core because his new role as wage earner in a highly structured, highly visible sector of society requires a corresponding change of roles within his family, changes in the nature of his participation in the community, and changes in his role vis-à-vis the major institutions of mainstream society—the police, courts, welfare, and credit systems.

Role conflict leads to stress. In some cases the tension may be immediate; in others it may take months to develop. During this period the hard-core seeks to control the social forces creating the stress, first by modifying his roles in the conflicting systems. The effectiveness of this strategy varies with the ingenuity of the individual and the number and intensity of his conflicts. As it becomes apparent that modifying his work role won't help, he moves toward role consistency by a more deliberate, often dramatic, alteration of roles, the quickest, most decisive of which is quitting the job. Some of the trainees did just that. For those who continued on the job the second, more involved, longer-term phase of conflict began. Again, the time it took to become critical varied with the individual and his situation, but in most cases the crisis peaked about the sixth month. In a few cases it took almost a year, and in two cases it took over a year. Conflict outside the job became more intense during this phase because the burden of accommodation shifted to existing relationships in the family and community and with mainstream institutions. But, whether the conflict was short- or long-term, the issue was the same, becoming an integral part of mainstream society or regressing to a consistently marginal position outside the labor market.

In more sophisticated terms, we conceptualize male marginality as a network of interrelated statuses occupied by the individual and a network of interrelated roles enacted by the individual in accordance with these statuses. Thus, if we use the term "role" to cover both status and role, male marginality implies a *system* of ongoing roles the individual performs. Change in one role in this system—e.g., change in economic role from chronically unemployed to stably employed—implies a change in all roles in the system. This model is consistent with the patterned conflict situations and adjustment processes experienced generally by the 28 hard-core trainees. Although there was variation among them in terms of the number and degree of conflicts, every trainee had at least two well-established marginal roles in conflict with his newly developing, economically integral role in industry, which in our framework of analysis is the key variable in the model.

GROUP PROFILES OF ROLE CONFLICT AND ADJUSTMENT

Since work role impact was most pronounced with respect to the family system, we will discuss this area of role adjustment first by analyzing the job anniversary profiles of the trainees' family households (see Table 12).

This and the following summaries cover the reference year which ended for each man one year after hire. They are based on intensive observations of each trainee in the factory, and at home whether he was retained or terminated. Definite trends appeared even in what might be called abortive cases. However, the year was not sufficient in every case for trends to stabilize.

If we divide the households in Table 12 on the basis of the four domains before hire, with female dominated households defined as those having more F cells than M cells, male dominated households as the opposite, and J cells as being neutral, we would draw a line separating the F and M groups below Galvão, thus giving us 18 female centered households, nine male centered households, and one joint household.

In the 18 F households, job role/family role conflict was a major factor in 15 cases. Barreca's, Fry's, and Cox's female dependency was so complete that job role conflict did not erupt in any visible way in social interaction.

In the 15 cases where visible conflict developed, there were decided role shifts within the family context in seven cases—Cooper, Banks, Wolf, Jewell, Till, Timbers, and Galvão. Eight of the 15 regressed to achieve role consistency, but only after considerable effort was made to surmount the stress without giving up the job. This effort ranged from short-term attempts on the part of Boice and Porter to the long and complicated struggles of Nolan, Walters, and Johns. Carter, Brown, and Hunt fell somewhere between these two extremes. Thus, in the 18 female centered households, family/job role conflict was hypothetical in three cases, and real and operational in 15 cases. Of greater significance is the evidence that visible progress toward adjusting family roles occurred in seven cases.

Male dominated families are harder to summarize because they conflict less with the cultural norms of the working middle class than do female dominated families. In addition, even when dysfunctional to the family, this male role is more inherently consistent with the culturally prescribed male role of family breadwinner. However conflict did develop in most of the male dominated households, because dominating the wife and family was a full time activity with which the job interfered.

Table 12
JOB IMPACT ON FAMILY SYSTEM ONE YEAR AFTER HIRE

Trends in Role Differentiation

	Stress in Pre-Job Domains	Inter-personal Dominance	Control of Finances	Authority over Children	Housework	Conflict Now	Jo Sta
Barreca	No	F/No chg	F/M	F/No chg	F/M	—	C
Cooper	Yes	F/M	F/M	F/M	F/O	less	C
Boice	Yes	F/O	F/O	F/O	F/O	less	J
Banks	Yes	F/M	F/M	F/M	F/M	less	C
Fry	Yes	F/No chg	F/No chg	F/No chg	F/No chg	less	J
Brown	Yes	F/No chg	F/No chg	F/No chg	F/No chg	less	J
Cox	No	F/No chg	F/No chg	F/No chg	F/No chg	—	J
Wolf	Yes	F/M	F/M	F/M	FC/M	less	J
Timbers	Yes	F/M	F/M	F/No chg	FC/M	more	J
Walters	Yes	F/O	F/O	F/O	O/O	less	J
Hunt	Yes	F/O	F/O	F/O	O/O	less	J
Carter	Yes	F/No chg	F/No chg	F/No chg	M/O	less	J
Nolan	Yes	F/No chg	F/No chg	O/No chg	M/F	less	J
Jewell	Yes	F/M	FC/M	F/M	M/No chg	more	C
Till	Yes	F/M	FC/M	M/No chg	F/M	less	C
Marcus	Yes	F/No chg	J/No chg	O/No chg	M/No chg	same	C
Porter	No	F/No chg	O/No chg	O/No chg	O/No chg	—	J
Johns	Yes	FC/O	FC/O	F/O	FC/O	less	J
Galvão	Yes	FC/M	FC/M	FC/M	FC/M	less	C
Smith	Yes	FC/No chg	M/No chg	F/M	M/No chg	more	C
Little	No	J/No chg	M/F	O/No chg	M/No chg	—	C
Manners	Yes	MC/M	MC/M	MC/M	FC/O	less	C
Greer	Yes	MC/No chg	M/No chg	F/No chg	M/No chg	same	C
Martinez	Yes	M/No chg	MC/F	F/M	O/M	less	C
Hughes	Yes	M/F	M/No chg	O/No chg	O/M	less	C
Davis	Yes	M/O	M/O	M/O	O/No chg	less	C
Sanchez	No	M/No chg	M/No chg	M/No chg	O/No chg	—	J
Hill	Yes	M/No chg	M/F	M/No chg	M/No chg	less	C

NOTES: Symbols left of the / signify the situation obtaining before hire, as per Table **11**.
Symbols right of the / signify as follows:

F = increased importance of female   M = increased importance of male
No chg = no change from picture presented in Table **11**
O = a cessation of interaction in that domain, in most cases due to separation or
partial separation from the household of the male, or in one case (Manners),
the female

Summary of Adjustment in Terms of
Job Role/Family Role

Job/family conflict minor
Separated and began dating each other again, this time with husband in
more dominant role
Quit job and regressed to absent father role
Man increasing status by legal methods; wife on the defensive
Quit job regressed to dependent son role; active in street crowd
Quit job and regressed to dependent son role; active in hippie variant
of park crowd
Quit job and regressed to dependent son; unable to function, mentally ill
Entered another on-job program and began asserting self at home
Quit job but gaining status at home; looking for another job
Quitting job helped him to escape wife who mothered him; now living with
real mother
Quit job and regressed to park crowd; wife returned to mother
Quit job and regressed to park crowd and jail; went back to his welfare-woman
Quit job and regressed to dependent child-lover role and drugs
Man beginning to fight more with wife and to diminish wife's career-mother role
Both accepting the fact he has the job
Conflict developing over her jealousy, his self-image
Quit job and regressed to playboy role; living with mother
Job brought conflict to a head; quit and regressed entirely to streets;
separated from wife
Wife allowing husband more say but conflict still unresolved
Conflict as a result of husband's hustling activity coming to a head
Job/family conflict minor
Wife in jail receiving psychiatric counseling; possible separation
Family strife and wife assault problem not resolved; possible separation
Conflict about mooching crowd resolved by death of closest friend and
jail sentence
Job helped give him financial and moral independence; less conflict with wife
Withdrew completely; sees his children at his house and is father there
Quit job and regressed to role of sole decision maker at home
Allowing wife more say; bought another car and she is driving him to work

This was the case for Davis, Hughes, Hill, Manners, Greer, and Sanchez in that order of ascending intensity. Thus, six of the nine had *direct* job/family role conflict. Resolution of the conflict developed naturally. Davis, Hughes, Hill, and Manners immediately began shaping an identity at the plant which distracted their attention from the home. Greer took his job seriously, but his home activities never decreased, and by the end of the year his conflict had intensified. Sanchez's domination of his wife and her reciprocating submission were so stably balanced that his conflict was basically a personal dilemma which he tried to solve by staying at home about a third of the time. By the third month, under fire for absenteeism, he quit and went back to caring for his chronically sick wife.

Job/family role conflict developed indirectly in the case of Smith and Martinez. As discussed in chapter 5, Smith was pimping on the side which was the direct conflicting factor, and the conflict was resolved when he gave up his outside business.

With Martinez, the conflict involved job/family/street crowd. The job was indirectly involved, because it was this that gave him the wages he was supposed to share with his unemployed friends. The conflict was resolved in favor of the job abruptly and dramatically when his closest friend was killed during one of their barroom brawls.

For Kenneth Little, there was no job/family role conflict. In fact, his wife was his greatest asset in his occupational rehabilitation.

Thus of the nine male centered households, eight had conflict—six direct and two indirect. Five male heads modified their roles at home in favor of the job, one quit and regressed, and in two cases pressure was mounting, and the outcome was undecided.

This summary emphasizes the fact that the marginal male family system is closely tied to hard-core unemployment. The percentage of families in conflict with the job and the fact that in every case successful role fulfillment on the job implied significant role modification at home illustrates that male marginality in the family is one of the major consequences of hard-core unemployment.

In addition to its impact on the family, the job affected male marginality in society at large, because there is a social incompatibility between occupational status in industry and status in marginal society.

This fact is supported by our before and after observations (see Table 13), and to a greater extent by the trainees' experiences through time. The pattern for the year was general and basically the same as it was in the case of family/job role conflict: job/street conflict, stress, and efforts to resolve the tension by the accommodation of first one set of roles and then another. The see-saw adjustment became a trend which tended to favor one set of roles over another. Although each decision in response to a conflict event may have been conscious, the net consequence of decisions in the aggregate was generally unconscious except in the case of counseling intervention by such persons as foremen, committeemen, coworkers or professional, occupational counselors.

Moreover, there are additional and less obvious generalizations that can be derived from their experiences which pertain to general differences between the job terminated (JT) and the on-job (OJ) trainees. A decisive factor in the trainee's job success was the ability to separate problems or conflicts. All hard-core with few exceptions entered the factory with a *set* of interrelated problems. The JT's tended to view their sets of problems as a synthetic mass which they met on an *ad hoc* basis from one crisis to another. For them work stresses tended to be fused with their complex of outside problems making the one large problem even larger. OJ's, on the other hand, began to understand and resolve stresses singularly. They were able to separate the job problems from the stresses in their private world. OJ's seemed interested in mastering the job for its own sake. In the private world they tended to concentrate on one problem at a time with perhaps one problem remaining for long-term solution. But job role and family-society roles are indisputably linked and perhaps what the JTs' experience reveals is that their network of marginal roles was simply too extensive to surmount, or the conflicts were too intense, or both. Further social-psychological study would be required to answer these questions definitively.

From a total of 28 men, 15 were still on the job in the same factory after one year and *were* in various stages of adjusting to their new roles in industry. If we include Wolf who was working in another factory, the total would be 16 out of 28. But what the experiences of these men

Table 13
JOB IMPACT ON MALE'S MARGINAL ROLES IN SOCIETY
ONE YEAR AFTER HIRE

	Job Status	At Hire					Anniversary				
		Police and Courts	Credit	Drugs and Alcohol	Street Groups	Hustling	Police and Courts	Credit	Drugs and Alcohol	Street Groups	Hustling
Cox	JT	+	−	+	−	+	−	−	−	−	−
Boice	JT	+	−	+	−	+	+	+	+		+
Nolan	JT	+	+	+	+	+	+	+	+	+	+
Carter	JT	+	−	+	+	+	+	−	+	+	+
Hunt	JT	+	−	+	+	+	+	−	+	+	+
Fry	JT	−	−	+	+			−	−	+	+	−
Johns	JT	+	+	+	+	+	+	+	+	+	+
Brown	JT	+	−	+	+	+	+	−	+	+	
Sanchez	JT	+	+	+	−	−	+	+/−	+	−	−
Porter	JT	−	+	+	+	+	−	+	+	+	+
Walters	JT	+	+	+	+	−	+	+	+	+	−
Timbers	JT	+	+	+	+	+	+	+	+	+	+
Wolf	JT	+	+	+	−	−	−	+/−	−	−	−
Greer	OJ	+	−	−	−	+	+	+	+	−	−
Smith	OJ	+	−	+	+	−	−	−	+	+	+
Till	OJ	+	+	−			−	−	+/−	−	−	−
Marcus	OJ	+	−	+	+	+	+/−	+	+/−	−	−
Hughes	OJ	+	−	−	+	+	−	−	−	−	−
Martinez	OJ	+	+	+	+	−	−	−	+/−	−	−
Davis	OJ	+	+	+	+	+	−	−	+/−	+/−	−
Manners	OJ	+	+	+	+	+	+/−	+/−	−	+/−	+/−
Hill	OJ	+	+	+	+	+	+/−	+/−		+/−	−
Galvão	OJ	+	+	−	−	−	−	+/−	−	−	−
Jewell	OJ	+	+	+	+	+	−	−	+/−	+/−	−
Little	OJ	+	−	−	+	−	−	−	−	+/−	−
Barreca	OJ	−	+	−	−	−	−	+/−	−	−	−
Cooper	OJ	+	+	−	−	+	−	+/−	−	−	−
Banks	OJ	−	+	−	−	−	+	−	−	−	−

NOTES: + = problem with or active participation in
        − = no problem with or active participation in
       +/− = diminishing problem with or participation in

Table 13 *(Continued)*

Summary of Trends in Marginal Status or Activity

mentally ill, unable to function
marked increase/fugitive-parole violation
marked increase/especially hard drugs
general increase/especially hard drugs
general increase/especially alcohol
general increase/especially alcohol
general increase/all areas
general increase/active in hippie variant of street crowd
generally the same/basic problems family conflict and drunk driving
generally the same as indicated
generally the same/especially alcohol
generally the same/especially alcohol
general decrease/entered another on-job program and doing well
generally the same/basic problem family conflict
generally the same/job and family conflicts coming to a head
general decrease/reduction in credit problem
general decrease/one setback in burglary but paying back
general decrease/relating to different crowd more compatible with job
marked decrease/moving away from old crowd/reduction in drinking
general decrease/moving away from old crowd/limited use of soft drugs
marked decrease/setting limits for himself not as easily led by friends
general decrease as indicated
general decrease/better control of financial problems
marked decrease; drinking problem still evident/moving out of drinking crowd
general decrease/moving more and more from old crowd
general decrease/basic problem family conflict/reduction in credit problems
marked decrease/all areas
marked decrease/beginning to solve problems legally

tell us is that assuming status in one sector of mainstream society does not mean an automatic cessation of social activity in marginal society. An individual may be active in both sectors for a long period of time. The new status must begin to pay greater financial, social, and psychological dividends before the role transfer can be begun. In addition, where the choice is clear, it takes time to extricate oneself from old commitments. Therefore, this process may continue indefinitely and if an observer looks at a given population of ex-hard-core at an arbitrary point in time, he will find a continuum of patterns of adjustment to industry with varying degrees of participation in such activities as drug use, and hustling, and varying incidences of police problems and credit problems, just as he would find in a mainstream population. However, one thing is clear: when the job does take hold, it tends to dissolve participation in or at least require a major modification of participation in marginal society.

To develop a more detailed understanding of the dynamics involved in this adjustment process, year-end analyses of a few selected cases are presented here. Family and society are intermingled in these analyses with one or the other appearing generally as the primary locus of conflict for the individual. However, family was the most common major source of conflict.

The technique of discussing cases in oral dialogue, recording them on tape, and later transcribing them is used. What follows is the edited transcript of five cases.

ROLE CHANGE

Lester Banks

PADFIELD. *What was the basic problem in Lester's social personality situation that had to be solved before one could say he was beginning to be converted to industry? We list him under household conflict, and his relationship to Joan appears quite important in this respect. We have a reverse male role for him: his wife managed the finances, dominated him, and had authority over the children, while he helped with the cooking, cleaning, and baby-sitting.*

WILLIAMS. *So what we're saying is that he made a switch*

somewhere, or that's what happened to him in the factory. I feel the job gave Lester the status he needed to overcome the role he was playing. I believe he had the basic equipment to do a good job, but because of his poor educational background he could never succeed. So when this NAB program began hiring people like him, it gave him that chance.

PADFIELD. *He reminds me of the people that predominate in any agricultural community of Mexican-American farm workers. Their chief characteristic is probably their illiteracy, and because of this they tend to be very dependent, and in a sense exploitable. But this dependence extends into everything, including the household, particularly if they are married to women who can read and write and are educationally superior to the men.*

WILLIAMS. *Joan is hardly more literate than Lester, but the fact that she is white would give her added leverage. Lester often told her, "The only reason you're higher up on the ladder is because you're white!" Before the job I don't think he had the nerve. But when he began working in the factory, he began to function and see himself as a man.*

PADFIELD. *What you're telling me is that in Lester's case his social family situation didn't interfere with the job as much as the job enabled him to change his family situation. He was a good worker at menial jobs to begin with, but the industrial situation gave him added leverage and strengthened his personality and self-image so that he could begin to change things at home . . . .*

WILLIAMS. *He began using the same weapons that the middle class uses. We often say that the middle- or working-class man has the advantage when it comes to the money, and with the unemployed, the woman has it. Banks didn't have this advantage before, and we see him now using the advantage that the job gave him.*

PADFIELD. *This brings up a question which I think is basic to our discussion in the book. Why is Lester, who was incompetent at home and dominated by a woman, different from Tim Carter who was also incompetent at home and dominated by a woman? In Carter's situation it affected his capacity to work. In Lester's case it didn't.*

WILLIAMS. *We talked about maturity factors. Tim took the route of escape, and Lester had more stamina to take this punishment. Tim used the street crowd and dope; Lester didn't.*

PADFIELD. *Take what punishment?*

WILLIAMS. *The punishment that was put on him. They both took punishment from their women. Joan dominated Lester; she put him down.*

PADFIELD. *She did in many ways, she manipulated him, and, or course, she was manipulating a volcano in this case. You might say she used child psychology; you could see her scheming all the time, but she never knew exactly the extent to which he would react. She tried to manhandle him, like you would a heavy object . . . .*

WILLIAMS. *The region of rearing might contribute to this situation.*

PADFIELD. *How do you mean?*

WILLIAMS. *In the South, Banks developed attitudes that Carter didn't develop in the West. He was taught a passive attitude—to be polite to his superiors, to obey.*

PADFIELD. *It's a good point. In other words his personality had internalized habits which enabled him to endure and to cope with domination. Where Tim had never had these habits engrained in him. And you think his regional environment was a significant influence?*

WILLIAMS. *Yes.*

PADFIELD. *In other words you're saying he's part of the black culture of the South, and Carter is not. We could have a key distinction here among the hard-core that we're dealing with. We readily recognize the important distinction between white and black when talking about the population of chronically unemployed people. Now within the black group maybe there is another key distinction to be made between Southern-reared and Northern- and Western-reared.*

WILLIAMS. *If we took this NAB program to the South and put it into effect, we would find more Lesters than we would Tims. We wouldn't find Bobby Hill, because there the treatment of blacks is different. They would squash Bobby; they wouldn't allow him to manipulate.*

PADFIELD. *Ironically you wouldn't get a program like this as readily in the South, because all the Lesters down there are going to take it the way its been . . . . The Lesters are not responsible for the inception of this kind of program, right?*

WILLIAMS. *That's right. When have you seen a man like Lester burning down a neighborhood? . . . And then we have to consider his age.*

PADFIELD. *That's part of the pattern of acquiescence—the older a person gets the more resigned he tends to become. When Lester began to feel his new status, he began to carry home a new self-respect.*

WILLIAMS. *It changed his self-image, because he saw himself as one who could work in an industry like Southwestern.*

PADFIELD. *In the case of Darrell Johns and Tim Carter, the most profound realization of the job was the fact that it was a job. The most important hurdle for them was getting up every day and committing themselves to work. In Lester's case that wasn't a problem, because he had been working for years. The new experience for him was the higher level of prestige. When that began to affect his personality, he began to carry that effect home . . . . We noted that then the antagonism between him and Joan began to take on a new dimension. We have conflict increasing over finances, the children, and his baby-sitting. Did he continue to help with the housework and children, or did they fight over this?*

WILLIAMS. *No. He continued to do the small things, which was reasonable I would say. If a screen needed fixing he would fix it. The main issue was the baby-sitting.*

PADFIELD. *And that he stopped.*

WILLIAMS. *He stopped to the point that he left the children at home and went to the bars and brought Joan home.*

PADFIELD. *The conflict began to go in his favor at the end of the year. So really the dramatic story in this case took place almost entirely in the home, not in the factory . . . . Do you feel that regardless of how this conflict will be resolved, Lester's job will be secure?*

WILLIAMS. *It's not going to be threatened by that. If she made him leave home, he would still keep his job.*

PADFiELD. *Well what about the gun Lester bought? You*

can't murder and go to work so what about the gun?

WILLIAMS. *Do you remember what he did with the gun? He told me he didn't keep it two weeks, because he was afraid that he* could *get mad enough to use it on Joan. He put the gun in the pawnshop and gave the ticket to a friend and let the friend get it out so it would be charged to him.*

PADFIELD. *But in a moment of weakness he made a decision and then rescinded that decision, which again is a commitment, and the job is part of that commitment. We have also noted that Lester started using the ultimate weapon, money—withholding money and controlling Joan's activities with it. Didn't you say you saw a counterreaction developing from Joan who wanted to leave him and get back on welfare?*

WILLIAMS. *She tried; she applied, but they wouldn't allow her.*

PADFIELD. *So she tried to get back on welfare. This welfare thing is very involved. It is not a matter of whether someone wants to work or be lazy. It involves all kinds of intimate relationships with other people. The welfare check or the job affects these relationships, and in Lester's case we're witnessing another chess game between two intimately related people.*

WILLIAMS. *Lester did something; he went to Vic Hilgenberg's office* (the factory attorney) *and asked him if he would tell the welfare people not to put his wife on welfare, because he was able to take care of his own family.*

PADFIELD. *I bet Hilgenberg liked that!*

WILLIAMS. *You better believe it!*

Bobby Hill

PADFIELD. *Roy, I'm still convinced, intuitively, that there's a lot to Bobby that we don't know. Of course this is a cliché in a way, because there's a lot to everybody that we don't know. But I don't have that feeling about Lester Banks. There's a lot in Lester's life that we don't know, but if we did find out more about him it would probably fit with what we already know. I have the opposite concern about our knowledge of Bobby.*

WILLIAMS. *Let's put it this way. Lester doesn't put on a show for you or me, nor do many of the guys. Bobby does.*

PADFIELD. *So what we're finding out about Bobby, and it did surprise me although maybe it hasn't surprised you, is that Bobby isn't the uncomplicated person I thought he was. As a matter of fact, all of our data on him centers on his conflict with authority: tyrannical abusive father, the hostility and aggression that came out in school and was later directed toward the police, and the police getting back at him. It's an easy explanation. But toward the end of the year it was apparent to me that Bobby is a pretty complicated guy.*

WILLIAMS. *So what we're saying is that we may be looking at only one side, the side that he deliberately wants us to see.*

PADFIELD. *That's true. Not only that, but I think he's conducting business, I mean engaging in social interaction with perhaps several kinds of elements or cultures.*

WILLIAMS. *We know this. He does business this way. I believe that Bobby's personality would allow him to walk right down with the potblowers, or the pushers, as he says he does. He's versatile that way. He said to me the other day, "I know how to talk to those people."*

PADFIELD. *So what we're finding out now is that he can move among the police and interact in a positive way with them.* (Referring to his cooperation with the FBI, see Chapter 5) *So that means he's not just fighting the police, he's one of them or was one of them, and when you find this out, it makes you wonder about the validity of all his hostilities toward them.*

WILLIAMS. *This police cooperation could have been exactly what he resented and this resentment is what he was expressing . . . . Everybody will assume some roles sometimes, even though they are in conflict with his basic personality. You can make one child tattle on another even if he really doesn't want to. Bobby could have been in the position where he didn't have any choice, because he did have a lot of traffic tickets. That could have been a weapon the police held over his head.*

PADFIELD. *Okay, what I find out from you is a logical contradiction in the social personality of Bobby Hill. Person-*

ality A: enemy of the police to the bitter end; personality B: a cooperator with the police. These are contradictory, and you're explaining the contradiction in a way that preserves one theory of Bobby's personality and preserves his personal integrity.

WILLIAMS. *Maybe I'm being biased here. Let's say it this way. Bobby plays roles. We know he played them with me, and he played them with you. Only when you were able to talk to Bobby beyond this play-role did you see what he had on his mind. When he first came to us, he couldn't work math. To keep us from finding out, he went through all kinds of motions to show how smart he was.*

PADFIELD. *There are many reasons that explain Bobby's hostility toward the police without saying it stemmed from the fact that they were making an unwilling accomplice out of him. His stepfather's treatment of him alone would explain a lot of . . .*

WILLIAMS. *. . . his resentment for authority.*

PADFIELD. *So his hostility seems to me to be relatively common and fairly normal for the experience that he's had. That's why I'm curious why you look for that, because I don't agree with you. I would say that if he cooperated with undercover agents of the FBI or the police, he did it willingly to achieve some selfish objective which he had.*

WILLIAMS. *What would that objective be?*

PADFIELD. *Money, and getting 57 traffic tickets taken off the book.*

WILLIAMS. *We don't doubt that.*

PADFIELD. *But my understanding of the situation seems to be different from yours. I feel that Bobby would be willing, as a matter of fact you might even say that Bobby solicited, the cooperation so that he could lose his record. Or put it this way, maybe the police put out a little bait for him, and I'll bet he jumped at it.*

WILLIAMS. *We don't doubt that either . . . .*

PADFIELD. *He wanted to. I thought you were saying the police were threatening him.*

WILLIAMS. *It could've been either way. They could've put pressure on him, because they had legitimate means. But on the other hand, I would say Bobby's personality allowed the police to use him. They wouldn't have to use pressure, because Bobby is basically for Bobby and anything that will give him favors.*

PADFIELD. *Okay. This could be the very thing that explains why Bobby is succeeding.*

WILLIAMS. *Manipulation.*

PADFIELD. On *the job. Because he's found a new tool, the same tool that 90 percent of the white people in that factory had—good old selfish capitalism. He's joining the middle class. He's just doing a little bit more screwing.*

WILLIAMS. *And he's doing it legitimately.*

PADFIELD. *The way we all do.*

WILLIAMS. *That's right. He has learned to play the game like white society has.*

PADFIELD. *Because it's the same game he's always been playing only now he has a better position . . . . Then we could say that he was not required to make as basic a role change as Tim Carter and Darrell Johns, and he was able to make this relatively superficial change by shifting his weapons—the tools of success—from one game to another.*

WILLIAMS. *Then all the job taught him was the legal way to do the things he wanted.*

PADFIELD. *And his personality is exactly the same.*

WILLIAMS. *Exactly the same.*

PADFIELD. *No* basic *change?*

WILLIAMS. *No. The job just taught him a legal way and gave him the legal tools. He still doesn't like the cops, in a sense.*

PADFIELD. *Well precisely what did he learn?*

WILLIAMS. *He learned to keep his mouth shut; he learned that when he got a ticket, he shouldn't stand behind the car and throw a rock; instead he should talk to the captain about it, even though he never learned not to give him too much lip. So that's a change . . . .*

PADFIELD. *Bobby has an uncanny ability to smell out sources of power for manipulating his environment. As soon as he got on the job that's what he began to do, and he was astute at it. If we say that, then there was no basic personality change. He simply came into a new environment and used his* same skills in another set of roles.

WILLIAMS. *He sharpened them . . . .*

PADFIELD. *How was he manipulating his environment before he came to work?*

WILLIAMS. *One environment we know about was the honor camp. He knew they were looking for tough guys, guys who could run a crew.*

PADFIELD. *Then you're telling me that for all of Bobby's hostilities, he does get along with the guy at the very top, the head cop, the principal of the school, the superintendent of the camp. He doesn't have a basic blind conflict with authority, because a person with an authority hang-up could never succeed in any organization because he would fight the guy at the very top.*

WILLIAMS. *The cop on the beat who has no authority, he's the guy Bobby's going to fight with.*

PADFIELD. *What you're saying then is, that to make our theory consistent, we have to reevaluate the meaning of Bobby's hostility toward the police. We can't describe Bobby as a man who's trapped by his hatred, and then begins to learn how to work out of it. There are altogether different premises involved here. You're saying that if he needed rehabilitating, which we don't know, he still wasn't able to accept it.*

WILLIAMS. *Well only to the point of learning to channel his aggressions in the right direction . . . .*

PADFIELD. *He learned how to manipulate in a new environment here . . . I really don't know, but I felt that he was kind of helpless.*

WILLIAMS. *I never got that feeling.*

PADFIELD. *I don't mean that people were abusing him, but I felt that he was being trapped by his own hostilities.*

WILLIAMS. *I always felt that if you confronted Bobby with a source of power, he would back off, and you would see what he really was. I got that feeling from the things I did with him, because I saw him put on a show for you all the time. If you came around he was like a kid, telling you, "Damn this!" and "Damn that!" and if you listened to him you would think, "That's a tough guy." But when Barbara clamped down on him he was a different man, subtle and mellow. He bullied me until I walked out there and cursed him out.*

PADFIELD. *So these were not blind temper tantrums. They were calculated, and although they didn't always achieve the thing he was trying to do, nevertheless he felt it was creating a certain impression.*

WILLIAMS. *If I went to a Black Panther meeting with Bobby, he would blend in with them; he would be standing there hollering, but when the action started, he would be standing off on the side.*

PADFIELD. *In other words, if you took away his audience, how would Bobby act?*

WILLIAMS. *What I really believe you would find would be a scared man who compensates with all of his antics for his inability to move around as other people do. The Bobby that you see is a tough guy. You could twist his arm, and he would never cry. But when he was put down in court and the judge said, "Six months!" Bobby broke down and cried. When he can't manipulate people, he is beaten.*

PADFIELD. *I think you're getting at something a little bit deeper here. Let's don't say that his demonstrations of hostility were a direct result of being scared. Let's say that they were part of his strategies of manipulation. What really shows that he was scared is that the only way he felt that he would succeed in a group was by manipulating people.*

WILLIAMS. *And by dominating them.*

PADFIELD. *He doesn't turn this domination on and off?*

WILLIAMS. *Yes he does. Right now Bobby has learned which of the judges to bad mouth and which ones not to.*

PADFIELD. *But the point is he still bad mouths.*

WILLIAMS. *Right.*

PADFIELD. *But if he does, he's not doing it because someone else is using pressure . . . . I think that a person has to have success to learn, and Bobby had been successful in using his force.*

WILLIAMS. *Because he feels that force has been used against him. He sees that the police have used force, and he sees what they have accomplished; so he learned from a master teacher. But he also taught himself when not to go too far, because he's been crushed before for using that same tactic . . . .*

PADFIELD. *I still think that Bobby also saw the effects of cooperation.*

WILLIAMS. *Bobby is smart, let's not take that away from him. He can out-think a lot of people, and he learned how to bully. Take Morrison* (his foreman). *Bobby knows Morrison's weak nature, and he will actually go in and dominate him and get a 15-cent raise. But if he went into Gore's office* (North Plant general foreman), *and Gore said, "Damn it, shut up," Bobby would back off like a kid. So he has learned how to read people in the subtle environment of the factory.*

ROLE REGRESSION

Carl Brown and Gary Nolan

PADFIELD. *To summarize Brown, we find that there is a personality conflict revolving around his relationship with women. He's really incapable of having a normal husband-wife relationship with a woman. This was true before the job, and the fact that he got a job took away his excuse for not marrying the woman he was going with. When she pressured him to assume a husband's role which he was incapable of doing, the conflict developed. It wasn't his relationship with the woman that conflicted with the job as much as it was the job throwing the existing relationship out of balance.*

WILLIAMS. *That's right. But I don't think that Brown could have held a stable job because of his background.*

PADFIELD. *I agree with you. Remember when we talked to him the last time—we saw him with his mother—he had gone all the way. The various clues he had revealed on the job were now full-fledged. He dressed like a hippie and talked like a hippie. It was apparent that work, in terms of status and the psychological and social meaning associated with it, had no place in his world.*

WILLIAMS. *Brown completely rejected that type of thinking. He often said, "Who ever said that work was the best thing for me?"*

PADFIELD. *Suppose he had been given a higher, more professional status? Suppose he was asked to be an employ-*

ment counselor at the service center. Do you think that he would have been more motivated?

WILLIAMS. *I doubt it. I say this because of a theory of mine. To do that type of job, you have to achieve some part of the status yourself. Everyday I get letters from people who say they like working with people, and they feel that what they have suffered through will qualify them to do this. To a degree this is true, but if you are still in the position where you need the help, then you can't help others. I think a high status job would frustrate Brown, because he would find that he couldn't really help others because of his own needs. Now if you put him in a position, such as a writer, where he could let the thoughts, particularly rebellious thoughts, come out, and he could see himself getting even with society for his own suffering, I would say he could be comfortable. He could write about the hippie element and how he felt, and he would feel he was really making an impact . . . .*

PADFIELD. *In this study the job is the key yardstick against which we are measuring all the important characteristics the trainees reveal. We saw the way the job affected Carl's relationship with the woman he was living with . . . . Brown has changed since last year. He began changing on the job, and he's changed even more since quitting. In what way did the job precipitate, aggrevate, or aid this change?*

WILLIAMS. *It's what I term ghetto speculation—what a job means to a ghetto resident. Society has said a job will solve all of his problems, and Brown had these expectations when he entered Southwestern's work force. First, he didn't expect the interviewers to hire him. He said to them, "You are holding me out of the job, because I am who I am."*

PADFIELD. *So what you're saying is that when Carl was interviewed for this job, it was as if the interviewers were saying, "Carl, do you want to go to Australia, or Africa, or some exotic place to get away from your problem?"*

WILLIAMS. *Let's say Brown thought it was a solution to his problems.*

PADFIELD. *What did it do to his problems?*

WILLIAMS. *When he came in, the experience let him know that what he was seeking was not found in a job. It took away the fantasy world the job was supposed to provide . . . .*

PADFIELD. *I think we have a major point emerging here. That is that job deprivation may cause a lot of these problems, but that job status doesn't necessarily solve them right away.*

WILLIAMS. *Right; in fact, it* doesn't *solve them.*

PADFIELD. *And the fact that it solves nothing still doesn't mean that job deprivation didn't cause the problems. It's like a person being deprived of a critical nutritional element for a long time and then suddenly getting it. His illness isn't going to clear up immediately.*

WILLIAMS. *. . . because it went too long before treatment started . . .*

PADFIELD. *Name one personality problem that Brown had that the job aggravated other than his not being able to assume a husband role with a woman. What was the problem pinpointed in counseling?*

WILLIAMS. *In Brown's case, the counselor began to unravel his family as part of his being a problem to himself.*

PADFIELD. *Without getting too psychoanalytical—because both of us are amateurs in that—he did have a lot of fear, didn't he?*

WILLIAMS. *Yes.*

PADFIELD. *Specifically, he had a fear of heights. Would you say generally he had a fear of inadequacy?*

WILLIAMS. *Yes.*

PADFIELD. *It would seem that success on the job would strengthen his feeling of adequacy.*

WILLIAMS. *It would if he had been left alone, but he had other pressures during this time that made him fail on the job.*

PADFIELD. *What you're saying is: (a) We're talking about a man being under pressure and wanting to get out from under it. The first pressure leading to the deterioration of the job was that he did not want to marry the woman because of his basic inadequacy, the feeling that he wasn't strong enough to be a father and husband. So he quit work to stop that pressure. (b) And after he quit, he then had to rationalize in his own mind why he quit. He wouldn't permit himself to admit that he quit work to keep from marrying this woman. So what he did was to reject the job and everything it stood for.*

WILLIAMS. *As not being the thing for him.*

PADFIELD. *Yes. He had to build up a whole wall of rationalization. Of course Brown is very verbal, very insightful, very creative. I could see the progression, because when he quit, he didn't have the rationale worked out. He just quit and then worked it out in the intervening weeks. He changed his dress, his hair-do, and everything, and that served as a public explanation of why he quit. But of course the real reason, he couldn't face.*

WILLIAMS. *If you go back in time, you will find that he started having problems about the time the baby was conceived. Until then, Brown had been a good machinist. The job was providing the money to do the things that he wanted to do. But suddenly this other role loomed up, and the pressure started.*

PADFIELD. *In other words, if that woman and the whole issue of his being a father before he was psychologically ready had not entered the picture, he would probably have accepted the job.*

WILLIAMS. *As a last resort.*

PADFIELD. *Did you ever tell him that?*

WILLIAMS. *No.*

PADFIELD. *I wonder what would happen if someone he thought a lot of sat down and faced him with that?*

WILLIAMS. *It might be a wise thing to do . . . .*

PADFIELD. *What did he do?*

WILLIAMS. *As a last resort, he went to the plant about the time the baby was due to be born and said he had solved his problems and was ready to go back to work. He was still shaking, but he went. When they didn't hire him, and the baby was born dead, he was relieved because he was free again, and he wanted to leave everything behind. He kept saying he needed money to get out of town.*

PADFIELD. *But he quit the job first.*

WILLIAMS. *Yes. The only reason he tried to come back to work was because he had accepted the fact that he would have to support the baby. He admitted he would only have stayed long enough to get enough money to leave town.*

PADFIELD. *So now he has this all worked into a*

philosophy . . . . How does Brown's pattern differ from Nolan's? Nolan had the same situation of quitting the job to avoid marrying Mary. He did exactly what Brown did up to that point but he didn't develop an anti-job philosophy. What do you think?

WILLIAMS. *Nolan knows why he quit. The counselor stayed with him long enough to unravel the problem between him and Mary. So Gary knew. But the counselor didn't get that far with Brown, because Carl ran off. Nolan quit when Mary started pressuring him. He deliberately went out, took dope, and wouldn't see anyone from Southwestern. He could have kept his job, but he deliberately fired himself.*

PADFIELD. *Step two is quitting the job to avoid coming to grips with the original problem, but the third step that Brown went through was inventing an elaborate philosophy of rejection . . . . The crucial difference between Nolan and Brown is the reason for quitting. Brown had it all worked out, he's rejecting the whole war-mongering society. But how did Nolan . . . see his quitting?*

WILLIAMS. *Nolan didn't go the third step. He sees it as his blowing a chance.*

PADFIELD. *What's his future like? Noboby can accept chronic failure, so what he's got to do is stop trying. He has to protect himself. Brown stopped trying and more significantly he had a half way respectable reason for not trying. What worries me about Gary—and maybe he's worse off than Brown, I don't know—is that Gary is still going to try.*

WILLIAMS. *But he can go one of two ways. He can either go back to the job and make it, or, as I would predict, he can escape with drugs.*

PADFIELD. *In other words, just work like a wino, just enough to get by.*

WILLIAMS. *That's what he's doing now.*

PADFIELD. *That's what he was trying to tell me the last day we went to his house. He said, "Look, maybe dishwashing is better for me." What he was saying was he was really going to be an anglo-isolate, i.e., deliberately lose his social identity.*

WILLIAMS. *But in that world he'll constantly feed that ego by using drugs.*

PADFIELD. *Don't say feed the ego, say separate the ego from what he knows about failure. In a way I'm more worried about Gary than I am about Brown.*

WILLIAMS. *Because Brown will go out and join the hippie movement, and their philosophy will be his reason for quitting his job.*

Floyd Hunt

PADFIELD. *What emerged as the crucial social or social-personality pattern in Hunt's case that conflicted with the job? We have a lot of potential areas, hustling, old crowd, alcohol, and intense conflict between him and his wife. Which was most incompatible with his job?*

WILLIAMS. *At the time he was terminated, it was his wife and his parents.*

PADFIELD. *We've recorded conflict over finances, children . . . . Did that conflict affect his work? How?*

WILLIAMS. *It sent him into a deep depression, and it gave him an illness that he didn't really have.*

PADFIELD. *You mean psychosomatic. Was this diagnosed by a doctor?*

WILLIAMS. *Yes, by two doctors. Floyd called it "the strains." He would come down with something in his groin; it would tighten up like a nerve condition.*

PADFIELD. *I've encountered it among blacks in the rural areas, that and "back" I heard a lot . . . .*

WILLIAMS. *He became ill, I noticed, whenever he was put under intense pressure. He showed us something that is prevalent in the ghetto children, and that is the expectation placed upon them by their parents to succeed, to get out of the ghetto. I think you will find this in Hunt's case because his father has a history of working for over 20 years for one company, and he preached to Floyd and his brother* (who is turning out just like Floyd) *constantly saying, "Look at me." His father was the model. I think Floyd rejected what his father was. The fact that he married a woman who had high* ideals and who preached to him as his father had done put an additional burden on Floyd.

PADFIELD. *That's how it affected his performance, but what about the job affecting his home? Was it a neutral factor, or did it increase stress?*

WILLIAMS. *Hunt had picked up some habits that he couldn't let go automatically, and he was never given enough time to drop his old crowd. When he first started he intended to make the job work, but when he went home in the evening his wife kept telling him, "You're not going to make it anyway." So he was programmed for failure before he ever started. He told me this constantly.*

He kept saying, "When I get my foot on the bottom rung of the ladder, I keep sliding back. I want to go up, but look like everytime I go up somebody step on my head and slide me right back down."

PADFIELD. *In other words, the job didn't help him any at home. Did it increase stress?*

WILLIAMS. *Yes, because while he wasn't working, his wife relaxed the pressure. She worked in an office where she could see men succeeding. She gave this pattern to Floyd constantly, and he could never fulfill her ideal. This is something we should note: In the ghetto there are two extremes of thought that parents drum into their children—some will tell their children that they are going to fail; others will make the expectations so high that the children are unable to fulfill them . . . .*

PADFIELD. *There is no realistic acculturation going on. There's a breakdown in that process.*

WILLIAMS. *If these children were to go to a white school with all of its advantages more of these expectations could be realized. But because they are going to ghetto schools surrounded by deprivation, they cannot achieve the goals set for them by their parents. Now some make it despite this disadvantage . . . .*

PADFIELD. *You're still telling me about the stress that Floyd brought to the job. Did he carry any effects of the job back to the house?*

WILLIAMS. *The job stimulated him for maybe five days.*

PADFIELD. *Were there any mechanical scheduling conflicts that the job brought to the household?*

WILLIAMS. *Yes, it put Floyd on a schedule, such as coming to work in the morning, which he was not accustomed to. The job also created a conflict about who was going to use the car. Also, the moment Floyd got a job, his wife wanted to go out and purchase furniture and improve their position. This upset Floyd, because he felt that it was like his parents pressuring him all over again . . . .*

PADFIELD. *Was there a tendency to fight more about finances since the check was in his name?*

WILLIAMS. *Not really. His wife never accepted him as being a stable employee, so she never considered Floyd able to succeed. She told him, "It's going to be just like one of those other tries you made; you won't make it anyway." She told me that; she predicted his failure.*

PADFIELD. *In this case he was hurt on the job because of the household, and the job didn't take hold so he could take anything back from it to the household.*

WILLIAMS. *First of all it wasn't the kind of job that enabled him to meet his expectations.*

PADFIELD. *Explain.*

WILLIAMS. *The job that Southwestern gave Floyd required welding, and the company does not certify welders who have not had experience. Floyd was taking government training for welding and felt that he was doing well, but the course was discontinued. Again his expectation of achieving was taken away from him. When he came to Southwestern, they didn't have enough to offer him. The job never turned Floyd on. He was on the job maybe four months, if that long. His absentee record is phenomenal.*

PADFIELD. *Did it do* anything? *We have a pattern before the job, and increased stress on the job. So the job was a source of some contention?*

WILLIAMS. *Yes. When he wasn't at work his wife expected him to be baby-sitting, which he didn't want to do, and when he took the job he rejected baby-sitting. It also provided a kind of shelter for him because his wife thought he was at work sometimes when he wasn't. Whenever she discovered that he wasn't, she became furious . . . .*

PADFIELD. *As far as the job, he didn't begin to act in that arena at all. He completely regressed. Was there any other conflict between the job and any other pattern of his where he had to make a choice?*

WILLIAMS. *With the crowd. And he chose to go back to them . . . .*

PADFIELD. *He didn't go back to his wife; they finally separated. Why did he quit the job? It wasn't to resolve the stress at home. He was beaten down so much that he didn't have any psychological strength left, and he just quit.*

WILLIAMS. *His parents and his wife constantly teamed up against him. They would say, "Floyd you should straighten up." When he was at Southwestern, his mother told his wife, "If Floyd doesn't make this job I'll help you to divorce him."*

PADFIELD. *He did resolve something by quitting—the nonsupport he was getting at work. He related back to his crowd, because they probably supported him more than the job. The job was an extension of the hostile environment at home. At least he put himself out of misery by quitting.*

WILLIAMS. *And he went back to the only area that he knew he could compete in.*

PADFIELD. *It did give him some kind of social support.*

WILLIAMS. *They did because he was the biggest guy in the crowd, and everybody looked up to him. They called him "Jungle Boy." . . . That is why I rejected the theory that says a man loves that environment. Floyd objected to the name "Jungle Boy," but in the end he accepted it, because by their calling him that they gave him the support he needed.*

THE JOB AS REHABILITATION

Both as cause and remedy a meaningful, stable job is the most important single factor in male marginality. From the standpoint of the participants in the culture of marginality, including heads of households, wives and children, actual job training and placement is a more viable remedy for marginality than rehabilitative inputs *without* occupational status such as vocational training, public welfare, counseling, and special educational programs for the disadvantaged.

The issue of direct job placement or compensatory opportunity is not as much a question of its cost-effectiveness relative to other rehabilitation programs for the identified "beneficiaries" as it is a question of its impact upon the "benefactors"—business, industry, and those presently assured of jobs in the existing system. Therefore, we cannot discuss this issue properly without first rearranging the conventional class-centric concepts of beneficiary and benefactor, because this dichotomy implies a number of false propositions, one of which is that the economically efficient, functional, and healthy people are helping the inefficient, dysfunctional, and pathological people.

The findings of this study (see Chapter 8) support the proposition that the existing industrial occupational system is dysfunctional, and that the hard-core unemployed are conveniently identified as the misfits in this system, which mines human resources and protects class interests in the name of rewarding individual virtue. But as we have shown, the culture of marginality is an integral part of the national social system. Therefore the question is not simply one of asking innocent bystanders, business and organized labor, to make sacrifices to rehabilitate their fellow citizens. We are asking a system that helps create the condition of the hard-core unemployed to help compensate for its actions by making basic changes within itself to allow for the recycling of its misused human resources.

The benefactors are part of the beneficiaries' problem not only because they helped to create it, but also because permanent economic rejection of people as individuals leads to socially dysfunctional families, making the likelihood of economic rejection of their children almost certain. An increase every generation of a factor of four in the population of hard-core unemployed sooner or later will seriously affect the welfare of everyone. Whether this population is now one million or ten million makes little difference in terms of the long range implications of this type of trend. Conversely the economic rehabilitation of individual heads of households must be multiplied by four in terms of its ultimate impact upon the society.

Compensatory job opportunity is a realistic policy not only from the standpoint of national welfare, but also from the standpoint of viable rehabilitation, because it enables the hard-core unemployed to operate in real as opposed to contrived and hypothetical situations. As the experiences of the trainees have been shown, adjustment is an unavoidable consequence of the experience of job status. In education, reality systems for learning skills are taken for granted. A student works on a lathe to learn machine took operating. He works with chemicals under laboratory conditions to learn chemistry. But social rather than motor behavior is the crux of the hard-core adjustment problem—not only within the factory, but also in the outside social systems in which he is operating. To be effective, reality training for the hard-core must extend beyond learning motor skills for hypothetical jobs to the practice of the real roles involved in real job status.

Is a job alone enough? For a small percentage of those defined as hard-core unemployed it is. Trainees Kenneth Little, Robert Barreca, Nelson Jewell, and Jack Davis could perhaps have made the adjustment with the normal amount of personnel services available at Southwestern. Since all of the 28 trainees, including these men, did get special training and counseling, we can only speculate. One thing is clear: If the true definition of hard-core unemployed is adhered to in the hiring process, the percentage of people in this category will be very low.

Counselors and counseling should be an integral part of the interaction systems in the factory. There is a constant flow of conflict events which become the natural fabric of adjustment, and which constitutes a pre-eminent counseling situation. But counseling by outsiders, as professional as they may be, is not enough. From screening to supervision, both the issue of compensatory opportunity and the social intrusion of hard-core unemployed in the factory, challenge existing attitudes and practices. The basic task of counseling or education must be to help the total factory population—including interviewers, instructors, foremen, management, and workmen—to change.

In addition, the public agencies that are inevitably involved in conflict events tend to have stereotypic views of the hard-core that reinforce old identities. Although it is absurd to expect counselors to try to change these systems, they do have a vital role to play in adjusting these stereotypes to fit the man's new situation.

Real occupational status combined with rehabilitative counseling within the total social context of the plant is a decisive factor in the occupational rehabilitation of the hard-core unemployed and as such is a decisive agent of change in the culture of marginality.

8

The Post-Hard-Core Contract

The first round in the union-management skirmishes over the training and placement of the hard-core at Southwestern ended with a clear victory for management in terms of keeping the trainees on the work force despite layoffs of senior workmen. In terms of the larger principle of providing access to industrial occupations for ghetto people as opposed to providing access merely for a given quota of ghetto people, management had been less successful. From our perspective of the microcosm at Southwestern this larger principle was being eroded.

Even in terms of how the existing quota of hard-core were being handled, erosion had taken place. As a consequence of union pressure and management tactics to circumvent this pressure, the general helper-learner concept had been weakened because trainees were not allowed to use tools. In addition, shop instruction was no longer directly related to job assignment, and the transferring of trainees to protect them from layoffs had increased confusion and undermined morale on the part of both trainees and supervisors. The polarized atmosphere resulting from these actions generated an identification with management as opposed to the work force and distorted the trainees' industrial socialization. Lines of communication between management and labor, which were faulty to begin with, deteriorated during the hard-core program to an even more superficial, hence deceptive, level. But in the final analysis, these erosions were secondary, not primary issues, because the hard-core involved were given special access to jobs, and personnel trained them, counseled them, and upgraded them. The primary issue was one of access. Without special systems of access such as out-of-labor-force recruitment, and special benefits of on-job training on the basis of need as opposed to "qualification" or work seniority, these erosions could not even have become issues. The crux of the NAB-JOBS program was compensatory opportunity, and the primary erosion was the weakening of commitment to this principle.

From the beginning of the NAB program at Southwestern until the eve of the new contract negotiations, management's public position was that the compensatory opportunity issue had been settled. Harper, vice president of Personnel, and other company representatives rejected any suggestion that the union was attempting to kill the NAB program. Instead they developed plans for the usual pre-hard-core type of union-management contract negotiations. However, to the union the issue was far from settled, and since management had won the first round of the hard-core conflict under the ground rules of the 1966-1969 (pre-hard-core) contract, these ground rules became the main target of union strategies for the 1969-1972 negotiations.

LOCAL 289 PREPARING ITS HAND

To union leaders at Southwestern, management's handling of the hard-core represented a public demonstration of union weakness. However, to understand this attitude and ultimately the union's reaction to the NAB program, we must consider union-management relations and the internal politics of the union at the time the program was initiated.

Southwestern Union Local 289 of National Aerospace Workers (NAW) is managed and served internally by a president, vice president, recording secretary, financial secretary, treasurer and three trustees. But the vital dimension of its operations involving wage and fringe benefits and the safety and security of its members is conducted by its business representatives and key committees. The business representatives consist of one shop committeeman for each department; three shop stewards, one for each shift; a deputy chief shop steward; and a chief shop steward. All of these offices are elected annually. In addition, there is a special business representative, elected every three years to serve on the negotiating or contract committee and grievance committee.

The grievance committee is made up of the union business representative on the contract committee, the chief shop steward, and one additional member selected by the chief shop steward. The general committee is composed of the chairman of the contract committee, the chief shop steward, and one additional member selected by the chief shop steward. The safety committee consists of one elected safety spokesman and each departmental committeeman. Thus, it is evident that the positions of chief shop steward, union business representative, and chairman of the contract committee are critical positions.

The NAB program was begun during internal political struggles within Local 289 that made it imperative for their key leaders to prove themselves. There was a feeling of being had among the younger and more vocal members which dated back to the ratification of the 1966-1969 contract.

The 1966 negotiating committee for local 289 was composed of old line, senior employees. After less than a week of negotiations, the committee called a general meeting to present the company's offer. Approximately one-fourth of the union's membership attended, most of whom were the younger, more vocal members. This group soundly rejected the company's offer, voting three to one in favor of a strike if their demands were not met. After another week of negotiations with little change in management's position, a strike date was set, but the union officers called another mass meeting on the eve of the strike. This time about four-fifths of the total membership attended, with the negotiating committee actively campaigning before and during the meeting for acceptance of the offer. The session was bitter and divisive, with the young militants pitted against the negotiating committee. When it became clear that the majority was playing a passive role, many of the younger members walked out, calling the session a "sell out" and threatening that next time they would call the shots.

The company's offer was accepted by a four-to-one majority, the strike was averted and within 18 months the contract committee chairman who had played a prominent part in winning union acceptance of the offer, was promoted to a management position in the company as employee relations representative, thus adding substance to the militant's allegation that the negotiating committee had sold out to the company. During the 1966-1969 contract period, the militants had succeeded in taking over key positions in the union, and by the time the NAB program was launched at Southwestern, the quiet transformation of union leadership was well underway.

This was the context in which the NAB program was begun. While it was inevitable—given the added factor of layoffs—that Line Relations and the union would clash over the program, and while perhaps is was also inevitable that ultimately the program would become a casualty of this confrontation, initially there was naiveté on both sides. The union's new leadership paid little attention and the hard-core and Line Relations paid little attention to what was happening in the union. But beyond their polite naiveté, union leadership did nothing to help build grass roots support for the NAB program, which later gave them a strategic advantage when they did begin their opposition. Initial resentment that had accumulated about the training facility and command procedures Line Relations had used in implementing the program could then be released with no awkward about-face.

However, the layoffs and the tactics used by Line Relations to keep the hard-core and enforce the layoffs signaled an end to union naiveté. It was at this point that issues posed by the hard-core and issues still smoldering from the 1966 contract abruptly converged, providing the first major test for the new union leadership.

One sensitive issue left unresolved after the 1966 contract was the lack of specificity in job descriptions. This deficiency was recognized by both union and management, and by verbal agreement, job descriptions were to be redefined during the course of the three-year contract. However, Line Relations did not follow through on the agreement, and prior to the NAB program, this issue was the focal point of numerous union grievances. To management, lack of specificity was desirable because it insured flexibility. Conversely the union felt such vagueness was undesirable because it gave management the right either to lay people off or not to hire them in certain classifications, and then to give these jobs to people in other classifications. A typical example of this was a grievance the union filed alleging that management was using assemblers to do the work of dispatchers who had been laid off.

When the hard-core became an issue, vagueness in job description gave Line Relations the advantage in manipulating work assignments, especially in the helper-learner categories. Repeatedly Miller, the DOT director, and sympathetic foremen and lead men deliberately assigned jobs stretching the interpretation of job descriptions in order to provide meaningful training. From the union point of view, this practice eroded the value of seniority. Lack of specificity in the contract put the union at a tactical disadvantage because it had to fight each individual incident, laboriously collecting evidence and preparing cases on an *ad hoc* basis.

In addition to reinforcing union sensitivity to disadvantages that it *was* aware of, management's tactics exposed disadvantages in the 1966 contract that it was *not* aware of. The focal point of the union leadership's frustration, of course, was the inability to protect senior people from layoffs in the face of new hires. They were confined by contract stipulations that seniority held only in specific occupations, e.g. plumbers, carpenters, aircraft assemblers, and so on. The company was free to place new people in other categories as long as those categories were not experiencing layoffs.

Another feature frustrating to union leaders was the upgrade plan. Under the 1966 contract, upgrades were awarded at the discretion of management. For example, if a senior man fearing layoff in his present category, filed an upgrade or change of classification request to another occupation, management had the prerogative of rejecting his request although it might be recruiting journeymen, or learners from the ranks of junior workers, or even new hires for the job. Thus, Line Relations was free to assign hard-core trainees as "machine-tool operator-learners," as it was in fact doing, even though it might be rejecting upgrade or change of classification requests from senior people facing layoff. In addition, the union could not use upgrade and change requests as an effective tactic even if management was obligated to honor them for the simple reason that Line Relations had the advantage of prior knowledge of personnel requirements. Thus, a score of positions could open and be filled before the existing work force knew about them. These three features, inherent or implicit in the 1966 contract, gave management a decisive advantage in its confrontation with the union over layoffs and the hard-core. Conversely, they sensitized union leaders to new issues and helped prepare them for the 1969-1972 contract negotiations.

Another, altogether new, issue that arose was subsidized training, in this case the benefits of government subsidized training specifically denied senior employees by virtue of their seniority and experience. Special training for the unemployed did not measurably threaten the union blue-collar worker as long as trainees then had to compete with more experienced and better trained people for available jobs. But, when the hard-core were *given* jobs and union status as an integral part of their training, the threat became obvious. When the benefits of subsidized training were combined with management's prerogative in interpreting vague job classifications, the existing rules restricting seniority rights in layoffs, upgrade and job-change procedures, and management's foreknowledge of job openings, the hard-core unemployed suddenly loomed as formidable competitors for the rich but limited benefits of industry that dues-paying labor was supposed to capture.

Thus, the smoldering issue of job descriptions, new sensitivity to some standard provisions in the pre-hard-core contract, and the altogether new issue of subsidized training set the stage for the union's strategy in the coming 1969-1972 contract negotiations.

NEGOTIATIONS AND THE NEW VS. THE OLD CONTRACT

The negotiating team for Southwestern was headed by Harper, vice president of Personnel and Jerry McClure, director of Line Relations.

On the eve of negotiations, Harper expressed the conviction that the union was not gunning for the hard-core program. On separate occasions, McClure had also rejected unequivocally any suggestion of union opposition. Whether Harper or McClure were actually convinced of this, or whether in fact they anticipated and prepared for it privately, it is clear that this concern was not reflected in the negotiating team's formal preparation. Judging from our interviews with Harper and McClure as well as accounts of union participants, Southwestern's negotiating team approached the negotiations prepared for the usual issues—wages, pension, medical and other fringe benefits, as well as local issues from past negotiations such as contracting work to outside nonunion contractors, absenteeism, plant rules and regulations, and so on.

As it turned out these were not the issues uppermost in the minds of the union negotiators. Rather, union demands corresponded to those contract provisions which had made it most vulnerable in its fight with the company over the hard-core.

To union negotiators rewriting job descriptions had top priority, and they wanted to start with the general helper-learner category. Of equal importance were demands to extend seniority rights across job categories for layoffs, upgrade, and change of classification requests coupled with a demand for advance notification on all changes in personnel requirements.

Looking at union demands and company concessions in greater detail gives indisputable evidence that the union had in fact "won the (hard-core) war," with a victory so complete that the rights to training were preempted in the process.

The first union demand called for a redefining of job descriptions, beginning with the category of general helper-learner. This category they said had allowed the company to have work performed by unqualified personnel. The union had compiled a list of incidents to prove this point, virtually all relating to the hard-core in jobs as general helper-learners. This particular job description originally written in June, 1958, was never disputed until 1968.

As McClure stated, "The latitude it allowed management during these years gave us the opportunity to introduce many a young person to industry. Many of the people who are doing semiskilled and sometimes skilled jobs began with us as general helpers."

The general helpers job description as written in 1958 was divided into three sections as follows:

A. *Summary:* To perform routine manual work, maintain good housekeeping, and assist skilled and semiskilled workers.

B. *Tasks Performed:* To perform such typical work as maintaining good housekeeping, normally in an assigned factory area by sweeping, wiping and cleaning machines, equipment, tools, work benches and floors, working from verbal or written instructions.

 Remove and clean chips and scraps from machines, keeping various types of scrap segregated in separate containers, and make proper disposition.

 Assist skilled and semiskilled workers by supplying workers with tools, supplies, parts, and materials.

 Load and unload hand trucks, pallets and racks; move, stack, clean parts and assemblies. Identify items such as raw materials, bar stock tools, parts and assemblies by such methods as color coding, steel stamping, etching, rubber stamping, and stenciling. Prepare stencils by use of stencil cutters.

 Perform other related duties incidental to the duties described herein, such as fluxing parts to be welded, and loading and unloading equipment and machines such as hydro-presses and drop hammers by positioning material, pads, and rubber strips as directed.

C. *Materials, Tools and Equipment Used:* Materials worked with: various types of raw materials, parts and assemblies; sweeping compounds, cleaning solutions, oil, solvents, and rags.

 Tools used: Hand tools.

 Equipment used: Hand trucks, cleaning equipment, oil spray guns, stencil cutters, brushes, and brooms.

In the new contract the name "general-helper" was changed to "general utility worker." Specifications now consisted of two sections. In section B the phrases "make proper disposition," "incidental to the duties described herein," and "flux part to be welded" were removed.

Section C relating to the use of tools was deleted entirely. It was the interpretation of this section that had caused the most disagreement between the union and hard-core supervisors.

The second order of business was management's foreknowledge of available job openings. The union had not been fully aware of this advantage until Miller's skillful use of it in keeping the hard-core placed in positions not yet checkmated by the union. It now wanted equal access to this information. In the new contract the company agreed to furnish the following information to the chief shop steward:

(1) Notice of payroll additions (daily).

(2) Seniority lists by classifications (6) copies monthly.

(3) Layoff recall drop list (1) copy as required.

(4) Anticipated surplus information list (1) copy weekly.

(5) Layoff list (6) copies as requested.

(6) Recall list (6) copies as requested.

(7) Union dues reports, showing dues deductions, terminations and dues cancellations or members transferring out of the bargaining unit (monthly (1) copy to union hall and (1) copy to chief shop steward).

(8) Terminations tab cards (1) copy weekly.

(9) List of employees entering bargaining unit from nonrepresented jobs (1) copy weekly.

(10) Organization change notice, showing changes in department and division numbers, etc. (1) copy as occurs.

(11) Minutes of general safety committee meeting (2) copies monthly.

(12) List of employees retiring (2) copies monthly.

(13) Suggestion awards list showing award of each individual in bargaining unit (1) copy monthly.

(14) Names of deceased bargaining unit employees (1) copy as occurs.

In the past, part of this information had been provided to the union as a courtesy, but now it became a *contract agreement*.

Other issues such as wages and fringe benefits, according to the union negotiating committee's unofficial report, were agreed upon quickly with only minor complications. The most controversial issue that arose during negotiations was that of having union members with years of seniority laid off while management was training *new* people for available jobs. To prevent all such layoffs in the future, the union demanded that seniority be the binding rule in any layoff or regression situation. Negotiators contended that seniority more than justified keeping most workers since they already possessed some skills, and retraining them was less costly than training novices.

To effect its demands for plant-wide, cross-job seniority rules, the union administered the *coup-de-grace* in the form of a comprehensive layoff and upgrade plan. Called the "Job-Family Progression Plan," it would preempt by seniority virtually all avenues of opportunity in Southwestern's production occupations. Seniority rights to subsidized training were *defacto* because if the company was bound to grant upgrade and job change requests by seniority as opposed to expertise, some form of training, retraining, or learning grace period was inescapable.

An illustration of how the Job-Family Progression Plan works is as follows: We use the maintenance family, for it was the primary area of on-job training of the hard-core. It contains 13 different types of jobs from janitor to air-conditioning mechanic. The function of this work group is servicing Southwestern properties and machinery.

Consulting Figure 4 and keeping in mind the seniority rule, it is clear that for men from the ghetto with very few skills, the only realistic starting point in this work group would be in the category of janitor. If by accident they had some experience as a garage attendant and could qualify for a step 2 job, it could not be offered until every janitor who was at the top of his pay scale for 90 days was offered the job opening first, regardless of his qualifications. Thus if he accepted, the employee with no qualifications at the top of the list would be given the job and a 30-day training period to prove his ability to retain the job in tnaι nigher classification. The same procedure would continue until the employee reached step 4, the maximum pay rate in the maintenance utility worker classification. At this level, he would be interviewed by management to determine his qualifications for the next

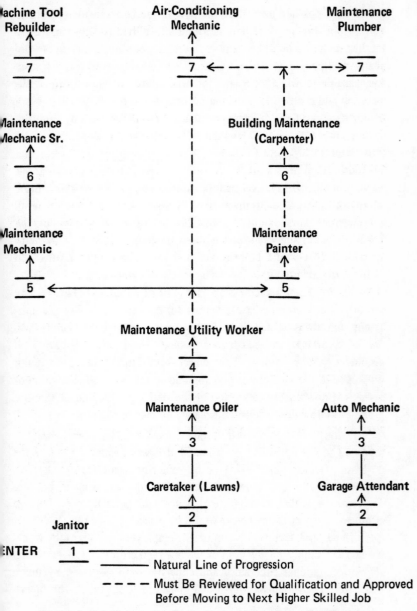

Figure 4—Job Progression Paths in the Maintenance Family

set of higher skilled jobs (note the dotted line between the step 4 and step 5 jobs, Figure 4). If he was found unqualified to advance, a copy of his review would be sent to a joint committee of union and managerial people who would instruct him what steps to take to insure his acceptance when the same job was offered at another time. His name would then go back to the bottom of the list. Only when every senior person on the progression list had been determined by this joint review procedure as being unqualified for that step job opening, would consideration be given to hiring the new applications on file for that position. There are six other job family groups under this plan. Without exception their entry level qualifications require skills far above those of any of the hard-core trainees hired by Southwestern. Therefore, even if new hires were admitted at the bottom of these six families, the hard-core could not begin there without training, and if training were to be provided, it would be provided first to senior people in other job families who had requests for change of classification on file.

The Job-Family Progression Plan also provided for regression by seniority—an even more costly feature for the company's. For example, if any employee in step 7, at the top of the maintenance family, was facing layoff, he regressed to the next lower position having an employee junior to him. That employee in turn bounced a junior employee in the next lower position and so on. Thus, the net effect of laying off one worker at the top of the step 7 level would be to move workers all down the line and ultimately bounce one janitor.

Obviously this plan ran into some opposition. Management was not opposed to the upgrading provisions, but it was firmly opposed to the regression feature that layoff be by seniority regardless of job class. Agreement with this provision meant that the company would lose expertise in which years of experience had been invested because senior employees facing layoff would be placed in jobs they had never performed, and technically competent employees in those jobs would be laid off simply on the basis of the one rigid criterion o date of hire. Thus occupational experience and expertise were displaced by union longevity. The Progression Plan had made provisions for this problem—

training. Not training for the hard-core unemployed, not even training for the union worker *per se,* but training for the worker who had paid the most dues to Local 289. The NAB principle was thus neatly reversed. Instead of training benefits allocated in proportion to time *un*employed, they were to be allocated in direct proportion to time *employed*—in effect to the hard-core *employed.*

It is not clear how strongly management negotiators opposed this plan, but the fact remains that it was adopted virtually intact.

Certainly there were other issues involved in the negotiations, some resulting from the NAB program and some not. For example there had been an agreement between union and management granting the hard-core a 30-day immunity from union membership. When the program became controversial and thus visible to Larry White (chief shop steward), he reversed his position and Harper conceded the issue even before negotiations. The 1969-1972 contract contained provisions that did away with the 30-day immunity privilege.

In addition, the old issue of job shoppers was also attacked. It had been Southwestern's practice during "labor-short emergency situations" to hire independent contractors who worked in the plant for a set period of time and produced a set number of items. Since the contractors were not under union control and, therefore, not subject to union dues, the practice was hotly contested in the 1969 negotiations and management conceded. But even in this issue the specter of the NAB program could be seen in the union's hardening attitude concerning what training could and could not do. If street people could be transformed from excons to skilled workers, similarly, surplus workers on layoff could be trained to do specialized, short-term jobs.

The new post-hard-core contract signaled an end to union naiveté regarding the uses and benefits of training. Moreover when compared to the pre-hard-core contract of 1966-1969, it is abundantly clear that despite Harper's statements to the contrary, job opportunity for the ghetto unemployed *was* the major union concern. In fact as analyses below will illustrate, this issue was the crux of a major industrial relations setback for management.

MAJOR CONSEQUENCES

Compared to the Job-Family Progression Plan, all other changes in the new contract were insignificant. The Family Progression Plan was not simply an erosion, but a major assault on the NAB principle of compensatory opportunity for the ghetto hard-core unemployed. Except for introductory paragraphs paying lip service to the principle of nondiscrimination on the bases of race, sex, age, religious and political beliefs, or union activity; and another image-conscious paragraph pledging the company's continuation of its present non-discriminatory practices; the new contract made no implicit or explicit reference to the hard-core unemployed. Such reference was unnecessary. The criterion "qualified" absolved everyone. In fact, it could be argued that the company was guilty of discrimination when they hired hard-core unemployed racial minorities while rejecting or laying off qualified white people. But the new contract ended hard-core training more decisively than by inference, as a projection of the logical consequences of the Job-Family Progression Plan will illustrate.

Under conditions of static or declining employment, the only available entry positions for new hard-core unemployed would be janitor. Any other position would require training, and training opportunity was now allocated on a seniority basis. In addition, if a recently hired janitor wished an upgrade, he was forced to compete with seniority. Even under expanding employment conditions, a hard-core unemployed would find his opportunity little improved, because all job openings would have to be filled first by senior people already in the plant. Thus, the employment boom would have the effect of opening to outsiders without experience only those positions at the very bottom of the pay scale. Conceivably under these conditions, openings to the hard-core unemployed could expand in the process, but only at the very bottom, in positions such as caretaker or garage attendant.

Thus, the progression plan closed the door for hard-core only, and not qualified blue-collar workers, mostly white, for they were still allowed the privilege of entering the labor force without starting at the bottom of the ladder as janitors.

Since the new contract there have been no more NAB programs at Southwestern for hiring new hard-core. In fact since December 1968, when the last contingent of Southwestern's original quota of trainees began on-job training, the company has taken a new approach in filling vacancies (replacements) in their existing hard-core program. In addition, Southwestern received another quota of ten trainees, which the parent corporation transferred to it from another subsidiary plant. It is significant to mention that this subsidiary plant requested cancellation of its program because of layoffs. In all, Southwestern hired and trained 24 more hard-core beyond the 28 cases we have analyzed. However, these 24 were of a higher caliber than the original 28. Although technically certified as hard-core, their education level was higher, averaging about 11.5 years as opposed to less than 10 years. In addition, there was a much lower arrest profile, and their employment backgrounds marked them as much brighter prospects than the original 28. Basically, they were technically and temporarily handicapped people already attuned to industry. Thus, even before the 1969 contract negotiations began, management concessions had signaled an end to hiring the hard-core unemployed, and with the 1969-1972 contract, the end of the program was formalized.

In addition to closing the doors to the hard-core, there were direct and indirect consequences of the Job-Family Progression Plan in terms of costs to the company. First in layoff situations, there were the direct costs of laying off trained, junior workmen and replacing them with senior workmen, who then had to learn new skills. These costs developed either in the form of training as such, or loss of efficiency during retraining or to a lesser degree in deferring layoffs. In a hiring situation the direct costs could be greater, since the company had to fill the open positions with senior people, and either train them or give them 30 days to learn while recruiting unskilled or semi-skilled workers to enter the progression system at the bottom.

Indirect costs developed in the form of human factor consequences. The upgraded or transferred worker had 30 days to be notified by his supervisor whether or not he was qualified to stay in the new position. Many of these workers did not make it and were transferred back to their original classification. Such a worker was stigmatized. He tended either to blame himself or the company for his failure. Both reactions were costly since the former affected the worker's self-confidence, hence his performance, and the latter caused him to file a grievance with the resultant loss of time for some highly paid people who had to investigate his complaint. These were actual, not hypothetical instances, and they are as amenable to cost accounting as are training costs. At the two-year mark of the new contract, no study of either direct or human-factor costs had been undertaken, but instances were numerous and dissatisfaction at the managerial level was obvious and increasing.

IMPLICATIONS

Was the Job-Family Progression Plan linked to the hard-core program? Beyond reasonable doubt the sequence of events at South-western established that it was. But these events posed an even more involved set of questions. If the union was seeking an end to the hard-core program, why didn't it simply demand this without resorting to the elaborate Job-Family Progression Plan? And if management was willing to sacrifice its commitment to the NAB principle, why didn't it simply accede to the demands necessary to accomplish this end without accepting the union's costly plan? The answer lies in the complexities and subtleties of discrimination. Like every other institution in society, racial and cultural discrimination continues to evolve. It has evolved from a superstructural to an infrastructural issue. The rules of discrimination have evolved to keep pace with efforts to liquidate discrimination and to postpone the increased competition for opportunity that liquidation implies. Hiring the hard-core unemployed is one program designed to help end the consequences of discrimination. Industry is given a stake in the program and costs to ownership are provided for. However, the program precipitates a crisis by confronting the union with the economic realities—the costs to them—of assimilating the ghetto unemployed into the labor market.

To union workers, programs for the occupationally disadvantaged are acceptable as long as these programs do not interfere with their own opportunities. From their perspective, the basic threat of the NAB program was that, in effect, it was an occupational redistribution program, and it was this fact that made it an effective and, to them, socially formidable program. As every blue-collar worker knows, working is not all that difficult. Making jobs pay is half the struggle, who get the jobs is the other half, and together these interests form the basis for union policy. It is one thing for the government to support people who are learning to work or to teach them how to work, or even to support them when they refuse to wash cars and sweep floors. It is quite another to place them in union jobs which have economic and social significance.

If Southwestern's union leaders were not initially aware of these ramifications to the hard-core program, they were quickly aware of them after layoffs. But the solution to their problem was complicated by the changing legal and moral rules of discrimination. It was complicated also by a sincere belief in the abstract principle of equal opportunity, varying in degree, of course, from one blue-collar worker to the next. *How to demand continuation of the benefits they realize from discrimination while at the same time going on record as being opposed to discrimination is not an easy task.* It is difficult to accomplish, and that was where the Job-Family Progression Plan became effective. It was not against hiring the hard-core; it was simply *for* seniority. Seniority had a moral acceptance equal to if not greater than equal opportunity.

On the other hand, the hard-core did not pose any real threat to the company. Although there were some costs to hiring and training the hard-core, even with the government subsidy, these costs were not overwhelming. Rather it was the costs and threat of costs imposed by organized labor in reaction to the program that appeared decisive in management's concession to the union. Yet, prior to and even after negotiations, Harper steadfastly insisted that the hard-core program was not an issue. Moreover, management negotiators did prepare for wage and fringe benefit demands, and from all accounts did not prepare for demands relating to hard-core issues.

Were such actions a result of naiveté, or were they deliberate? We can only conclude that they were deliberate. Again as in the case of the union's dilemma, the solution to the crisis of equality was not simple. Management, more exposed to public scrutiny than labor, felt a strong moral obligation to support work opportunity for the disadvantaged. On the other hand, there were limits to the costs it would bear. How far should a company go in pursuing a public policy designed to benefit society generally, but not the company specifically—such as training unskilled manpower when skilled labor was in abundance? Up to the time of negotiations, Harper had given a number of signals that Southwestern had reached its limit. He had withdrawn from the operations of the training center and took no active part in Miller's efforts to find jobs for the trainees. He conceded to the union when it insisted that general helper-learners should not use tools. Moreover, he was beginning to favor the union's position of protecting seniority. Harper's actions, plus the negotiations themselves, indicated to us that the company had gone as far as it would go in protecting the NAB program from the union. Its obligation to the hard-core had ended in keeping those still in the program from being laid off. The future of the program was an incidental issue, and if necessary, it would be conceded. If Harper acknowledged this as an issue, he would then have to explain why he conceded it. It was simpler for both union and management to ignore the existence of the moral issue they were both willing to sacrifice in the name of another moral issue—seniority. Thus, in the endeavor to maintain the public image of *not* openly opposing job opportunity for the disadvantaged, management semantics and union semantics were mutually supporting.

The question still remains: If management was prepared to concede the NAB principle, why did it do so at such enormous costs to the company? First, the full implications of the Job-Family Progression Plan were not immediately apparent, even to the union. The plan was experimental, and only when union members began taking advantage of the regression feature in unanticipated numbers did the cost implications become apparent. Second, the cooperative management and union tactics of keeping the real issue with its racial overtones submerged rather than out in the open made analysis even more difficult. The union viewed itself as protecting sacrosanct seniority and little more. Management tended to view the Job-Family Plan as little more than a thrust against the hard-core. Most likely, if this plan had been treated like any normal demand and brought out into the open,

Harper would not have approved it. Thus the hard-core program was not just a basic issue underlying the issue of seniority, it was a deliberately avoided issue. And, one of the consequences of avoiding it was a miscalculation of the cost to the company of the Job-Family Plan.

Finally, the dynamics of union-management interaction which unfolded at Southwestern revealed basic economic and social realities peculiar to industry as a whole. The impact of compensatory opportunity for ghetto unemployed, in theory at least, tested every union contract in every industry. The more unemployment increased, the greater the test. The NAB thrust itself has shifted from emphasizing hiring *new* hard-core to emphasizing instead, upgrading hard-core already in industry and finding jobs for Vietnam veterans. In the face of diminishing job opportunity, higher incomes for labor, increasing technology, and increasing numbers of people looking for work, the issue of protecting equity in the infrastructure of discrimination in the name of seniority will probably be a major feature in union-management negotiations for some time to some. Any effective policy to bring the ghetto back into mainstream society will find this dysfunctional system far more formidable than the so-called pathology of the ghetto.

APPENDIX:
A Note on Background and Methods

This study was conceived and organized in the spring of 1968 as a project of the Bureau of Ethnic Research, Department of Anthropology, University of Arizona. It was funded by the Rockefeller Foundation that same year.

Exploratory investigations of job training programs in the San Diego area were conducted in June and July, 1968; one program in one factory was selected for intensive longitudinal study and this case was observed uninterruptedly from late July, 1968, beginning with its first screening interviews of hard-core applicants until the end of 1969, which was one year after the last class of trainees had been hired and 18 months after program initiation. Although January 1970 marked the end of systematic, comprehensive observations and the beginning of analysis, information regarding union and management activity relating to the hard-core was still being processed through the spring of 1972.

Participants and their roles in the project were as follows: Harland Padfield, with a research background in the social anthropology of minority groups in the context of economic development and technological change, initiated the project, conducted exploratory surveys, obtained the cooperation of the case factory, organized the case study, and conducted observations and interviews in the factory primarily and the community of Southeast San Diego secondarily throughout the course of the study. His field contact was continuous through the summers and falls of 1968 and 1969, intermittent through the winter and spring of 1969, and occasional through the spring of 1972.

Marianne Padfield with a background in counseling and guidance conducted family interviews in the Southeast San Diego community in the summer of 1968 and assisted in interview analyses in the summer of 1969.

Roy Williams with a background in family and industrial personnel counseling joined the project in August, 1968. A resident of San Diego for 15 years and a local leader in the black community of Southeast San Diego, he conducted observations and interviews of trainees and their families, public and private agencies including policemen, welfare workers, job placement counselors, probation officers, and courts through 1969. He also assisted in the observation and interviewing of trainees in the factory context until the phasing out of the hard-core training facility in the case factory in early 1970.

Roy Williams and Harland Padfield collaborated in all phases of the project including the analysis of the data, the write-up of the report and the editing of the manuscript.

The study was designed initially to focus on one set of people—the hard-core unemployed—faced with a unique experience—entry level occupational employment in the labor market. After an initial survey of job programs in the San Diego area, the researchers planned to construct a sample of trainees in a number of programs and study their work-related adjustments both on and off the jobs by observing them on the job and interviewing them and their families off the job for a period of six months. San Diego was chosen because of its situation in the Southern California industrial megapolis. Although Los Angeles with the highest concentration of industry and low-income minority populations in the West had received and was continuing to receive considerable attention, little inquiry had as yet been conducted in the San Diego area. This statement is somewhat oversimplified, but it nevertheless provides for discussing the changes which evolved in the early stages of the investigation.

Four basic changes in the design were made, partly as a result of accident and partly as a result of an evolution in theoretical organization resulting from the feedback of the information being processed. First, quite early in the project, the researchers decided to concentrate on a set of trainees in *one* firm rather than construct a set from multiple firms, because they were encountering a variety of job programs in the survey each differing in its objectives and rules. At the same time they learned of the existence of a rather large NAB effort in San Diego that had just recently begun. To control for the former and take advantage of the latter they decided to concentrate on the NAB-JOBS system. This is where the accident of timing was instrumental. The decision to use the NAB system was reached in about mid-July, 1968. At that time numerous plants had already initiated NAB programs but the researchers learned of one factory that was preparing to launch its NAB program at a time which coincided with their timetable.

They contacted the firm, found them in the early stage of organization with no apparent structure and no trainees yet interviewed or hired, which was ideal for the purposes of their study. Moreover the company was congenial to the idea of a study and expressed willingness to cooperate, giving researchers the run of the plant, access to interviews and organizational meetings, access to personnel records and even the privilege of interviewing trainees on the job with prior approval of their supervisors. In addition to the factors of timing and access, the selection of this company was ideal in other respects: It was medium-sized, well-established, and typical of the profile for San Diego industry generally, and its quota of trainees was within the range of the number of cases that two researchers could be expected to handle.

The other changes in design could be regarded as consequences of this initial change. For example when the full extent of the reactions of union workers to the trainees was learned, the researchers decided to shift from the single focus on trainee behavior to a dual focus giving equal emphasis to the behavior of two sets of people—the hard-core and the factory—each having, hypothetically at least, a distinctive system of propositions. Observation schedules then had to be modified to pursue blue-collar worker behavior beyond the context of interaction with trainees.

The third modification evolved rather quickly when it became obvious that the forces impinging upon the trainees *outside* the plant were more significant than factors in the plant in terms of explaining their work adjustments. Therefore the theoretical framework and the objectives of the study were elaborated to observe the trainees systematically in two social settings—the plant and the ghetto community

The fourth modification extended the duration of data gathering

This was an inevitable consequence of the case factory's program of hiring trainees in five five sets a month apart. A year of observation was then planned despite the risk of an incomplete set of data. But with the contribution of matching resources from cooperating organizations, overtime contribution of the researchers and the hope of obtaining supplemental funding the study was begun. As it turned out a six month set of data on the factory and the first class of trainees indicated that the most significant adjustments were just then beginning to take shape, so in January of 1969, the researchers decided to operate within a time frame of one calendar year for every trainee which clearly meant that data gathering could not be phased out for a year and a half and in some categories like union management relations, decisive adjustments would perhaps not emerge until contract renewal time in 1972. Nevertheless, all of the major modifications in research design were made in rather rapid succession and schedules and routines within this new framework were fairly well-established by September, 1968.

The theoretical framework was general with specificity evolving as data were gathered and analyzed. Thus it is much easier to say what was being done in retrospect than it was when observations began.

Quite simply and generally the study began as a longitudinal interaction study hypothesizing the interaction of distinctive sets of people in two discrete settings—the factory and the ghetto. Within the factory setting four sets of people were observed—management, supervisors, union workers and hard-core trainees. In the Southeast San Diego setting the interaction of trainees with their families, social networks and strategic public agencies like law enforcement, courts and welfare was observed. The relevant groups were identified by this framework but there was too little basis for analytical explanation hence too little discrimination for data gathering. Because of the latter problem in particular, observations were soon restricted to probing responses to key events, such as the interplay of management and union responses to layoffs and the interplay of supervisor, workmen, and trainee responses to absenteeism and infractions of shop etiquette. This focus and the event of lay-offs stimulated the researchers to develop the framework of the sociology of benefits-over-costs of compensatory training for the hard-core unemployed.

This proved to be a useful overall framework for the factory vis-à-vis the hard-core, but in the continuing probe of hard-core adjustments in both the factory and community setting, much of their response behavior appeared irrational in these terms, either short run or long run. Clearly if this framework was viable, another dimension of gain/loss had to be postulated and demonstrated. However it took six months for this to evolve, and again, it evolved as the trainees' natural interaction situations evolved through time. Inevitably the researchers found themselves analyzing this data within a social-psychological framework. They began concentrating on role behavior and obtained uniform data in earlier cases retroactively. Hence the sociology of cost/benefit framework was elaborated in their cases to include gain of social-psychological satisfaction in role systems associated with job status, over loss of social-psychological satisfaction in role systems associated with economic alienation and marginality.

Methods and techniques consisted of observation routines, in which all trainees were visited in their work locales at least twice a week. The researchers conducted casual interviewing of principals in the course of this visitation. In private they conducted routine depth interviewing of hard-core trainees and family members for standard information like family, occupational, educational, residence, and arrest histories. In addition they conducted depth interviews in all special event circumstances affecting work performance such as absenteeism, reprimands, citations, conflicts in the plant, complaints or any felt need on the part of the trainees. Finally, when possible they observed and communicated with trainees and associates under traumatic circumstances such as during family fights, job termination, jail, and blowups at the plant.

The researchers also interviewed factory personnel in private to probe attitudes toward important events. Although these contacts were not made uniformly throughout the plant as a whole, the information from the three perspectives of blue-collar worker, supervisor and management was systematized. Standardized plant data consisted of attendance records of hard-core trainees and the control group, merit reviews, progression histories of the trainees, and weekly diaries summarizing the trainees' situations.

Basic techniques consisted of on-the-scene observation of natural interaction situations recorded in diaries at the end of each day and tape-recorded depth interviewing to probe significant events observed firsthand or reported secondhand as soon after the event as possible. Standardized, topical guides rather than schedules and questionnaires were used for observation and routine interviewing and the observation of interaction behavior and nondirect interviewing were relied upon to construct role differentiation rather than formalized test instruments.

NOTES

1. *Report of the National Advisory Commission on Civil Disorders* (New York: New York Times Company, 1968), pp. 112-116.
2. *Ibid.*, pp. 42-108.
3. Charles L. Sanders, "Industry Gives New Hope to the Negro," *Ebony,* 8 June 1968, pp. 193-195.
4. William L. Henderson and Larry C. Ledebur, *Economic Disparity: Problems and Strategies for Black America* (New York: The Free Press, 1970), pp. 151-154.
5. *Ibid.,* pp. 142-148.
6. *Ibid.*, p. 185.
7. See Henderson and Ledebur, *op. cit.,* pp. 175-192; and Allen R. Janger and Ruth G. Shaeffer, *Managing Programs to Employ the Disadvantaged,* Studies in Personnel Policy, No. 219 (New York: National Industrial Conference Board, Inc., 1970), pp. 3-9.
8. Janger and Shaeffer, *op. cit.,* p. 9.
9. Henderson and Ledebur, *op. cit.,* pp. 151-154; Lawrence A. Johnson, *Employing the Hard-Core Unemployed,* American Management Associates, Inc., U.S.A., 1969; and Mentec Corporation, "Considerations in Employing the Disadvantaged in the *JOBS-Program,*" prepared for the Office of Manpower Administration, U.S. Department of Labor by the Mentec Corporation, Oakland, California (Washington, D.C.: Government Printing Office, 1969).
10. Janger and Schaeffer, *op. cit.,* pp. 9-11.
11. Henderson and Ledebur, *op. cit.,* pp. 126-127.
12. *What Can You Do About the Hard-Core Unemployed?* (New York: The Research Institute of America, June 18, 1968), Preface and pp. 1-2 (italics added).
13. Janger and Shaeffer, *op. cit.,* p. 11.
14. *Ibid.*, pp. 41-114.
15. In addition to all references above, see "How to Turn Dropouts into Steady Workers," *Business Week,* 31 August 1968, pp. 64-68; Kenneth C. Field, "A New Life: Unemployables Hired by Detroit Car Firm Surprise Their Bosses," *Wall Street Journal,* 12 August 1968; Jerome P. Frank and Walter Rayher, "Can You Manage the Hard-Core Workers?" *Mill & Factory* 83, 2 (August 1968): 41-50; Richard C. Halverson, "Ghetto Plants offer Hope for Hard-Core Black Unemployed," *The Christian Science Monitor,* 19 July 1968; Ulric Haynes, Jr., "Equal Job Opportunity: The Credibility Gap," *Harvard Business Review* 46, 3 (May-June 1968): 113-120; "Negro-Owned and Managed Plant Fills Big Ghetto Need—Jobs," *Modern Manufacturing* 1, 4 (September 1968): pp. 80-81; Herbert R. Northrup, "On Hiring Hard-Core Jobless," *U.S. News & World Report,* 14 October 1968, pp. 82-86.
16. See especially, Johnson, *op. cit.,* pp. 55-197.
17. Janger and Shaeffer, *op. cit.,* pp. 14-15.

18. James D. Hodgson and Marshall H. Brenner, "Successful Experience: Training Hard-Core Unemployed," *Harvard Business Review* 46, 5 (September-October 1968): 148.

19. *What Can You Do About the Hard Core Unemployed?*, p. 15.

20. Janger and Shaeffer, *op. cit.*, pp. 6-7.

21. Frank and Rayher, *op. cit.*, p. 42.

22. Janger and Shaeffer, *op. cit.*, p. 42.

23. See Harland Padfield, "New Industrial Systems and Cultural Concepts of Poverty," *Human Organization* 29, 1 (Spring 1970): 29-36; also in Richard M. Hodgetts and Fred Luthans, eds., *The Responsibilities of Business* (New York: The Macmillan Company, 1970).

24. *Ibid.*, p. 34.

25. For an excellent theoretical exposition of this cultural phenomenon see Anthony F. C. Wallace, *Culture and Personality* (New York: Random House Press, 1965).

26. See Elliot Liebow, *Tally's Corner: A Study of Negro Streetcorner Men* (Boston: Little, Brown and Company, 1967); Kenneth B. Clark, *Dark Ghetto: Dilemmas of Social Power* (New York: Harper Torchbooks, 1965), pp. 21-62; Hyman Rodman, *Lower Class Families: The Culture of Poverty in Negro Trinidad* (New York: Oxford University Press, 1971), pp. 190-200.

27. See *Report of the National Advisory Commission on Civil Disorders* (New York: New York Times Company, 1968); John Hersey, *The Algiers Motel Incident* (New York: Bantam Books, Inc., 1968); James P. Spradley, *You Owe Yourself a Drunk* (Boston: Little, Brown and Company, 1970); "Question Remains," *Time,* 25 May 1970, p. 26.

28. "The Rising Problem of Drugs on the Job," *Time,* 29 June 1970, pp. 70-71.

29. *San Diego Union,* 15 October 1968.

30. For verification of the "attempted murder" charge, see "Steelworker Charged in Hoe Assault," *San Diego Evening Tribune,* 16 October 1968.

31. *San Diego Union,* 27 October 1968.

32. See Liebow, *op cit.;* Herbert J. Gans, *The Urban Villagers* (New York: The Free Press, 1965), pp. 229-249; Clark, *op. cit.,* pp. 63-80; Charles Keil, *Urban Blues* (Chicago: The University of Chicago Press, 1966), pp. 1-29; Ulf Hannerz, *Soulside: Inquiries into Ghetto Culture and Community* (New York and London: Columbia University Press, 1969), pp. 70-104; Oscar Lewis, "The Culture of Poverty," *Scientific American* 215, 4 (1966): 19-23; and Rodman, *op. cit.*

33. Henderson and Ledebur, *op. cit.,* p. 152.